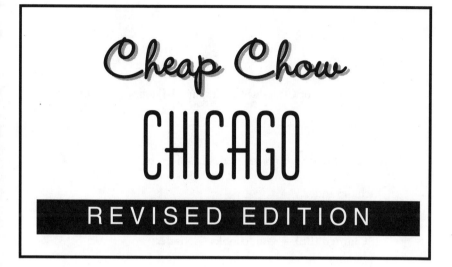

Cheap Chow CHICAGO

REVISED EDITION

A LaBan

Library of Congress Cataloging-in-Publication Data

LaBan, A.
Cheap chow Chicago / A. LaBan. —Rev. ed
p. cm.
Includes index.
ISBN 1-55652-293-2 (alk. paper)
1. Restaurants—Illinois—Chicago—Guidebooks.
2. Chicago (Ill.) —Guidebooks. I. Title.

TX907.3.I32C472 1998
647.95773'11—dc21 98-20442
CIP

Revised edition
Published by Chicago Review Press, Incorporated.
814 North Franklin Street
Chicago, Illinois 60610
ISBN 1-55652-293-2
Printed in the United States of America

5 4 3 2 1

To my frequent dining companion Eric.

Contents

Introduction

Does the inside of your refrigerator look like mine—fully stocked with door food/an assortment of condiments and a good supply of cold beer? Do you dread grocery shopping? Hate maneuvering through crowds up and down aisles, buying expensive items you don't need and forgetting important staples you should have remembered? Waiting in endless lines because the only time you have to shop is on the weekends when everyone else is out there too?

Do you ever just not want to cook? One of my friends says there's nothing better than a home-cooked meal. I agree; I just prefer that someone else cook it. It's not a matter of being able to function in the kitchen. After all, any relatively literate individual can thumb through a cookbook and whip out some risotto. OK, maybe a lasagna. Probably a burger is doable. Certainly Kraft Macaroni & Cheese. But what's the point if it's just me (or us)?

You're so busy, right? You're trying to balance long hours at work with maybe a family or maybe a social life or school or something else-and wouldn't it be easier just to go out and grab something to eat? But you're so busy trying to do it all that you rarely have the time to sample any places new to eat. And then there's the money thing. All that eating out begins to add up after a while, doesn't it? Not necessarily.

Cheap Chow Chicago is a way of helping you through a busy time. It's a way of acquainting you with the multiple opportunities that exist in your own backyard to eat well for less. *Cheap Chow Chicago* points you in the direction of a myriad of dining establishments where the food is, at minimum, pretty good and, always, relatively cheap.

The concept here is "Taste for Less." *Cheap Chow Chicago* uses a two-tier price-rating system to deliver to you satisfying meals including tax and tip (but not appetizers and desserts, alcohol, or cappuccino) for either:

$10 or less

$15 or less

Restaurants are organized by themes ranging from ethnic cuisine to a focus on a Chicago neighborhood to a type of food—maybe ribs or vegetarian—to a type of dining—all-you-can-eat or late night—or just whatever I felt like writing about. To enhance the dining and guidebook experience, each chapter has an informative and chatty lead-in editorial designed to truly capture the designated theme.

So you may be asking, "What gives her the right? What does she know? Why should I spend my hard-earned money on this book and take her advice? And, after reviewing some 300 restaurants, how much does she weigh?" Well, *Cheap Chow* was a successful (at least financially) monthly newsletter for three years before it became a book, and we're now publishing updates. I've honed my talents as food editor at the now defunct, hip Wicker Park 'zine *Chicago's Subnation* and, more recently, at *NewCity*. I've seen my share of criticism of my work (some of which one of my former editors gleefully published for the public), and, frankly, it's all helped work the kinks out.

You know, people find out you review restaurants, and they want to ask you all kinds of questions. Challenge you. "What's your favorite cheap restaurant?" I hear that all the time. You know, that's proprietary information—it's worth money. As a restaurant writer, I hate people who just want to pump me all night for free advice. Hey, here it is—all of it. Buy this book. Or if you can't do that, here's my short list of faves. Photocopy the pages and save some bucks:

The Best of *Cheap Chow Chicago*

That's Italian Anna Maria's. Forget all those expensive trattorias in Lincoln Park or downtown. A once nondescript storefront has spiffed itself up and still houses an extraordinary kitchen within.

Stick to Your Ribs Hecky's. Winner of *Cheap Chow Chicago*'s first (and only) Reader Poll. "It's the sauce."

Get Stuffed the $1.50 junior vegetarian burrito at the Taco & Burrito House. Locations open late night at Irving Park and Broadway and Fullerton and Ashland.

Go Fish the $7.95 sushi deluxe at Shiroi Hana. Nine pieces and a maki roll, accompanied by the inevitable miso soup and hot towels. A small price to pay for the nightly wait.

Where Everybody Knows Your Name J. T. Collin's Pub. Almost the perfect neighborhood bar where you can lounge by yourself or comfortably with a room full of strangers. Great chicken flat bread.

Oodles of Noodles Penny's Noodle Shop. How do they continue to do it so good, so fast, and so cheap? Furama for dim sum daily. Or, Thai This if you need to Thai one on.

The Cutting Edge Bite, Leo's Lunchroom, or Twilight. Choose any one, you can't go wrong. The most creative, hippest food in the city at the right price.

A Room with a View The Signature Room on the Ninety-Fifth. $8.95 pig-out buffet makes this one of the Mag Mile's hidden gems.

Oktoberfeast, Ja Resi's Bierstube. Cheap sausages served in a classic biergarten.

And The One We Keep Going Back To Jim's Grill. Grab a stool at the counter for a cheap diner breakfast or a Korean specialty. Have an invigorating ginger tea on me.

A Few Notes About Using This Book

This book does not purport to identify every budget restaurant in the city. This is the new and updated version of *Cheap Chow Chicago*. Version 2.0, if you will, with all new restaurants, new chapters, new reviews, and updated pricing. But no, I still haven't eaten at every dump, dive, diner, and cheap buffet deal that's out there. There's simply not enough space in my week, my year, or my stomach. For those of you who are competitive, who want to righteously point out a place I missed, feel free. You could be an excellent source for some good finds.

The bottom line is that this book's just indicative of what's out there. It's here to point you in the right direction. It doesn't feature every restaurant it could; it certainly doesn't have write-ups on many of those eateries you should know about anyway if you get out at all. Feel free to explore on your own. Read the competition—I do. Of the periodicals, I recommend *NewCity* over the *Reader* or *Chicago* magazine, because, well, *NewCity* publishes my stuff, so you can read it for free. Also, talk to others who are themselves adventurous eaters who go out a lot. Some of my best tips have come from my own outgoing brother and sister-in-law, dedicated eaters whose habits have only been altered by the arrival of my nephew, the most special small person in the world, by the need now to find not only cheap and interesting eateries, but ones that are also kid friendly.

Yes, I know how to spell! But, each restaurant has its own ambiance, its own flavor, its own way of spelling dishes on their menus. So the spellings in each review are true to these nuances, to help preserve the ambiance, you know.

In spite of all efforts to keep up-to-date on pricing or even places being in business, things change. I've done a good amount of research on each chapter's subject matter and restaurants, and it's only due to an active lifestyle and a high-stress corporate job that some of my research—some of the eating part, that is—isn't too noticeable. But, if you've got to know for sure whether that risotto is still $9.95, give the place a call. Who knows, maybe the place isn't even serving risotto any more. In some hopefully isolated and very sad situations, the place itself might not be serving anything any more (as in no longer in business). It happens to even the best of places. If you're the anxious type, phone first.

These are restaurant reviews, so they are, after all, a matter of opinion. The reviews in this book are based solely on my own personal point of view. Reviews are done from the angle of the average eater (there were no free meals here, and restaurants were reviewed after "mystery shopping"), but they are subjective. They're how I see things. Although I rarely write about a place I think is just terrible (what's the point in wasting the space?), I'm not adverse to pointing out the warts. You might expect some for $15 or less. Remember, this is a value deal here. If you're expecting Le Francais, you'd better drive to Wheeling. Regardless, keep in mind that you may disagree with me. Go ahead and express yourself. If you've got particularly strong opinions about something, feel free to write me a note. Why stop there? If you're really adamant, feel free to write your own book. There's nothing stopping you. Have fun.

Latin Fling

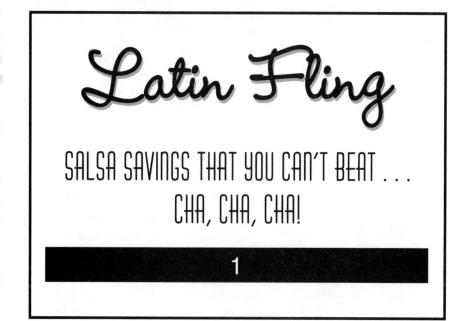

SALSA SAVINGS THAT YOU CAN'T BEAT . . . CHA, CHA, CHA!

1

Dateline, 1492—in Italy, there is no such thing as tomato sauce; the Irish aren't able to enjoy potatoes with their meat in shepherd's pie; and Mexicans have never heard of a burrito with cheese. Five hundred years ago though, with the arrival of Columbus and subsequent Iberian explorers, menus began to change globally as the world became truly well rounded. An exchange of flavors from the old to the new accompanied the movement of ships as the indigenous ingredients of the Americas mixed with the spices and foodstuffs of Europe and Asia to create new dishes in the Old World and completely nuevo cuisine in the New World.

The Spanish explorers' first port of call was the Caribbean where Columbus, and ultimately the rest of Europe, first tasted four of the five most economically important New World crops: maize, sweet potatoes, chili peppers, and manioc (the fifth, the potato, was later unearthed as the Spaniards moved south into the Andes). The Spaniards added cattle, pigs, and other livestock to this picture, and a new cuisine was cooked up in the tropical kitchens of Puerto Rico, the Dominican Republic, and Cuba.

In 1519, the Spanish left Cuba and moved inland into Mexico and Central America where they encountered the culinary traditions of highly developed Indian civilizations. The Aztecs introduced Cortes to chocolate, beans, corn tortillas, tamales, and deep-fried insects (one of the Aztecs' primary sources of protein). In turn, the Spaniards brought the Indians beef, chicken, pork, dairy products—and voilà . . . the burrito supreme was born.

> "Tita knew through her own flesh how fire transforms the elements, how a lump of corn flour is changed into a tortilla, how a soul that hasn't been warmed by the fire of love is lifeless, like a useless ball of corn flour."
>
> —*Like Water for Chocolate*, **Laura Esquivel**

As the Spanish influence spread farther south, many Peruvian traditions managed to coexist with, rather than be subverted by, the Spanish invaders. The world outside the Andes mountains is indebted to Peru for both the potato and the tomato (although the world chose not to take advantage of the Incas' other major food source, the guinea pig).

Chicago is home to a broad range of Hispanic cultures, and by the year 2000, it is estimated that one in every four Chicago residents will be either Mexican, Puerto Rican, Cuban, or of another Latin or South American nationality. Today, there are four primarily Hispanic wards in the city: the Southwest Side's Mexican barrio neighborhoods of Pilsen and Little Village and the predominantly Puerto Rican communities of West Town and Humboldt Park. Other Hispanic groups tend to be spread throughout the city, with smaller concentrations of Cubans in Logan Square and the Far North Side Edgewater community. With such a strong Hispanic presence, Chicago is able to offer some fine examples of Cuban, Peruvian, Central American, and, of course, Mexican cuisine. Plenty of opportunities to grab a cold Dos Equis, a Xingu, or a Negra Modelo and journey off on your own culinary voyage. ¡Mucho Gusto!

Café Bolero & Grill

2252 North Western, (773) 227-9000

Cuban food incorporates the cuisine of the Spanish conquistadors that "discovered" the island with the influences of the black slave population that supported the colonists. Marked by a neon sign that can be seen all the way to Logan Square and matches the blue neon bar inside, Café Bolero is an airy little café that serves fine examples of these hybrid island dishes. If you don't know a fried plantain from a tamale from a stuffed yucca, you might try ordering from the tapas section of the menu and grazing your way to awareness (tapas are $2.00 to $7.99). Combination platters, including a vegetarian combo plate, are available for $7.50 and under. Entrées start at $5.99 and are served with rice, black beans, and sweet plantains. Good-sized sandwiches run $2.25 to$5.99. Three kinds of flan are available for dessert: de leche (plain), de mamey (tropical fruit), and de coco (coconut). A sidewalk patio with a nice shady trellis is also here.

Open daily. Full bar. Sidewalk seating.

Ambassador Café

3605 North Ashland, (773) 404-8770

A fine example of Cuban cuisine found at the corner of Ashland and Addison, Ambassador is a homey little place with an inviting lunch counter and autographed pictures of the Cubs covering the walls. The specials are posted in Spanish (you'll have to ask for a translation if you no hablas), and a case full of flan, plain or coconut, greets you as you sit down. Boasting the famous Cuban sandwich—ham, turkey, and pickles on flat rectangular bread that tastes like a French baguette—the Ambassador also offers a good number of meat (particularly pork and chicken) entrées and a large selection of fish and seafood. All dishes, except seafood, are priced under $10 and are served with white rice, fried sweet plantains, and black bean soup. Start your meal with one of the tropical fruit shakes and end it with sips from a tiny cup of thick, sweet Cuban coffee.

Open daily. BYOB.

El Tinajon

2054 West Roscoe, (773) 525-8455

Dishes from the land of the Maya, which melded with Spanish influences to form Guatemalan cuisine, can be sampled at El Tinajon, a brightly decorated restaurant named after a handleless clay pot traditionally used to hold fresh drinking water. Guatemalan specialties accompanied by frosty mugs of Gallo (Guatemalan beer) include pepian antigueno, a spicy Indian stew with pork, quisquil chunks, and green beans ($7.50) and jocon cobanero, chicken simmered in special green sauce ($7). The menu has a number of other offerings that may seem similar to Mexican but are served with a Guatemalan twist, including chorizos, pork sausages prepared with Guatemalan spices and served with black beans, rice, broiled tomato sauce, and salad. Vegetarian dishes, along with pricier red snapper and shrimp dishes, are also available.

Open daily. Full bar.

Rinconcito Sudeamericano

1954 West Armitage, (773) 489-3126

Chicago's premier establishment for Peruvian cuisine is this unpretentious storefront in Bucktown that more than makes up for its lack of ambiance with its quality meals. Take time to find out what excellent Peruvian cuisine tastes like ("be patient, our food is made to order") and be prepared to haul home a big doggy bag—the portions here are huge. Entrées start at $8.50, with most being under $10 except seafood. Try the arroz con mariscos (Peruvian paella, $10.90) and don't miss the house specialty aji de gallina ($8.90), shredded chicken in a nut cream with potatoes, Peruvian spices, and rice. There's a large selection of other chicken, seafood, and other interesting dishes, including cau-cau (honeycomb tripe and potatoes, $8.50). Don't pass on the side dish of plantains. Go easy on the spicy green stuff that comes with the bread. That's not guacamole!

Open daily. Full bar.

El Nandu

2731 West Fullerton, (773) 278-0900

At El Nandu, "La Casa de Las Empanadas Argentinas" (the House of Argentine pastries), stuffed flaky pastry pouch empanadas ($1.95) are the name of the game and come in a variety of stuffings including:

Criolla—ground beef with onion, tomato, olives, raisins, and hard-boiled eggs

Ticumana—diced steak with onion, tomato, olives, and hard-boiled eggs
Pollo—chicken with white cheese and tomatoes
Jamon y queso—ham and white cheese
Queso—white cheese
Camarones—shrimp with white cheese
Pescado—cod with white cheese
Maiz—corn with white cheese
Espinaca—spinach with white cheese and hard-boiled egg

If you've got room after all those empanadas, entrées start at $8.95. Try the pollo con chimichurri, chicken breasts smothered in the signature sauce made from garlic, parsley, oil, vinegar, and spices. Argentine slides flash on screen during the week, while live Latin music throbs all weekend.

Open daily. Full bar. Music on weekends.

Las Tablas

2965 North Lincoln, (773) 871-2414

Most of the entrées at this Colombian steak house are too expensive, but the few options that qualify make Las Tablas worth the trip, even if you find yourself breaking your budget. Las Tablas specializes in slabs of thin tender steaks and chicken, marinated and served on butcher blocks with potatoes, plantains, fried yuca, and tangy chimichurri sauce, as well as assorted fish and seafood. Those trying to eat cheap can still sample the churrasquito ($9.95), the smaller but ample chargrilled New York strip. A marinated chicken breast, the pollo al ajillo, a number of rib eye and flank steaks, red snapper, king fish, and beef tongue are all also somewhat doable at $10.95.

Open daily. BYOB.

Tango Sur

3763 North Southport, (773) 477-5466

Tango Sur is a small storefront of an Argentine steak house serving parrilla (barbecue), various cocina (entrées), and pastas con salsa Argentina (pastas served with Argentine tomato sauce). Some of the beef options push the price barrier, but there are still a good number of chicken and veal dishes and a breaded beef topped with two fried eggs that make cutoff and let you enjoy the food of the Pampas. Pastas can be ordered with estofado ($2.90), a beef stew in a tomato meat sauce that "goes great with any pasta!"

Open daily. BYOB.

Food For Fast Feasts

quick bites

Irazu

1865 North Milwaukee, (773) 252-5687

Head west on North Avenue and take a right on Milwaukee. The neighborhood suddenly becomes barren, populated only by boarded-up warehouses with none of the ambiance of chic Bucktown just west. In this demilitarized zone, Irazu, a Costa Rican oasis beckons. Originally a fast food stand, they have recently expanded for more seating. On a nice day, you can relax on the patio, admire the scenery, and sip a refreshing tropical fruit shake (fifteen different flavors, $1.50 with or without milk). Or, tuck into a giant, spicy Central American–style chicken burrito ($3.10) or a cilantro-and-pepper–laden steak taco ($1.40). Specials, including pork chops with rice and beans, are $5.50. A new dining room was finally opened, giving patrons an eat-in alternative to the patio.

Closed Sundays. BYOB. Patio.

French Connection

Bargain Bistros That Are Really Nice!

2

We'll always have Paris . . . and its stuffy haute cuisine restaurants flaunting their haughty Michelin stars. But, there's more to French cuisine than a tiny medallion of veal drizzled in some sublime but sparse sauce and garnished with a single sprig of parsley and exactly two baby carrots. Non, the real France, la France profonde, offers heartier fare as diverse and varied as the country itself. As different as the beaches of Normandy are from the glittering sands of the Côte d'Azur, regional French cuisine reflects not only the geographic but ethnic diversity of a country that has blended the influences of Germany, Scandinavia, Italy, Spain, and Africa since before the reign of Charlemagne to long after the time of de Gaulle.

Nobody knows the truffles I've seen . . . The French were seemingly less successful than their European neighbors—the Spanish, English, and Portuguese—in their mad dash to colonize the world. Although they were able to occupy troublesome territories in Africa and Southeast Asia, the French were summarily booted out of North America and most of the Caribbean after losing the French and

Indian War in the mid-1700s. In spite of their sometimes abrupt departure, the French did make a lasting impact on a number of regional and national cuisines. In Indochina, French influences helped Vietnamese dishes develop into the most subtly sophisticated in Southeast Asia, and in Northern Africa, the impact of the French helped push desert dishes from the sustaining to the sublime. In the Western Hemisphere, French influences not only had an effect on the foods of the Caribbean but also contributed heavily to both the evolution of the Creole dishes of cosmopolitan New Orleans and the Cajun fare of the backwoods Louisiana bayou.

> "I've discovered something: if I give the dish a name, or translate the repulsive name it already has into French, my family can't tell my cheap concoction from gourmet fare. I've decided the key to successful food presentation is arrogance."
>
> —*The Cook's Journal*, **Linda Henley**

The French had an influence on the Chicago area long before the doors of Le Francais opened. In 1673, Che-kau-kou, an Indian word meaning "Wild Onion," was discovered by French voyageur Louis Joliet. A year later, Père Jacques Marquette stepped ashore at Gross Pointe Bluff, looked at marshlands, and declared, "Merde, this land is worthless." Although Père Marquette established a campsite at the present location of Damen Avenue and the Chicago River, it wasn't until 100 years later that trader Jean Baptiste Point du Sable, the son of a French merchant and a Haitian woman, became the first official non-Indian resident of Chicago.

Today, Chicago boasts a number of nouveau bistros serving regional French cuisine along with other international and regional flavors that evolved under French influences—Vietnamese, Moroccan, Caribbean, Cajun, and Creole—bistros that Parisians would be happy to frequent at twice the price. Oh merci merci me, some of the best things in life are brie. Bon Appétit!

Merlot Joe

2119 North Damen, (773) 252-5141

"A casual French joint," Merlot Joe has one of Bucktown's best front porches for dining, one of Bucktown's best back patios, and entrées all under $10. With an attractive one-room bungalow that serves as the dining room when you can't sit outside, Merlot Joe offers a changing seasonal and holiday menu of French bistro and Mediterranean-influenced options. "Cajun Nights" include crawfish etoufée, blue corn catfish, jambalaya, barbecue shrimp, and the "bonjour platter," a mixture of all the other Cajun stuff (all $10). Bistro selections, $8.00–$10.00, range from quiche du jour to the peasant dinner, duck confit and Alsatian sausage on a bed of mixed greens and lentils tossed with garden tomato, red onion, carrot, and raspberry vinaigrette. Pastas, $8.00–$10.00, include vegetable couscous and linguine à la bouillabaisse. Specials may be over budget.

Open daily. Full bar. Sidewalk and patio seating. Brunch. Free parking.

Le Loup Café

3348 North Sheffield, (773) 248-1830

So maybe you won't be one of the lucky sun worshippers on the sparkling beaches of the Côte d'Azur or French North Africa, but at Le Loup you can eat like one. Entrées, big enough for "howling appetites," are a little on the expensive side, starting at $8.95 for the vegetarian dishes, crêpes and ratatouille. A number of the chicken dishes, including poulet roti aux herbes, poulet Louisiana, coq au vin, and chicken couscous, look and taste almost exactly the same, but, since they taste good and you get a huge plate of whichever one you choose, does it really matter? Also available are cassoulet (duck, veal sausage, and white beans), civet de porc (marinated pork), and boeuf bourguignon (beef stew), all of which, be warned, push the limit in terms of price. As an added benefit, the back of the menu provides a detailed treatise on "the Wolf Society," which you can review as you relax amongst the numerous wolf posters and bumper stickers claiming, "Red Riding Hood lied." There's a nice, predator-free patio to enjoy during the summer.

Open daily. BYOB. Patio.

La Crêperie

2845 North Clark, (773) 528-9050

The grande dame of Chicago bistro dining, La Crêperie has been around for over 25 years serving good-deal dinner crêpes and plush you-definitely-don't-need-to-eat-that-too dessert crêpes in its original smoky front room containing a dark bar that's frequently haunted by accordion music. Large pillows of buckwheat crêpes are folded in squares around broccoli and cheese, spinach crème, ratatouille, chicken curry and rice, or other fillings ($3–$8). Dessert crêpes sport descriptions like crème de marrons, Grand Marnier, and Suzette à la Germain and shouldn't be had for $3 to $6.50. Noncrêpe entrée items include orange roughy or steak frites, both $8 à la carte.

Sometimes closed Mondays. Full bar. Patio dining. Brunch.

The Red Rooster Wine Bar & Café

2100 North Halsted, (773) 929-7660

Located in the heart of trendy and bustling DePaul, The Red Rooster is a quiet oasis of French provincial cuisine. A cabin-like bistro and the sister restaurant and next-door neighbor to the fancier Café Bernard, a good portion of the menu chalked up on the wall will allow you to stay under the "fork and knife" limit. Try the mustard chicken, a quarter poulet with vegetables, all for the right price of $8.75. Or, be a little adventurous and sample the smoked chicken and apple sausage over angel hair pasta with tomato coulis for $7.95. Other good bets are the pork scaloppini ($9.50), the duck à la orange ($9.75), and spinach fettuccini with sea scallops ($9.75). Remember, you're responsible for the consequences to l'addition (that's your check) if you should be driven to savor your meal with a glass of vin.

Open daily. Full bar.

Heaven on Seven (the original)

111 North Wabash, 7th floor, (312) 263-6443

Woo, doggy! Every East Loop worker's favorite lunch spot, we've got to give a nod to the original legendary Cajun lunch spot. This diner packs 'em in to close-pressed tables (not a lot of extra room for shopping bags or coats) and diner stools every day. Cajun selections are a little pricey, averaging between $8.50 and $9.95, but most devotees feel it's worth it.

Closed Sundays.

quick bites

Paris Pastries

2421 North Clark, (773) 296-2857

Similar to Le Paris Croissant, Paris Pastries is a small bakery with tempting desserts that also serves light bites, including quiches, French pizza, and potato soufflé ($2.45), hot sandwiches such as French grilled cheese ($4.75), and cold sandwiches such as saucisson and pâté with cornichon ($4.75). All sandwiches are served with chips and cornichon.

Open daily.

Provence Market

3232 Lake, Edens Plaza, Wilmette,
(847) 853-9155

Owned by the chef of Winnetka's Provence restaurant, Provence Market sells takeout that is "fresh, fast, and French." The market serves many of the restaurant's entrées for $6 to $11.75 a pound, and supplements those meals with salads, soups, sandwiches, and desserts. A perfect place for those who don't want to dine out every night. "Time is short, yet palates are demanding."

Open daily.

quick bites

Heaven Can't Wait

Join the Local Ragin' Cajuns at the new Heaven on Seven

Years ago, I went for lunch with a friend at the original Heaven on Seven, or the New Garland Coffee Shop as it was originally known. I still remember . . . It was a cold day, so we hiked a couple blocks through the pedway, the catacombs of Chicago, and made our way into a dingy, overheated elevator in the Garland Building. We exited on the seventh floor to a dingy, overheated coffee shop kind of joint (the kind with the long counter where your grandmother used to take you for a tuna sandwich and pie). We waited in a long line of overheated customers and then wedged ourselves into a small table, where we sat elbow-to-elbow, cheek-to-jowl with our dining neighbors. We all shoveled Cajun food. I've got to admit, the place did have some charm.

The way people raved about it, you'd think Heaven on Seven was a missing piece of the bayou that had floated conveniently into the Loop. The only problem was the place was rarely open for dinner. That was fine if you worked downtown and could squeeze out for lunch, but what about those fans of Louisiana fare who didn't work just a pedway away? Those who maybe didn't even work in the city? Tourists, whose visit to Chicago might only be completed by a bite of the Big Easy?

Well, for those who couldn't find their way to Wabash, the gates of heaven are now open at a new location in the mall at 600 North Michigan. Nestled in the back side of Eddie Bauer, underneath eight wide-body movie screens, is the new, hot place, the new **Heaven on Seven**, now open nightly for dinner.

My coworker Alexa and I decided to go check the place out at lunch. We joined the hoards of fans rampaging up the back escalator off of Rush Street. And there it was, heaven looking like a scene right out of an Anne Rice novel that had somehow been mixed up with a genteel suburban truck stop.

A window, graced with an iron trellis and shutters flung open, beckons coyly to the would-be ragin' Cajuns pouring off the escalator, "Y'all come right in now, hear." Unfortunately, heaven must wait, and so did we. After putting our name on the long list, we clutched our vibrator and waited for the electric hum that would alert us of our turn to step through the gates.

Once buzzed, we scurried past a wall-to-wall, floor-to-ceiling rack of hot sauce to the back room, which is graced with a stuffed, grinning gator (or is it a croc?) mounted above the diners. Chandeliers, supposedly reminiscent of a New Orleans ballroom but probably filched from a local funeral parlor, are draped with Mardi Gras beads.

We were escorted to our table, which was stocked with no less than 22 different bottles of hot sauce, making it a tight squeeze for a two-top. The bottled brew ranged from your standard Tabasco to more exotic stuff like "Vampire," "The Bat's Brew," the curious "Ass in the Tub," and our favorite (although Alexa thought it tasted kind of odd) the "Hot Bitch at the Beach," a product whose label touted, "She's all natural and all mighty hot n' delicious . . . she's got the hots for you!"

Woo doggy, we were hoping the food could live up to the condiments. We stoked our appetites with a couple of starters, although Alexa had to avoid the gumbo since she's allergic to shrimp. So

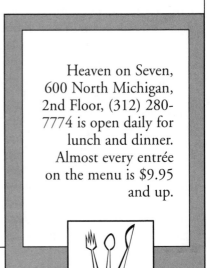

Heaven on Seven, 600 North Michigan, 2nd Floor, (312) 280-7774 is open daily for lunch and dinner. Almost every entrée on the menu is $9.95 and up.

many options, with openers like potato-crusted jalapeno peppers, sweet potato moss, fried Alabama rock shrimp, and andouille sausage sweet potato polenta, it was difficult to choose.

We skipped the "lagniappe" (a little something extra), sides like jalapeño cheddar corn muffins and parmesan-reggiano cheese grits, and moved straight to the main event. We agreed that the po'boy sandwiches weren't for us—soft shell crab, "angry" chicken, catfish—but at $9.95 a pop, nothing poor about them. We figured if we were going to spend $15 on lunch, we wanted a real meal.

I went for the "Southern classics" and got the Louisiana crab cakes, which were tender and tasty. Alexa chose from the linguinis and ordered the chicken voodoo, which we both agreed had rather a strange peanut-coconut flavor. Since I obviously got the better deal, she's going to order the Louisiana soul deluxe next time—a Southern sampler plate with Mardi Gras jambalaya, red beans and rice, and other good spicy stuff.

We resisted the blandishments of the various paraphernalia for sale—shirts, private-label hot sauce, etc.—and headed back to the office with a Cajun fried shrimp carryout for a coworker. As we drifted down the moving staircase, we were sure we heard a whisper from above "A bottle of heaven . . . you can take it with you . . . for $4.95."

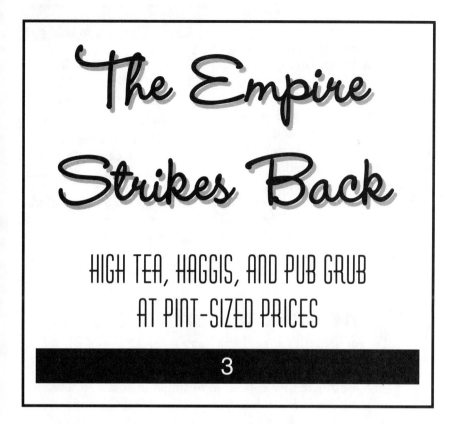

The Empire Strikes Back

HIGH TEA, HAGGIS, AND PUB GRUB AT PINT-SIZED PRICES

3

Even after having to play catch-up after their nearly century-late start, the British quickly made up for time lost to their continental cousins. Propelled by the voyages of Sir Francis Drake and, subsequently, the East India Company, the British managed to corner all the tea in China and had curried favor for the queen in India by the early eighteenth century. Even halfway around the world where they had kicked out the French, Dutch, and Native American Indians, the Red Coats were having their way in North America until they suddenly found the (tea) party over.

Don't tread on me . . . In spite of their ability to conquer and rule, the British were never really able to impose on the colonies one aspect of Britannia—traditional British cuisine. And, can you blame the colonials for resisting to the end? The British could take the furs of North America, the spices of the East, and diamonds of South Africa, but they couldn't force their new subjects to take bangers and mash, Welsh rarebit, or steak and kidney pie.

> "Take some more tea," the March Hare said to Alice, very earnestly.
>
> —***Alice's Adventures in Wonderland*, Lewis Carroll**

Not somebody to trifle with . . . Two hundred years later here in the heartland, Chicagoans continue their ancestors' resistance to Cornish pasties, black and white pudding, and parsnips and brussels sprouts. Even the few establishments in town that do specialize in authentic Irish, Scottish, and English dishes dilute their menus with American burgers, salads, and pastas, leaving a straight diet of beans on toast to mad dogs and Englishmen. But if you're set on pounding some mixed grill or corned beef and cabbage, opportunities do exist, although they are thankfully few and far between. God save the queen.

The Duke of Perth

2913 North Clark, (773) 477-1741

Chicago's premier Scottish pub with the Midwest's most extensive collection of single-malt scotch serves all-you-can-eat, beer-batter-dipped cod accompanied by peas and chips (that's fries to you colonials) for $6.95 on Wednesdays and Fridays from lunch until midnight. In addition to the ubiquitous batter-fried white fish, the Duke of Perth offers the delicacies of the Highlands, including the Scotch egg, a breaded sausage wrapped around a boiled egg with sweet chutney ($4.95), steak and kidney potpie ($7.25), shepherd's pie ($6.25), and sides of stovies, mashed potatoes, ($2.25). American-style burgers sport names dedicated to Scotch heroes with accompanying tributes, including the William Wallace cheeseburger ($5.95) for the brave heart who was "hanged, drawn, and quartered with his head then impaled on London Bridge." A patio with picnic tables is available during nice weather, and there's often live music on the weekends.

Open daily. Full bar. Patio dining. Live music.

The Red Lion

2446 North Lincoln, (773) 348-2695

Chicago's original English pub, the Red Lion derives its name from the heraldic device of Edward III, who ruled England in the mid–fourteenth century. And, the Red Lion serves a traditional English repast that has probably been around since then. You can start it all off with Welsh rarebit ($3.75) or beans on toast ($3.55). If you're looking for a lighter bite (does such a thing exist here?), you can move on to the pasties and pies—that would be Cornish pasties, shepherd's pie, and steak and kidney pie ($6.25–$6.50). For heartier fare, there's bangers and mash (sausages and potatoes, $5.95) and mixed grill (Canadian bacon, American "streaky" bacon, baked beans, mashed potatoes, and grilled tomato, $6.75). Finish it off with a proper English trifle and a Black and Tan.

Open daily. Full bar. Patio dining.

Abbey Pub

3420 West Grace, (773) 463-5808

Abbey Pub, one of the best-known Irish hangouts in town, offers both traditional Irish food and traditional Irish music. There are a lot of places around town where you can go see a hot, local band while you enjoy some standard bar food. But why subject yourself to greasy grill when you can savor mixed grill (Irish sausage, pudding, bacon, lamb chops, and fries for $8.95) along with some of the best shepherd's pie in town ($8.95) and other Irish delicacies and some traditional American favorites while you listen to that same band at Abbey Pub? At Abbey Pub, you can enjoy your imported Irish bacon and cabbage ($7.95) while you listen to the tunes of Irish bands on Wednesdays and Thursdays, folk, blues, or rock on Fridays and Saturdays, and a weekly Irish jam session on Sundays. Monday is the weekly barn dance, and Tuesday is an acoustic open stage. Cover varies at Abbey Pub, but is usually around $5. (For more information, see Abbey Pub in "Diversionary Dining.") Big screens in each room carry live broadcasts of Irish, English, and Scottish football—soccer for you colonials—all World Cup games, and rugby matches.

Open daily. Full bar.

Nevin's Pub

1450 Sherman, Evanston, (847) 869-0450

> "There are no strangers here. . . . Only friends who have not yet met."
>
> **—W. B. Yeats**

With Nevin's Pub, the owners of the Davis Street Fishmarket have attempted to bring the cheer of the traditional Irish pub to Evanston. It's also one of the few restaurants around that has actually dropped its prices in the past few years. "Pub Grub" offers the best of the Emerald Isle for $5.25 to $7.95, including corned beef and cabbage, garlic and pepper roasted pork loin, Dingle Bay sea cakes, shepherd's pie, Irish sausage rolls, and Irish lamb stew (available October 1 through April 30). Salads include smoked Irish salmon ($7.95), and fish and chips come in three different options. A ribeye is $7.95 and is served with baked beans and slaw or chips. Chips and gravy are available as a side, bread and butter pudding with whiskey vanilla sauce for dessert. Sunday afternoons, an Irish band jams Celtic favorites.

Open daily until 12:30 A.M. weeknights, 1:30 A.M. on weekends, and midnight on Sundays. Full bar.

The Hidden Shamrock

2723 North Halsted, (773) 883-0304

In between English football, international rugby, and live bands, you can order from one of the most extensive Irish-oriented menus in town. Along with the ever present shepherd's pie ($6.95), you can chow year-round—not just one day in March!—on beef stew ($6.50), bangers and mash (sausage, mashed potatoes, and baked beans, $5.75), Irish sausage rolls ($4.50), chicken curry ($5), and Irish fry, a traditional Irish breakfast with bacon, eggs, sausage, tomato, onion, mushrooms, and black and white pudding ($7.75) served all day. Top it all off with hot apple pie garnished with Irish custard. Slainte, laddie.

Open daily. Full bar. Live bands Thursday–Saturday.

The Outpost

3438 North Clark, (773) 244-1166

Harking back to the days when the memsahib wore white gloves, sipped afternoon tea, and bowled on the lawns of Raffles in Singapore, the Peninsula in Hong Kong, Rangoon, and Delhi, The Outpost pays noble tribute to the foods of the once far-flung British Empire. Designed to look somewhat like a wood-paneled library or smoking room at a men's club, The Outpost fuses flavors of the East and West. Pizzas are thin and crispy and enough for a meal; try the Thai pork with a black bean tahini sauce ($6.50) for an interesting combo. Salads are entrée size, with the spicy Mongolian shrimp on greens with black sesame seed dressing ($5.75) being a tasty light bite. Many of the entrées are expensive, but the woolloomoollo prawn ravioli in a pesto cream sauce ($10) is a good option, as are the penne pasta and Italian sausage marinara with shiitake mushrooms ($9.50) and the vegetables sautéed in sesame oil and teriyaki glaze, which can be served with grilled chicken, shrimp, or beef ($7.75–$8.75). Over twenty wines of the world are available by the glass.

Closed Mondays. Full bar. Sidewalk seating. Sunday brunch.

High *Tea*

INNOVATIVE EATERIES FOR THE FINANCIALLY FINICKY PALATE

Tea for two and two for tea . . . Unfortunately these days in Chicago, finger sandwiches, dainty pastries, and the other accoutrements of high tea run a lot more than $2. In fact, you have to leave the confines of the city to find a deal on high tea. The Mad Hatter tea at **Seasons of Long Grove**, 314 Old McHenry, Long Grove, (847) 634-9150, makes the commute worthwhile, though. *Tea*totalers don beribboned and flowered hats from a selection provided and then settle down for finger sandwiches, scones, biscuits, and pastries—all for $10 from 2:30 to 4:00 P.M., Monday through Saturday. It's a popular spot for young girls' birthday parties; Seasons even serves a children's tea made with berries, raisins, hibiscus, and honey.

In the city, only the **Inter-Continental Hotel**, where tea with all the fixin's is served daily for $11.75, comes close to making the price cut. If you're ready to break the budget, other teas can be found every day at:

The Drake Hotel $15.50/$21.95 with champagne/$8.95 for kids

The Fairmont Hotel $15/$19.50 with champagne/$22.50 with sherry

The Four Seasons Hotel $16.50—everyday except Sunday

The Ritz-Carlton Hotel $16.50/$20.75 with sherry/$23.75 with champagne

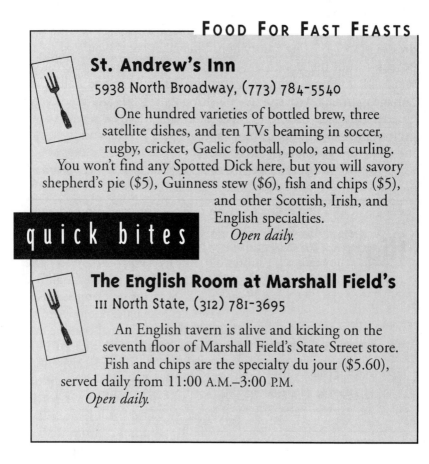

Food For Fast Feasts

quick bites

St. Andrew's Inn

5938 North Broadway, (773) 784-5540

One hundred varieties of bottled brew, three satellite dishes, and ten TVs beaming in soccer, rugby, cricket, Gaelic football, polo, and curling. You won't find any Spotted Dick here, but you will savory shepherd's pie ($5), Guinness stew ($6), fish and chips ($5), and other Scottish, Irish, and English specialties.

Open daily.

The English Room at Marshall Field's

111 North State, (312) 781-3695

An English tavern is alive and kicking on the seventh floor of Marshall Field's State Street store. Fish and chips are the specialty du jour ($5.60), served daily from 11:00 A.M.–3:00 P.M.

Open daily.

The Primavera Bar at the Fairmont Hotel

200 North Columbus, (312) 565-8000

The only place in Chicago that honors the old pub tradition of serving "yards" of beer, cold ones are literally served in yard-long glass tubes with a bulb on the end. Beers come in a variety of drafts from Bud to Guinness. A yard is $12 and a half yard is $7.

quick bites

Open Daily.

Fado

Bagpipe proficiency not required at Celtic eatery

I let off some steam every weekend in a coed soccer league. Sprinting up and down the field, or the court if it's winter, while skilled players, most of whom are a decade younger than me, dribble circles around me. So I may not be a great player, but I run hard.

I met Fergal through soccer. A young computer programmer, he came to Chicago from Ireland in the late eighties, and we hooked up when he was looking for a team. After eight years, Fergal went back to Ireland last fall. We're going to miss him on defense.

Fergal was a great source on what's "real" Irish in Chicago. Not much passed muster with Fergal. Abbey Pub and a couple other little places. So I'm wondering what Fergal would have thought of Fado.

Fado is astutely located in River North in an area that's visited by almost every traveler to our fair city, next to the Rock 'n Roll McDonalds and under the benign gaze of two Chicago landmarks, the Rainforest Café's giant tree frog and the Hard Rock's air guitar. To my pleasant surprise, no immense leprechauns or giant shamrocks loomed over the front door.

It was a little hokey, but Fado still seemed to be executed with an effort at good taste. The outside is designed to look like two traditional storefronts, one for "McNally & Sons" and the other "Ceol Agus Craic," which translates roughly as "music and fun."

The inside showcases the historical gathering places of the Irish people. *Fado* means "long ago" in Gaelic Irish, and the eatery has been decorated to illustrate "the story of Ireland's rich and celebrated pub culture."

Six different historical settings are featured. Upon entry, you see the massive wood tables and chairs of the fifth and sixth century Celtic chieftain. A stone dolmen, a monument marking the burial grounds of kings, wraps itself around this area of the bar, and crafted metals depict the work of Celtic blacksmiths who beat iron and bronze into weapons for the hunters and warriors.

You walk past a lattice screen on the bar that is reminiscent of the huts inhabited by workers in Ireland's cottage industries. This section is peppered with antiquated manufacturing devices, including looms, spinning wheels, a butter churner, and even a water pump. The floor becomes cobblestone and timber, and diners sit under an open loft.

The final first floor area is the post office/shop pub of the turn of the century, where villagers

Fado, 100 W. Grand, (312) 836-0066, is open daily for lunch and dinner. Meals are priced $7.25 to $16.95. Irish bands play Monday and Tuesday nights.

met to provision and gossip among the clutter of merchandise. From there it's a trip upstairs, passing under a currach fishing boat suspended from the ceiling to the world of St. Brendan's monks on the mezzanine, marked by a stone-carved cross and altar table and then up another flight to the "rural country cottage pub."

The country pub highlights the cozy world of the small pub proprietor, with more stone and timber materials and a raised floor in one corner for entertainment. It's a contrast to Fado's last setting of the Dublin Victorian pub, with its velvet curtains, stained glass, beveled mirrors, and brass.

Much of the interior decorating is done with "authentic" materials, like the 100-year-old bar in the Victorian pub that was shipped in forty pieces from Dublin and reassembled at Clark and Grand. The only incongruous note is the stools. Half the seats in Fado seem to be two-foot high stools. That may be authentic, but I'd find it uncomfortable hanging out all night with my mates at the pub squatting, frankly, on one of those, albeit nicely padded, stools.

The menu runs the gamut of classic Irish pub grub. Potato and leek soup is served daily, and four kinds of traditional Irish boxtys, Irish potato pancakes stuffed with corned beef, salmon with tomatoes and cream cheese, or other fixings, are also available.

My dining companion Alexa and I passed on the Irish-style bacon and cabbage, the Irish stew, the chicken cottage pie, and the all-day Irish breakfast in favor of the Guinness beer-battered fish and chips and the shepherd's pie. Alexa paddled through half of her currach of shepherd's pie before she had to pack up the rest to go, and I also ran out of gas on all of those tasty batter-dipped chips. The warm root vegetable mélange on the side was a nice touch that I managed to finish off.

Unfortunately, we ran out of room before we could tackle the brown bread ice cream or the whiskey trifle. We're going back for the fresh Galway Bay–style mussels, some dessert, and more Guinness. Slainte.

East of Eaten

A TASTE OF EASTERN EUROPE IN THE HEART OF THE MIDWEST

4

"The cliché endures: Chicago really is a city of neighborhoods—a vast mosaic of separate entities, each with its own history, personality, and particular landmarks and institutions. The neighborhoods originated most often as gleams in the eyes of ambitious land developers or as ethnic enclaves, which grew into towns and were in turn swallowed up by the swelling, 19th-century city. The result was and continues to be a diverse and colorful sprawl of traditional and newly hybrid communities and cultures.

While the idea of 'neighborhood' conjures up notions of time standing still in a place where 'everybody knows your name,' the truth is somewhere between that bucolic image and utter chaos. Chicago's neighborhoods have been most strongly characterized by two forces: people moving in and people moving out."

—Sweet Home Chicago

> "Whatever you do, make it taste Polish. Put cabbage in."
>
> —***Household Management,***
> **Florence Nesbitt**

Like the sausages that have so come to symbolize this city's contribution to our national cuisine, starting in the nineteenth century, Chicago accepted waves of Eastern European immigrants seeking the American dream and stuffed them and their native customs and spices into a city that bulged under the restraints of its political and big business casings. Fleeing repressive imperial regimes, the people of Eastern Europe poured into Chicago and ended up supporting the local family dynasties—the hog butchers for the world, the tool makers, the stackers of wheat, the players with railroads, and the nation's freight handlers of Carl Sandburg's "Chicago."

Leaving behind the iron fist of the Austrian-Hungarian Hapsburg Empire, the Czechs, or Bohemians as they were known in Chicago (really Moravians, Slovaks, and Ruthenians, in addition to the Bohemians), were one of the first groups to migrate en masse in 1848 after the failure of a nationalistic uprising. The Czechs were some of the most literate and highly skilled Europeans to be processed through Castle Garden and Ellis Island, and they left their mark on Chicago. By the 1870s, the Czechs had established the Pilsen enclave on Blue Island Avenue between 16th and 22nd Streets and supplied workers to the McCormick Reaper Works and the Chicago, Burlington, and Quincy railroads. Anton Cermak, who was born in Prague but relocated to the Lawndale neighborhood, crushed the gangsters who were controlling local government during Prohibition and established Chicago's Democratic Machine.

Other Eastern Europeans made a substantial impact on the city's development. Antanas Kaztauskis, a Lithuanian èmigrè, was one of the many residents of Back-of-the-Yards working in Packingtown. His 1904 article, "From Lithuania to the Chicago Stockyards—An Autobiography," inspired a young journalist named Upton Sinclair to go undercover for a year to produce *The Jungle*, an exposé on Chicago's meatpacking industry that hit the nation squarely in the stomach. Today's ultra-hip Ukrainian Village was established by a wave of Ukrainian immigrants fleeing imperial Czarist Russia prior to World War I. These Ukrainians brought with them both the Greek Catholic church and the traditional foods of Kiev.

By 1920, the Polish community had become the largest foreign-born immigrant group in Chicago, with an estimated 31 percent of all European Poles becoming American citizens in the 1920s. Originally settling in small pockets on the Southside and around the intersection of Division, Milwaukee, and Ashland, the Polish community later moved north on Milwaukee to Avondale, the forty-first ward and home of longtime alderman, Roman Pucinski. You don't have to be the Pope to enjoy a plate full of pierogis and some of the cheapest and most extensive all-you-can-eat buffets around. A veritable Polish pig-out, a Baltic banquet, the Danubian dinner . . . there are all kind of options around town to Serb you right if Yugo out and find them—Czech one out!

Andrzej Grill

1022 North Western, (773) 489-3566

Found on the edge of the Ukrainian Village and once cited in a now moribund Wicker Park–based magazine by Bruce, owner of the Empty Bottle club, as "on the verge" and "Polish with attitude," Andrzej Grill has figured out that you can successfully capitalize on a seedy location as long as you serve huge, tasty meals for only $3.50 for lunches and $5.50 for dinners. A tiny place with exactly four small tables, four chairs, and three video arcade machines, Andrzej lists a large number of selections for either "lunches" or "dinners" on handwritten cards hanging in vertical rows on the wall. A lunch for three-and-a-half bits gets you a dozen pierogis smothered in fried onions (optional) and sour cream. Pierogis come in cheese and potato, meat, sauerkraut, plum, or blueberry. Dinners include potato pancakes, white sausage, white fish, chicken livers, and various chicken or pork dishes. For a light meal, try one of the many soups, including tripe stew, bean, potato, sauerkraut, and three kinds of borscht—Ukrainian, white, or red—with meat croquettes. In a hurry? Call ahead, and it'll be hot and waiting. As the grill advertises, "Be you waiting too long, call first."

Open daily. No alcohol.

Two other good bets for pierogis are **Caesar's Polish Deli,** 901 North Damen, (773) 486-6190, and **Halinas European Restaurant and Deli,** 6714–6718 West Belmont, (773) 685-8569. In business for over a half a century, Caesar's is a Polish grocery with a couple small tables and a refrigerator case full of twelve different kinds of pierogis (along with fifteen different kinds of homemade soups). Halinas serves pierogis in the standard cheese, meat, and potato versions, along with sauerkraut and plum, for $3.99 a pound.

Healthy Food

3236 South Halsted, (773) 326-2724

Lithuanians first came to Chicago in the late nineteenth century and settled themselves into the Bridgeport and Brighton Park neighborhoods located south and west of the Union Stockyards, or the area known as Back-of-the-Yards. Today, most of Chicago's Lithuanian community is centered around 69th (Lithuanian Court Plaza) and 71st between California and Western in Marquette Park, the last of the pre–World War II neighborhoods to evolve out of the Union Stockyards and Chicago's thriving meatpacking industry. Fortunately for Northsiders like me, you don't have to hike all the way down to 71st to enjoy some great Lithuanian eats. Located just west of the Comiskey Park/Bridgeport neighborhood is Healthy Food, where you can get a taste of Lithuania without having to drive all the way down to the current center of Lithuanian culture. Open since 1938 and the oldest Lithuanian restaurant in the city, Healthy Food serves up bounteous, filling portions of artery-clogging Lithuanian and Eastern European specialties seven days a week for prices that haven't been adjusted for inflation. Lithuanian specials include blynai, Lithuanian pancakes with a dozen different kinds of fillings ($4.95) including vsysniu (sour cherry) and spanguoliu (cranberry); koldunai, boiled meat or cheese dumplings served with sour cream and bacon ($5.50); kugelis, Lithuanian potato pudding ($5.50); and roast half duck ($8.95). Meals are accompanied by freshly baked dark Lithuanian bread. All these Lithuanian favorites include dessert—a choice of Jell-O with a swirl of whipped cream or kolacky, traditional fruit-filled pastries.

Open daily. No alcohol.

Other good Lithuanian bets that are more of a hike south include:

Neringa Restaurant 2632 West 71st, (773) 476-9026
Nida Delicatessen and Restaurant 2617 West 71st,

(773) 476-7675

Little Bucharest

3001 North Ashland, (773) 929-8640

Reputed to have been the home away from home for the Bulgarian World Cup team during their sojourn in Chicago, Little Bucharest offers a convenient taste of Eastern Europe, whether you're coming all the way from the Balkans or just five minutes from your Lakeview abode. Although a bit on the expensive side, Little Bucharest offers a huge menu that's guaranteed to deliver both a Romanian holiday and leftovers to anyone who stops in for the huge entrées and nightly accordion music. Although chicken, veal, sausage, pork, beef, and lamb dishes, along with goose and rabbit, are available in abundance, those who want something lighter will like the stuffed vegetables—green peppers, cabbage, eggplant (all $8.95) or the Romanian stuffed red peppers ($9.95). All "veggie" dishes are stuffed with a ground meat combination—vegetarians need not apply here. Most entrées are served with spaetzele, those tasty little dumplings. Daily specials are a great deal; Thursday night is mititei night ($6.95), small Romanian sausages. Don't miss Taste of Bucharest, held every September and seemingly attended by Chicago's entire Romanian population. Take advantage of the free limo service.

Open daily. Full bar. Sidewalk seating. "Taste" festival every September.

The Bosnia Restaurant

2122 West Lawrence, (773) 275-4100

Formerly the Bosnian Social Club, the Bosnia Restaurant caters to expats who gather to watch soccer and share their community, including a familiar cuisine that is a mixture of the foods served by neighbors in Hungary, Germany, Romania, Serbia, and the Middle East without any pork or alcohol due to the influence of Islam. The national dish is cevapi lepinja, a charbroiled hamburger made from ground lamb and beef sausages served on soft frisbee-sized, English muffin–like lepinja bread. A number of Bosnian calzone-like phyllo turnovers are also available, including burek (meat pie), sirnica (cream cheese), and zeljanica (spinach). In addition, the menu includes schnitzels, goulash, and traunichi sir, tart goat cheese designed to be eaten with bread or cabbages and peppers. Portions are huge, and no entrée costs more than $8.

Open daily. No alcohol.

Café Croatia

5726 North Western, (773) 276-2842

Marked by a cozy pink sign highlighting a brightly lit patio on north Western Avenue, Café Croatia serves a broad selection of Croatian specialties in the atmosphere of a European ski haus. The waiters all sport colorful, embroidered vests and will be more than happy to serve you one of the many entrées priced $8.95 and up. Along with the ubiquitous cervapcici, Café Croatia has cufte, skewered ground meat, and musaka, a regional version of moussaka made with mushrooms, noodles, and feta. Specialties from the Dalmation coastal region and Slovenia are also featured, and many of the dishes are flavored with sauerkraut and/or sour cream.

Closed Monday. Full bar. Sidewalk seating.

Argo, Inc. Georgian Bakery

2812 West Devon, (773) 764-6322

Opened in early 1997 by a former surgeon who emigrated to the United States, Argo is located on a stretch of Devon populated with shops serving Hasidic Jews, Russians, and other Eastern Europeans. Argo is a small storefront that's made up of one open room dominated by a large brick kiln-like oven in the middle where two kinds of Georgian breads—long, thin shotis ($1.09) and round breads ($1.49), along with puffed round cheese-filled hachapuris ($1.49)—are baked. Patrons, who can sit at two small tables and sip strong coffee, can watch the dough being kneaded and prepared for the depths of the beehive-shaped oven.

Closed Wednesdays.

Some of *Cheap Chow Chicago*'s other favorite feasts from the East featured in other chapters:

Old Warsaw
4750 North Harlem, (708) 867-4500

The Red Apple/Czerwone Jabluszko
3121–23 North Milwaukee, (708) 488-5781

Both restaurants boast huge, Polish, all-you-can-eat buffets. The Red Apple also features a deli. (For more details see "Chowing Down")
Open Daily

quick bites

Simplon-Orient Express

4520 North Lincoln, (773) 275-5522.
From Paris to Istanbul, meals tracking the Eastern route of the fabled Orient Express. (All aboard in "Taste of Lincoln Avenue.")
Open daily.

Beet Generation

Loosen up the borscht belt in Ukrainian Village

United by Milwaukee Avenue, the Ukrainian Village and other neighborhoods to the north have been the settling grounds for Eastern European immigrants for over a century. At one point, the intersection of Division, Ashland, and Milwaukee was the locus of a Polish community larger than any other gathering of Poles outside of Poland. While the Poles have moved north and west, and the evidence of their old neighborhood has been practically eradicated by the current owners, the original Ukrainian community, located roughly between Hoyne and Western on Chicago, fights to retain its identity.

Churches are the enduring landmarks of the Ukrainian Village. Dedicated in 1915, Saint Nicholas Ukrainian Catholic Cathedral at Oakley and Rice was modeled on the Basilica of Saint Sophia in Kiev (although only 13 of the original's 32 copper-encased domes were incorporated into the Chicago version). When Saint Nicholas switched to the Gregorian calendar in 1973, a split developed between the older members of the community and newer, more conservative immigrants. Because of the split, the traditional Saints Volodymyr and Olha Ukrainian Orthodox Cathedral (Oakley and Superior) with its gilded Byzantine domes and colorful, two-story-high mural on its facade was formed to maintain the older Julian calendar.

An even more striking edifice is Louis Sullivan's Holy Trinity Orthodox Cathedral (Leavitt and Haddon). Built in 1901, the church was patterned loosely on wooden octagon-on-a-square churches of the old country and was designed to blend mysticism and functionalism.

Unfortunately, the area's restaurants, important gathering points themselves, have had less staying power than the houses of worship. Galans, arguably the city's best-known Ukrainian restaurant, closed and is now in the process of going French country, leaving slim Ukrainian pickings on Chicago Avenue.

Sak's Ukrainian Village Restaurant is one of the few remaining proprietors of Old World Ukrainian cuisine.

The Ukraine, the region that was headed by the ancient trading capitol of Kiev and that adjoins Romania and Poland, was the breadbasket of the old Russian empire; it produced 25 percent of the staples consumed in the old Soviet Union, primarily wheat but also corn, rice, barley, potatoes, beets, and vegetables. The regional cuisine, incorporating a crazy quilt of ethnic flavors including Greek, Byzantine, Asiatic, Scandinavian, Turkish, and Germanic, is a substantial cuisine, a doughy, gamey, meaty, rooty, smoky menu—part comfort food, part indulgence. Overall, a nightmare for your cardiac system.

Its entrance way marked by a curvy wood retro bar back lit in red, Sak's restaurant area is accented with red—red vinyl booths, red formica tile, and red babushka-like table cloths covered with clear plastic, which seems appropriate, since Sak's serves, reputedly, the best borscht in town, along with some hefty platters of other Ukrainian dishes.

All dinners come with soup, salad, potato, and dessert. Entrée choices range from kapusta and kobassa (sauerkraut with Ukrainian sausage), to helubtsy (cabbage rolls with meat and rice) in either a mushroom gravy or tomato sauce, to plyatsky (potato pancakes). Varenyky, Ukrainian dumplings similar to pierogis, are stuffed with meat, cheese, sauerkraut, or potatoes and smothered in either mushroom gravy or hot butter with bacon bits. Chicken Kiev, schnitzel, and even hamburgers are available for the less adventurous. If you can't make up your mind, have the "family

Sak's Ukrainian Village Restaurant, 2301 West Chicago, (773) 278-4445, and Ann's Bakery, 2158 West Chicago, (773) 384-5562, are both open daily. Meals at Sak's range $5.95 to $8.95. Old Lviv, 2228 West Chicago, (773) 772-7250, is closed Mondays.

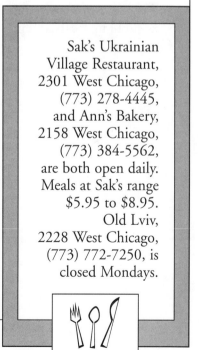

feast," which for $8.95 a person seems to include a taste of almost everything on the menu. Finish off your dinner with homemade apple pie, which at Sak's is more similar to a square, multilayer apple torte than it is to the American version. Cheese-filled dessert crêpes dolloped with whipped or sour cream are also a good bet if you've got any room left. Rinse it all down with a cup of Ukrainian coffee, which is enhanced with something special from the bar.

If you just want to get a quick and easy intro to the Ukrainian menu, try **Old Lviv Ukrainian Food Restaurant**. A small storefront with a bar and a couple tables, Old Lviv has a daily buffet for $5.99 that features nearly a dozen different hot dishes, three soups, and several salads. Varenyky can be ordered alone for $3. Soup is also served à la carte, and the selection will probably include borscht, cabbage, or chicken noodle.

Just a little east down the street, **Ann's Bakery** is another surviving neighborhood institution specializing in "European" rye bread, Ukrainian twist bread, fine pastries, and wedding cakes. Also a small grocery store with a small area set aside with tables and chairs, Ann's invites locals to hang out in the small café area, nibbling treats and gossiping in the language of the Cossacks.

Curry, Be Happy

An Affordable Passage to India

5

The Indian subcontinent. A huge kite-shaped peninsula stretching from the Himalayan and Hindu Kush Mountains, through fertile plains and stark deserts, down to steamy coastal jungles. As early as 2,000 B.C., the Indus River valley was home to a flourishing community. Since then, waves of invaders and conquerors have moved through the land, resulting in a broad diversity of cultures, languages, religions, and food. The food of the Muslims and Hindus of Kashmir and Bengal is typified by seafood and vegetarian dishes; the Northern Tibetan Buddhists of the Darjeeling tea region specialize in stir frys and plain and stuffed breads; the merchant Jews of Calcutta introduced Middle Eastern dishes; and the orthodox Jains, who wear face masks to prevent the accidental inhalation of tiny life forms, took vegetarianism to new heights.

As in the United States, a wide range of climatic conditions influenced the basic development of India's various regional cuisines. Dishes from southern and eastern India are almost always supplemented by rice, which thrives in these areas of heavy rainfall. Fried and stuffed breads are staples in the dryer north where wheat and barley can be grown. Coastal regions serve a variety of fish, seafood, and tropical fruits; inland, fruits such as apples, peaches, apricots, and strawberries are common.

> "How I should like to visit India!"
>
> ***—Vanity Fair,* William Makepeace Thackeray**

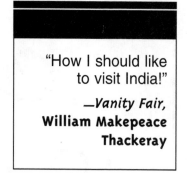

A common thread among these various subcontinental menus is an abundance of spices. Indian food, regardless of regional origin, is characterized by rich, complex spices, although not always hot ones. Chilies, the heat in many Indian dishes, are actually native to the Americas and were not introduced into India until the sixteenth century when they were brought in by Portuguese traders. Spices, long valued for their medicinal and preservative qualities along with their role as seasonings, have made a major contribution to both Indian and world history. In the days of King Solomon, India's Malabar Coast was a major trading center for spices and other luxuries. The Phoenicians, Greeks, Romans, and Chinese all found their way along the trade routes to India. It was the lure of the spice trade that gave rise to the Age of Exploration and Columbus and the other adventurers who braved falling off the edge of the world for the riches of India.

Like many other Asian groups, Indians originally came to Chicago in search of education and then stayed. Today the West Ridge neighborhood—a mile stretch along Devon Avenue—features silk and saris, 22-karat gold jewelry, and videotape copying. This is the hub of the city's Indian community of some seventy thousand Indian and Pakistani residents, making Chicago one of the two biggest concentrations of Indians in the country (New York has the other). On weekends, in particular, Devon Avenue is packed with locals hungry for both shopping bargains and traditional food. Most of the restaurants feature Northern Indian, Mughal-influenced fare (the Mongols who conquered much of the subcontinent in the sixteenth century were Muslim, and, therefore, ate meat), which many would assert is to true Indian cuisine what chop suey is to Chinese. Similar to Chinese communities that began serving Szechuan, Hunanese, and other alternatives to Cantonese once that cuisine became common and palates became educated, Indian restaurants are beginning to branch out and feature other regional specialties and many vegetarian dishes. So, start with tandoori and move on from there. Put some spice in your life.

Curry is a British term derived from the Tamil term *kari* meaning "sauce." Ethnic Indians do not use the term at all, nor do they use commercial curry powders, which are blends of several spices including coriander, cumin, red peppers, turmeric, and fenugreek. Instead, they make their own fresh blends called *masalas.*

Gandhi *Marg*

Devon between Kedzie and Ridge

INNOVATIVE EATERIES FOR THE FINANCIALLY FINICKY PALATE

Anchored at the intersection of Devon and Western is a nearly mile-long stretch of sari stores, jewelry shops, electronics and appliance outlets, and eateries specializing in $6.95 all-you-can-eat lunch buffets (with dinner often being available for a few dollars more) featuring chicken and lamb curries, palak or mutter paneer (homemade cheese with spinach or peas), naan (tandoori oven bread made with white flour), dal (thick porridge), salads, chutneys, and sweet desserts.

Welcome to India and the numerous restaurants that will try to curry favor with you. Anchoring the strip is the elaborate **Viceroy of India Restaurant,** 2516 West Devon, (773) 743-4100, one of the older restaurants in the area. Viceroy has a cheap lunch buffet, but is probably not cheap chow for dinner. Try one of the three daily chef's specials for a good intro to Indian food. Although its decor looks Italian, **Kanval Palace**, 2501 West Devon, (773) 761-7270, specializes in both Indian and Pakistani dishes. Entrées run $5.50 and up. The charga chicken, a whole chicken cooked with mango butter and spices, is the specialty of the house. One of the best all-you-can-eat dinner buffets in town ($8) is found at **Sher-A-Punjab**, 2510 West Devon, (773) 973-4000, and features naan along with paratha, roti (whole wheat version of naan), and other breads. **Dasaprakash,** 2511 West Devon, (773) 465-DASA, part of a family chain of restaurants in a half dozen locations throughout India and one in Dubai, specializes in Southern Indian Cuisine, but the street's king of Southern cooking is **Udupi Palace,** 2543 West Devon, (773)-338-2152, which specializes in "pure vegetarian" Southern Indian dishes. Try the curry with spicy okra, Madras-style cashew pakoras (savory vegetable fritters), dosai (crêpes made from rice, wheat, or lentils), or uthappam, thicker pancakes. Entrées are garnished with sauces, chutneys, and sambar. A more recent entrant into the Devon scene, **India House,** 2548 West Devon, (773) 338-2929, brings some interesting twists to the menu. "Kadhai" dishes ($6.95–$9.25) are prepared in a khadhai, an iron wok, and served in a mini copper wok. Other dishes are prepared on a tawa, an iron plate griddle. Tawa options come in lamb and various other organ meats. Try one of the twenty different versions of tandoori ($4.25–$11.25). Wash it all down with a mango shake. **Ghandi India**, 2601 West Devon, (773) 761-8714, the first Indian restaurant opened on Devon, features both Northern and Southern dishes cooked in the tandoori (clay oven) style. Ghandi has a large menu of entrées priced from $4 to $9. Desserts include payasam, thin noodles cooked in milk and honey with nuts and dried fruit. **Natraj Restaurant,** 2240 West Devon, (773) 274-1300, also specializes in Southern dishes. The Krishna Yoga Foundation meets here on Sundays. Buffet dinners are available on Thursday nights. If you want to bring some of this tasty stuff home, stop in one of the **Patel Brothers Groceries,** 2600 West Devon, (773) 764-1857 or 2542 West Devon, (773) 764-1853, after you're done eating and stock up on spices and basmati rice.

Star of India

3204 North Sheffield, (773) 525-2100

If you don't feel like hauling all the way up to Western and Devon, head for Belmont and Sheffield, which is the locus of a mini Indian restaurant community. The secret at Star of India is to go with a friend and order one of the three combination plates that will allow you a good graze through the menu. The baadshah (king) platter includes tandoori chicken, seekh kabab (lamb), chicken tikka, rogan josh (lamb curry), naan, rice, mixed vegetables, dalmakhni, and desserts for $12.95. The dil bahar platter adds fish tikka and a couple of other dishes to the baadshah platter. The begum (queen) platter offers a taste of seven vegetarian dishes, naan, and dessert for $11.95. Once you figure out what you like, you can go back and order each entrée on its own and really dive in.

Open daily. BYOB.

Standard India Restaurant

917 West Belmont, (773) 929-1123

The second of the Lakeview trio, Standard India has been around for over ten years. A side of naan is $.95 here, compared to about $2 and up everywhere else. Entrées range from $9.95 for the tandoori mixed grill down to $2.95 for some of the vegetarian dishes. The assorted appetizer platter, with samosa (triangular-stuffed pastries), pakoras, kabab, aloo-tikki (potato patties stuffed with lentils, peas, and herbs), chicken tikka papadum, and sweet and mint chutneys is a good way to start for $5.75. A buffet lunch is available on the weekends, while a vegetarian dinner buffet is spread Tuesday and Thursday evenings. Both are only $7.95.

Open daily. BYOB.

Raj Darber

2660 North Halsted, (773) 348-1010

If spartan ethnic storefronts make you nervous, Raj Darber, with its table cloths and elegant dining room, is the place for you. Tandoori chicken ($7.95) is well seasoned and juicy. Several biryani dishes, rice dishes made with basmati rice grown in the foothills of the Himalayas, are also a good bet. A number of vegetarian dishes, including several paneer (homemade cheese) dishes usually served with peas or spinach, are also available. All entrées are served with a side of basmati rice pilaf and a potato dish. Oven-baked breads are á la carte. Finish off your dinner with a serving of kheer ($2.95), rice pudding with pistachios.

Open daily. Full bar.

Zaiqa Indian Restaurant

858 North Orleans, (312) 280-6807

Zaiqa is the original eatery in the Orleans/Division area offering food from the subcontinent to legions of northern Indian and Pakistani cab drivers (a mosque is nearby). The restaurant is a spare storefront with an adjoining pool room and half the off-duty taxis in Chicago parked in the dirt lot next door. Zaiqa offers maybe a dozen Indian and Pakistani dishes on handwritten menus. Grab a spicy vegetarian plate and then grab a cab (if you can tear one of these guys away from the pool table).

Open daily.

Tiffin

2536 West Devon, (773) 338-2143

Tiffin, which means a light midday meal, stands out on Devon with its fancy decor and its "frontier" cuisine. The restaurant, with its circular interior and hollowed out "lid," is shaped like one of the stacked metal dishes that tiffinwallahs use to carry through the streets of Bombay at noon for lunch. Tiffin serves dishes from the various borders of the subcontinent, including Afghani chole peshaware ($6.50), a chickpea and potato combination; Southern Indian paper masala dosai ($7.50), rice crêpes filled with spicy onions and potatoes served with sambar and coconut chutney; Northern Indian Mughal specialty murg shai korma ($8.50), chicken pieces simmered with almonds in a cream sauce; hot and sour Goan lamb vindaloor ($8.95), a west coast specialty favored in the former Portuguese territory of Goa and in Bombay; and Kashmiri rogan josh from the northwest ($8.95), lamb pieces cooked in Kashmiri masala with saffron and yogurt, among others. While standing in line for the $6.95 buffet, you can watch a chef wrapping frisbee-shaped pieces of dough around his "pillow" and dropping them on the cook fires to make naan.

Open daily. Full bar.

Sultan Palace

6345 North Western, (773) 764-8400/5588

I was told once by a cab driver that Sultan Palace is the best Pakistani restaurant in Chicago. Marked by its gilded gold dome towering over Western Avenue, the family-owned Sultan Palace strives to recreate the atmosphere and the food of the Mughal emporers. One wall sports a specially commissioned mural of the Taj Mahal, which was built by the emporer Sultan Shah Jahan in 1721 when Pakistan and India were united under Muslim rule. The china, silverware, and wall rugs are all handmade in Pakistan and replicas of the Sultan Shah Jahan's own kitchenware. You can use these trappings of royalty to eat a variety of Mughlai vegetarian entrees priced $5.95 to $7.95 and tandoori, starting at $6.95. The restaurant serves only Zabiha meat, which I'm told is the equivalent of kosher meat for Muslims.

Open daily. No alcohol.

Food For Fast Feasts

Moti Mahal

2525 West Devon, (773) 262-2080

The original Lakeview location is covered in "Bagging It" For those who like to sample, good assorted platters are available here.

Open Daily.

Gaylord India

678 North Clark, (773) 664-1700

If you can't even make it up to Lakeview, but you're still craving tandoori and not at the prices charged by Bukhara or Klay Oven, head for Gaylord India. Some good standard Northern Indian dishes are available in a daily $7.95 lunch buffet for River North/Michigan Avenue–area yuppies. Gaylord India also has tasty kulfi (Indian ice cream).

quick bites

Tibet Café

Gourmet enlightenment attained at Asian restaurant

After numerous incursions, the Chinese invaded and occupied Tibet for good in 1959. The subsequent revolt of the Tibetans in the same year resulted in the Dalai Lama fleeing along with thousands of Tibetan refugees across the Himalayas to India, Nepal, and Bhutan. Since that time, Tibetans claim that over 1.2 million Tibetans have perished, more than 6,000 Buddhist monasteries have been demolished while irreplaceable ancient treasures have been pillaged, and over 110,000 have chosen to live in exile as so many Chinese have moved into Tibet that Tibetans have become a minority in their own mountains.

In spite of the country's troubles, Losar, the Tibetan New Year, is celebrated the last day of the year through the third day of the Tibetan calendar (February or March) with prayer flags flying over homes and incense wafting in the air. I decided to prep for the festivities by checking out Tibet Café. I thought it would be particularly appropriate to visit the restaurant with my friend Sue, a slim and fit individual who trains to climb mountains in her spare time. Leaving her clamp-ons behind, Sue and I trekked to Sheridan and Irving Park, currently a regular United Nations of the Chicago restaurant scene with Tibet Café in a storefront lineup that includes Nigerian and Moroccan eateries along with numerous Hispanic establishments.

Sonam Dhargye and Kalsang Dhonoup, two former Tibetan lamas, came to the United States in 1992 and founded the Tibet Café with a partner in 1996. Kalsang, the Café's chef, had sewn monks' robes back in the Gyoyo Monastery, and he used his talents to turn brightly colored, gilded sari fabrics into seat cushions and decorations that festoon the blond wood-paneled restaurant. The walls are also decorated with butter sculptures, creamy swirls of color traditionally made with yak butter and tsampa (roasted barley flour) that depict deities and Buddhist scenes that have been sculpted by Sonam, the host, who mastered the uniquely Tibetan art that serves as a form of prayer in the monastery. Prayer flags and, in a place of honor, a smiling picture of the Dalai Lama complete the interior.

We kicked off our meal with a pot of boe cha, traditional Tibetan tea churned with light salt, butter, and milk. I assume the natives get the real stuff with dairy products from the trusty yak, but our tea au lait, although delicately salty, seemed to be safely pasteurized and was interestingly tasty. We suffered no ill effects and later ordered another round.

Tibetan dishes borrow elements from the country's neighbors, particularly India and China, but relative to some of the other Asian palates, Tibetan seems to be a gentle cuisine served with salad, rice, or pita bread, with an abundance of vegetarian dishes. Spicy potato dishes, either shokog khatsa, served cold on greens with hot bread, or Himalaya khatsa, spicy potatoes also served cold with cauliflower, fresh peas, and tofu on greens with hot bread, are tasty vegan options.

One of the menu highlights is the tsel momo, supposedly the national dish of Tibet. Momos are pot-sticker look-alikes steamed and filled with mixed vegetables or fried (tsel momo ngopa) and served on a bed of shredded salad. More momos include those made with potatoes mixed into the vegetables (Tibet Café Special).

Entrées combine an extensive number of hot and cold options. Meat dishes feature beef versions of the momos, steamed beef dumplings (shaymo) or fried (shaymo ngopa). It seems like almost every culture has its own version of the hamburger, and

Tibet Café,
3913 North Sheridan,
(773) 281-6666,
is open daily, Saturdays and Sundays only for lunch. BYOB.
Vegetarian dishes range from $4.95 to $6.50; nonvegetarian options run to $8.95.

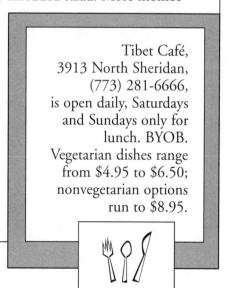

the Tibetan burger appears in the form of sha-bhale, beef patties seasoned with shallots and herbs. Even seafood is available, a shrimp curry made with a yogurt and herbs marinade. We weren't quite sure how this could be a traditional dish of the mountains, so we said *no to-je-che* (Tibetan for "no thanks").

Our only disappointment was the Tibet Café curry, a chicken curry made with what we assumed was the same yogurt and herbs marinade as the shrimp got. There was a lot of it, but it was relatively bland. We applied hot sauce liberally.

We wound dinner up with dysee, sweetened rice studded with raisins mounded beside a warm yogurt. Sated and feeling on top of the world, we relaxed under the benign gaze of the Dalai Lama and sipped another pot of tea.

Extra Chow: Ready for a field trip? Head to south suburban Lemont to the area's most important Hindu site, the Hindu Temple of Greater Chicago. This large, white temple, built at a cost of $4 million and sitting on twenty acres of land, is dedicated to the Hindu deity Rama. Other Hindu deities can be worshipped inside.

Out of Africa

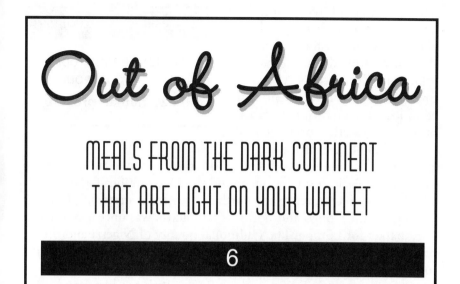

MEALS FROM THE DARK CONTINENT THAT ARE LIGHT ON YOUR WALLET

6

frica, a land of startling contrasts, from the Graceland of the south to the heart of darkness in the central Congo to the savanna and sands of the north. The African continent is over three times the size of the United States and contains some forty-nine countries. Within its varied geography, Africa has the world's largest desert, second-largest rain forest, and second-longest river. Africa is the birthplace of woman (and man, but the oldest skeleton discovered to date was nicknamed "Lucy" for a reason) and also the historic birthplace of coffee.

> "If I know a song for Africa—of the giraffe, and the new African moon lying on her back, of the plow in the fields, and the sweaty faces of the coffee pickers, does Africa know a song for me?"
>
> —*Out of Africa*,
> **Isak Dinesen**

Africa, the Dark Continent, a land of endlessly varied scenery, peoples, history, and, yes, even food. These days, with Chicago's increasingly international restaurant scene, you don't have to don your khakis and book your trip to the bush to experience the contrasts of Africa's culinary traditions. No, many of Africa's distinctive cuisines are well represented in local restaurants. A number of the city's eateries specialize in the spicy dishes of East Africa and Ethiopia, reflecting that country's positioning as a long time bridge between the African subcontinent and the Mediterranean and Middle Eastern cultures to the north. West Africa, stretching from the edge of the Congo and north to Timbuktu, was once a colonial breadbasket for Europe. The traditional bounty of Nigeria and the rest of that region, including yam porridge, fufu (cassava—also used to make tapioca), jollof rice (African rice pilaf), and goat stew, can be sampled at several Edgewater and Rogers Park neighborhood establishments. In addition, the couscous of Islamic North Africa and Morocco can be found rockin' the Casbah all over town.

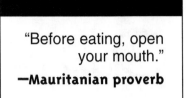

> "Before eating, open your mouth."
>
> **—Mauritanian proverb**

Over the course of a couple hundred years, West Africa, helped by a number of neighbors to the north, exported millions of its own residents. Though forcibly removed from their homes, these slaves managed to maintain aspects of their native traditions and helped to shape the Afro-Caribbean cuisine of the islands and the soul food of the American South. A melding of British and African influences gave rise to the cuisine of Jamaica, while Spanish and African cooking traditions combined to produce Cuban, and the whole mix—French, Spanish, African—resulted in the Creole and Cajun dishes of New Orleans and the Mississippi delta. These classic melting pot situations are probably best illustrated by a Jamaican saying, "out of many, one people." And, one cuisine. Direct from the sands of the Caribbean and Gulf Coast to the third coast of Chicago, there's plenty of opportunity around town to indulge in these hybrid dishes.

Talk Like an Ethiopian . . .

Enjera a thin pancake-like bread prepared from fermented teff flour

Berbere ingredient of wat prepared from red pepper and other spices

Wat a spicy sauce made from berbere along with meat, fish,

vegetables, or leguminous seeds
Awaze sauce made from red pepper and other spices
Mitmita powdered chili pepper seeds blended with other spices
Alitcha mild sauce made from turmeric and other spices, along with meat, fish, vegetables, and leguminous seeds

Vee-Vee's African Restaurant

6245 North Broadway, (773) 465-2424

The traditional bounty of Nigeria can be sampled locally at Vee-Vee's, a restaurant in the Edgewater neighborhood that offers a fine experience in traditional West African cuisine. Dining typically consists of one-dish meals made up of a starch—usually rice, millet, maize porridge, fufu, pounded plantains, yams, or cassava—served with a spicy "stew" or soup. The dish is often flavored with ground mango seed, melon seed, crayfish, or some tasty goat tidbits. For a number of the one-dish meals, ogbono or egusi (melon seed) soup, for example, the starches are in the form of sticky globs that the diner grabs in hunks and uses to get the soup to the mouth. Rice dishes that can be eaten with table utensils are also available. Chicken, fish, or goat can all be ordered with rice steamed in coconut milk and accented with pureed tomatoes, onions, pepper, and thyme. Our drums were really beating after tasting the coconut rice with chicken ($7.50). For those who have a hard time deciding between yam porridge (yam, meat, crayfish, tomatoes, and spinach in a sauce) and ngwo-ngwo (goat pepper soup), Vee-Vee's has an all-you-can-eat buffet on Sundays from noon until 6:00 P.M. for $9.99 where you can graze through the goat stew and yams prepared in various combinations in addition to jerk chicken, fried plantains, jollof rice, and more. Allow plenty of time here—service is very friendly, but excruciatingly slow. A word to the wise: Nigerian dishes, like the weather and current political situation, are hot, hot, hot. If you can't stand the heat, you'd better stay out of this West African kitchen.

Open daily (Fridays and Saturdays till 2:00 A.M.). BYOB. Buffet served Sundays only.

Suya African Grill & Bar

3911 North Sheridan, (773) 281-7892

Suya, a small West African restaurant across from the Sheridan/Howard Red-line El stop, anchors a United Nations restaurant lineup that includes Tibet Café and L'Olive next door. *Suya* is a beef marinated in either mild or hot spices, then grilled "African-style" and served with tomato and fresh onions (small, $2, *mallam* or medium, $3, and *minister* or large, $5). Dishes at Suya also feature either fufu, a pounded yam that tastes like dense, smooth mashed potatoes, and semovita, a white corn polenta, both of which are served with okra soup or egusi, a thick stew made from melon, spinach, or bitter leaf. Diners mold a piece of fufu, dip it into the stew, and rinse their fingers in the water bowl. The menu also includes fresh catfish soup ($4) and goat or beef soup ($3); joloff rice ($7) with chicken, white fish, goat, or beef—kind of an African jambalaya; and vegetable kabobs marinated in traditional African spices ($6).

Closed Mondays. Beer and wine. Open until midnight on the weekends.

Linette's Jamaican Kitchen

7366 North Clark, (773) 761-4823

In East Rogers Park, Linette's Jamaican Kitchen, a small storefront decorated with Jamaican seascapes and fishermen that contrast comfortably with worn wood floors, offers a cozy neighborhood atmosphere to those who want to enjoy peppered shrimp, red snapper, jerk pork and chicken, Jamaican beef, vegetable patties, or cow feet. Meals are $8 to $8.50, and combination plates with two options are $10. Dampen the heat with a sip of sorrel (a blend of wine) or Irish moss, a seaweed health drink.

Open daily. No alcohol. Serves breakfast on Saturdays.

Island Delight

1461 East Hyde Park, (773) 324-3100

On the South Side, well-known Jamaican eatery Island Delight serves spicy beef patties, along with spinach patties and vegetable versions that are loaded with carrots and other mixed greens for $1.25 each. Wash it down with a cola champagne or a Jamaican pineapple soda.

Open daily. No alcohol.

Mama Desta's Red Sea Restaurant

3216 North Clark, (773) 935-7561

Ethiopia, where thousands of years ago homo erectus first began to walk upright, has long been the conduit between the African subcontinent and the northern Mediterranean and Middle Eastern cultures. Ethiopia's food reflects these influences and can be sampled extensively through a "hands-on" experience at Mama Desta's. At Mama Desta's, you use strips of injera, a flat, spongy bread, to grab handfuls of doro wat, a spicy chicken in berbere sauce that is also Ethiopia's national dish; yebeg alitcha, a stew of lamb, onions, and green peppers; and yemisir wat, pureed green lentils blended with spices and herbs. A number of reasonably priced combination dishes (around $7 and up) offer the adventurous eater a number of opportunities to run your hands through various vegetarian, chicken, fish, and meat dishes.

Open daily. Full bar featuring Ethiopian beer.

Ethio Village Café & Restaurant

3462 North Clark, (773) 929-8300

Those who know Ethiopian tell me Mama Desta's is the best, but if you're struck by Mama Desta's lack of atmosphere but are still in the mood, two other Ethiopian options can be found just up the street. Ethio Village Cafe & Restaurant boasts the cheapest Ethiopian fare on the block—including a $6.95 all-you-can-eat vegetarian buffet, live music Fridays and Saturdays, and honey wine served by the carafe.

Open daily. Full bar featuring Ethiopian beer.

Addis Abeba

3521 North Clark, (773) 929-9383

The other option, Addis Abeba, located just north, offers more atmosphere than Mama Desta's but less amenities than Ethio Village. A good selection of sampler platters is available here where the motto is, "We cook for you . . . Just as we do for ourselves."

Open daily. Full bar featuring Ethiopian beer.

Caribbean American Baking Company

1539 West Howard, (773) 761-0700

The Caribbean American Baking Company in Rogers Park is Chicago's only source of Jamaican beef patties ($1.05 each including tax), spicy little turnovers that are as common in Jamaica as hot dogs and burritos are here. This bakery supplies all the local restaurants in town, popping an estimated 10,000 patties a week out of the oven. Other Jamaican specialties, including Hardough bread, plantain tarts, and Bulla cake, are also available here.

quick bites

Open Daily.

The Equator Club

4715 North Broadway, (773) 728-2411

Cap off an African dinner with an evening of African music and entertainment at the Equator Club. Cover is usually about $8. If you don't eat before you go, inexpensive tasty ethnic tidbits are often available for snacking.

Open Daily.

Seoul Food

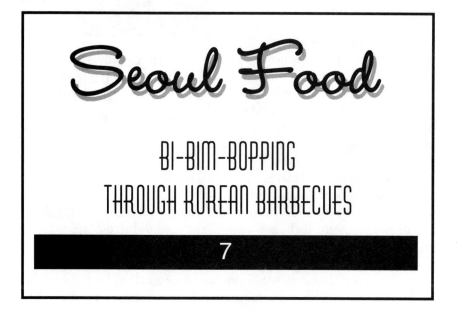

Bi-Bim-Bopping Through Korean Barbecues

7

Dateline, 1988—Seoul—for perhaps the first time since the fifties, the attention of mainstream America turns toward Korea amid the pomp and circumstance of the Summer Olympics.

Often called the "Irish of Asia," Koreans spent much of their history being conquered by neighbors. When not being subjugated by a country next door, Koreans were actively involved in kicking nonresidents out and keeping them out, thereby earning the nickname of "The Hermit Kingdom."

Even today, after the splash of the Olympics in Seoul and countless reruns of M*A*S*H, most Americans know little about Korea; that's too bad, since the Koreans, like the Irish, have a fiery and colorful heritage, which is expressed in every aspect of their culture. Take Korean cuisine; for example, take kimchi. The soul of the Korean people is pickled into kimchi, an incendiary side dish/condiment consumed at every meal and made by fermenting various vegetables in garlic and chilis. There are some two dozen different varieties of kimchi, and the average Korean family has numerous black kimchi pots perking away on the back porch.

Complimentary side dishes, or panch'an, are served at every meal (a great deal—no need to order an appetizer here!), and the number of sides increases as the day goes on. At a typical dinner at a local restaurant, it's not uncommon to be confronted with at least nine side dishes and soup to accompany your entrée. Some typical sides include sigumchi namul, blanched spinach with sesame oil and seeds; kejang, raw crab legs marinated in red chili sauce; and tubu, marinated tofu.

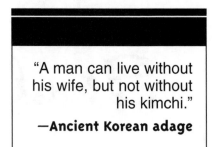

> "A man can live without his wife, but not without his kimchi."
>
> **—Ancient Korean adage**

Along with the abundant side dishes, Korean cuisine is also typified by "one-dish" meals, such as bi-bim-bop, a rice bowl traditionally topped with bean sprouts, bluebell root, blanched fern, spinach, a fried egg, and chili sauce on the side. Most local Korean restaurants do the "bop," although they may substitute carrots or zucchini for some of the traditional greens. Other dishes commonly found around town are galbi (beef short ribs); and bulgolgi (sliced beef); both marinated in a tangy sauce and often cooked at your table on a special grill resembling a Mongol helmet. In addition, as a country practically surrounded by water, it should be no surprise that much of Korean cuisine revolves around seafood, particularly sea skate, octopus, and squid.

Chicago has a fairly large Korean population. In 1965 immigration laws eased, allowing in a wave of Asians from politically unstable countries. Koreans settled in the old Albany Park neighborhood and established Chicago's Koreatown in the area lying between Pulaski and Foster to the north and west, Montrose to the south, and the north branch of the Chicago River to the east. Today, take a drive down Lawrence Avenue, and you may think you've suddenly crossed the international border. English practically disappears and is replaced with hangul, the Korean written language. But, you don't need to read Korean to go out and eat it and enjoy it. Go for it—bop till you drop.

Editor's Note: The romanization of the names of Korean dishes varies all over town—some of the common standards are used here.

Jim's Grill

1429 West Irving Park, (773) 525-4050

Also profiled in the breakfast chapter, "Early to Rise," Jim's Grill offers not only a great diner-style, short-order breakfast, but also a wide array of Korean options. Tiny Jim's, seating less than twenty at counter and tables combined, is home to Chicago's cheapest bi-bim-bop, often a $3.95 special on the weekends, $4.50 regular price for chicken, pork, beef, or vegetarian (shrimp a little more); $6.50 for "Dave's Deluxe"; and $4.55 on Tuesdays for the hyumi, bi-bim-bop made with brown rice and oats. Bop that! Also on the menu are great deals on standbys such as bulgolgi ($5.95), mandoo with fried rice (Korean dumplings, $4.95), maki rolls (Korean vegetarian sushi, $4.95), and soy vegetarian pancakes with seaweed soup ($4.55). Wash it all down with an assortment of traditional Korean teas, including barley and ginger, very good for your yin and yang. No little side dishes here—but at these prices, you can afford to splurge on a couple of appetizers.

Open Monday through Saturday for breakfast and lunch. No alcohol.

Korean Sam-Mee Restaurant

3370 North Clark, (773) 525-5050

Nestled among the Wrigleyville sushi houses on north Clark, Sam-Mee is a friendly little storefront that makes Korean cuisine easily accessible to those who refuse to go north of Addison unless there's a Cubs game. The hefty menu offers traditional favorites, including bi-bim-bop for $7.95, along with some specialties that may require some acquired tastes, such as koree guhn tang (cow tail soup) and woo jock tang (cow feet soup). The bindae duck bockum (fried pancakes, $7.95) is highly recommended (it's served with nine side dishes!). Fish dishes and fish stews, eight of each, are also available. To top off the good location and the good prices, the service at Sam-Mee is exemplary. As some research took place on a bitter cold night (which one?—so many, just can't remember), I was greeted graciously with a steaming glass of tea, and then ensconced in a booth with my own personal space heater at my feet. Now that's service.

Open daily. Full bar.

Korean Restaurant

2659 West Lawrence, (773) 878-2095

The heart of Chicago's Koreatown, Lawrence Avenue, is lined with restaurant storefronts where names are displayed prominently in hangul, the Korean written language, and English is often a second language. Korean Restaurant is one of the more established locations and is able to accommodate the language needs of "foreigners." Korean Restaurant offers over eighty different dishes served in huge portions, twenty-four hours a day. Four different types of bi-bim-bop range from $6.95 to $9.95. Bim nengmyon, hot spicy buckwheat noodles, is a fiery specialty, and hejang kuk, ox blood and chunks of beef boiled with vegetables at $5, is a real deal.

Open 24 hours. BYOB.

Cho Sun Ok Steak House

4200 North Lincoln, (773) 549-5555

Cho Sun Ok was once just another neighborhood greasy spoon, before its owners realized that their customers were more interested in ordering the Korean dishes relegated to the back of the hamburger menu. So, they got rid of the burgers and went with the Chinese and Korean dishes, although none of those dishes are steak. The specialties of the house—pheasant, quail, wild rabbit, and duck—are a little pricey for us at $20, but the rest of the menu is very reasonable, with the bi-bim-bop checking in at $6.95. Spicy bean curd is also a good option at $5.95. Enjoy your meal to the background entertainment of KTV, Korean TV—a constant stream of soap operas and talk shows.

Open daily. Full bar.

Bando Restaurant

2200 West Lawrence, (773) 728-7400

This is it—Chicago's Le Francais, the Ambria, the La Tour of the area's Korean restaurants. With its lobby waterfall and indoor, adjacent parking lot, you know you're not going to get chopped liver when you walk in here. And when you do walk in, you may very well find yourself in line in back of a large group in traditional Korean dress, because if you're Korean and you live in Chicago and you're getting married, this is where you want to come to party with up to four hundred of your nearest and dearest in Bando's large hall. In spite of its pomp and circumstance, Bando manages to keep the prices reasonable, with a good number of entrées running from $7 to $10. Three types of bi-bim-bop are served here, with the base version starting at $7.95. Galbi-tang (beef short ribs), one of the house specialties, is $8.95.

Open daily. Full bar.

Mandarin House

819 Noyes, Evanston, (847) 869-4344

Like many Korean and Vietnamese restaurants that pretend to be dining establishments offering more mainstream Asian cuisines, this dumpy little storefront masquerading as Chinese is actually a Korean eatery serving a range of traditional dishes made mainly with either beef or chicken. Chicken or beef bi-bim-bop is $6.50; both the bulgolgi and the galbi are comparatively good deals at $6.30. Try some tender, tasty san juk or Korean shish kebob for only $6.75 and $6.50 respectively. Assorted combinations for $6.50 to $8.20 offer the adventurous diner an opportunity to graze.

Open daily. BYOB.

FOOD FOR FAST FEASTS

quick bites

Gin Go Gae

5433 North Lincoln, (773) 334-3895

Gin Go Gae is upscale, expensive establishment, along the lines of Bando. Although a little pricier, the restaurant serves a huge assortment of side dishes with each meal. Gin Go Gae also takes credit cards, one of the few, along with Bando and Shilla, that do. (For more details, see "Taste of Lincoln Avenue.")

Open daily. Full bar.

Shilla

5930 North Lincoln, (773) 275-5930

If Bando has competition for the "godfather" of Chicago's Korean restaurants, Shilla is it. Specializing in Korean and Japanese food, Shilla offers a selection of eight private banquet rooms. Galbi, sashimi, and shrimp tempura, both Korean and Japanese style, are the house specialties.

Open daily. Full bar.

Extra Chow: If you're up enjoying the sights and tastes of Koreatown, make sure you check out the Bultasa Buddhist Temple, 4358 West Montrose. Chicago has five Buddhist temples, but the Bultasa is unique because of its "1,000 Buddha Temple Altar," the only one of its kind in the Midwest. It's open every day from 6:00 A.M. to 9:30 P.M., the monks will be happy to give you a guided tour.

In the Belly of Buddha

Awaken to Amitabul's vegan temptations

The corner of Southport and Roscoe saw more action September 3, 1997 than the Wrigleyville area has witnessed since the Cubs last won the division. That Tuesday night, driven by the promise of free food and rumors of a spontaneous performance by the Smashing Pumpkins, 750 hungry fans stormed the doors for opening night at **Amitabul**, a new Korean Buddhist Vegetarian restaurant opened by the owners of **Jim's Grill**.

Although just a tiny diner, Jim's itself has a huge following. At first glance, the 1429 West Irving Park storefront looks like a cheap, short-order grill; a second look, however, uncovers near-overflow crowds scooping rice dishes and noodles out of shiny, deep-bottomed metal bowls, snarfing up bites of strange grain-and-vegetable pancakes, and throwing sushi-like pieces of vegetarian maki rolls into heart-healthy guts. In short, Jim's is a gustatory Asian oasis hiding behind the facade of American grease. True believers have hoarded the knowledge to themselves, lest the word get out and the lines grow longer.

In September, rumors had spread that a new Jim's would be opening nearby. All through the long hot summer, one of the owners, Dave Choi, says he was peppered constantly for updates. "When, when?" pleaded the faithful, and Choi would just smile enigmatically and reply, "Soon, soon." If you were particularly lucky, he might share a construction tidbit or an anecdote about a tussle with city hall for a license. Then, details about the Amitabul concept began to leak out. Not just another Jim's, Amitabul, which means *awakening*, would be a forum for Choi and his family partners to let their talents with Korean Buddhist vegetarian food run wild. Devotees squirmed in anticipation.

And then the big night arrived. Although music was promised, Choi discouraged speculation that the Pumpkins, fans of the cooking at Jim's, would perform. Refusing to be discouraged, the crowds formed. Said co-owner Eric Kim, "We expected to cook for about three hundred. They were lined up all the way down Southport. What people will do for free food!"

But it was Amitabul free food—fat-free, cholesterol-free, animal by-product-free. And the faithful were rewarded for their patience. Glistening green piles of kim bop (maki rolls) in vegetable, "energy," kimchi, and jade varieties were inhaled, along with piles of vegetable pancakes—wholewheat, brownrice, kimchi, soybean, "energy," blackbean, and wholewheat with miso. Diners frolicked through noodle dishes, mandoo can do and kimchi du-bi-du, among other creative options. They finally found nirvana—a salad of tofu, seaweed, vegetables, and apples designed to take taste buds to the promised land.

Long past opening night, Amitabul remains kimchi hot—most dishes are served mildly spicy

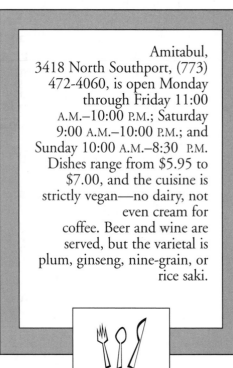

Amitabul, 3418 North Southport, (773) 472-4060, is open Monday through Friday 11:00 A.M.–10:00 P.M.; Saturday 9:00 A.M.–10:00 P.M.; and Sunday 10:00 A.M.–8:30 P.M. Dishes range from $5.95 to $7.00, and the cuisine is strictly vegan—no dairy, not even cream for coffee. Beer and wine are served, but the varietal is plum, ginseng, nine-grain, or rice saki.

to "you-probably-can't-handle-it" spicy. Lines continue to form for Amitabul energy nuts, various nuts stir fried with honey and tangy plum sauce served over whole-wheat noodles; maha pyogo, three kinds of mushrooms steamed with fresh garlic over rice; various selections of bi-bim-bop; and the ever-popular soy vegetable pancakes, which Amitabul serves with various grains and legumes. The list of daily specials is particularly popular; various menu selections are served with a choice of soup for $5.99.

With all the owners' positive energy being devoted to Amitabul, Jim's Grill is now open only during the week. Traffic at Jim's apparently spikes up on Fridays, when those who haven't been able, make a complete transition to meatless bi-bim-bop get their last fix of chicken or beef. But chef Choi has implemented a regular meal program for those who have pledged themselves to the true vegetarian path; he plans to offer monthly cooking lessons soon in his upstairs demonstration kitchen, perhaps prompting a citywide culinary awakening.

Oktoberfeast, Ja!

8

Oompah-pah, oompah-pah . . . Late September through October, people all over the Chicago area put on stupid Peter Pan felt hats, heft a cold plastic stein, and cavort to the big band sound of hairy-legged men encased in green shorts with leather banding. Oktoberfest season brings an opportunity every weekend to wave a brat, chug some hops while wedged between strangers at a picnic table, and let it all hang out while doing the chicken dance with two thousand other feather-capped partiers. Ja!

Chicago, of course, has deep-rooted German traditions that have led us to today's celebrations. The city's first German settler, Heinrich Rothenfeld, relocated here in 1825. By the early 1840s, the first German settlement, New Buffalo, was formed between Chicago and North Avenue. Germans later moved north into the Old Town area and then on up Lincoln Avenue to Lincoln Square at Lincoln and Lawrence. Critical to the development of Chicago's German community and, probably Chicago's persona as a whole, was the founding of the city's first brewery in 1836, which bubbled out six hundred foamy barrels a year. One of the original founders (sorry, not Berghoff; he didn't show up until the 1890s) then went on to expand his business in partnership with future mayor William B. Ogden. By 1856, Chicago's nine German breweries were churning out 16,270 barrels a year.

> "Things could be wurst."
>
> **—Traditional motto of master German butchers**

Oktoberfest evolved out of a wedding reception that got out of hand—the celebration of Bavarian King Ludwig I's marriage to Thérèse Sachsen Hildburghause, a festive event marked by a great horse race and much partying among the residents of Munich. In 1896 the first great beer tent was opened and local breweries began serving a special Oktoberfest brew just for the festival.

Today, the Munich Oktoberfest begins the next to last Saturday in September and continues until the first Sunday in October, luring nearly 6 million tourists from all over the globe to the largest public festival in the world, which is held on Thérèsienwiese (Thérèse's meadow). Although the party unofficially kicks off with a parade of local brewers riding in ornate carriages, brewery wagons full of beer, and dancing beer maidens on decorated floats, it's not until the Lord Mayor of Munich opens the first barrel of beer with the words "Ozapft ist!" (It's tapped!) that the festivities really begin.

By the end of the 16-day event, festival-goers will have drunk 1.4 million mabs (gallon-size steins) of beer in 14 giant beer tents seating up to 10,000 at a time that line the Wirtsbuden-Strasse (the main drag). They will have also consumed more than 75,000 roasted chickens, 70,000 sausages, 60,000 legs of pork, and 80 whole oxen.

Oktoberfest has evolved into a worldwide celebration customized by each local community. In New York City, Greenwich Village's Washington Park hosts a Dachshund Oktoberfest with hundreds of "wiener dogs," some wearing tiny leather caps, others in red sweaters. In Cincinnati, the annual Oktoberfest celebration features the world's largest chicken dance, where in 1994, 48,000 people flapped and wiggled right into the Guinness Book of World Records as the largest dance in the history of mankind

If you can't afford the ticket on Lufthansa or aren't able to get yourself to Cincinnati for a mass chicken dance, there are plenty of local options that you might want to check out. Oktoberfest celebrations in the Chicago area start in September, with some of the biggest being Lincoln Square's German-American Festival, with its accompanying Von Steuben parade, and the Berghoff Oktoberfest. If you miss those two kickoff events, there's still plenty of places to party. After all, you've still got the big daddy of them all, maybe one of the only reasons you'll ever have to travel west of O'Hare—Wheeling's own Hans Bavarian Lodge Oktoberfest, one of the largest celebrations in the Midwest. Starting mid-September and running through October 24, Friday and Saturday nights from 6:30 P.M. to midnight, you can join 2,500 other revelers who like to hang out in covered parking lots and pound plastic steins at endless picnic tables. $19 ($20 day of or $10 for admission no food) buys you admittance and dinner, a hefty platter of quarter chicken, bratwurst, Hungarian sausage, German potato salad, sauerkraut, rye bread and butter.

If you can't make it out to Wheeling, there are numerous local urban opportunities. The Chicago Brauhaus, a Lincoln Square anchor, hosts an Oktoberfest celebration starting October 7 and running through November 8, which features live music and dancing nightly except Tuesdays. Or, if you're a true devotee, check out the four-person band playing every weekend year-round at Edelweiss Restaurant on West Irving Park. If you're really searching, check your local churches—chances are, even they're probably having a little shindig where the faithful normally park. Just hunt around—any place you can set up a tent and tap a keg is a possibility for indulging in the spirit of Brüderlichkeit. Have fun and "auf die wies'n" (translation, "to the meadow").

Resi's Bierstube

2034 West Irving Park, (773) 472-1749

German food is generally not cheap chow. Yes, you usually get a lot for your money—complete meals so weighty they knock you out for, well, in some cases, maybe forty years (Rip Van Winkle, was he German or Dutch?). But all this bounty usually comes at a price. The true exception to this rule in town is Resi's, a snug little restaurant with an outstanding beer garden that really delivers for under $12. Complete dinners, excluding the schnitzels, with hefty main dishes and two sides hover between $7.50 to $8.95. Try the fried liver cheese and potato salad. A variety of sausages with side fixin's range from

$4.75 to $8.50. Wash it all down with a choice from among sixty bottled beers and eight on tap. This place gets crowded with regulars, and you may end up sharing your picnic table in the tree-lined, lantern-lit beer garden with fellow diners who don't know your name. Service is exceptionally friendly. Ask for our waitress, Edit, a fixture at Resi's for the past twenty years. (More on Resi's in "Gardens of Eat-in.")

Open daily. Full bar—choice of more than five dozen beers. Patio dining.

Edelweiss Restaurant

7650 Irving Park, Norridge, (708) 452-6040

Boasting its own Oktoberfest celebration where patrons are entertained by a four-piece band, Edelweiss is worth the drive for a truly solid meal. Complete dinners spanning the range of German offerings are priced mostly from $9.95 to $11.50. À la carte entrées, if several courses leave you numb, are $6.50 to $6.95. Hot and cold sandwiches are $4.75 to $8.25. At least three varieties of schnitzel appear daily on the menu—the one with Hunter's sauce is highly recommended. Check out the interesting stuffed animals draped over the band's drumset.

Open daily. Full bar.

Viennese Kaffee-Haus Brandt

3423 Southport, (773) 528-2220

A Viennese pastry shop that serves breakfast, lunch, and full-course dinners featuring traditional specialties, Viennese Kaffee-Haus Brandt brings memories of the Hapsburg Empire to this west Lakeview neighborhood and is one of the few establishments left in town that makes all its own pastry dough. Most dinners range in price from $7.50 to $9.75 and include a salad and side vegetable. None of them would be considered light. Try the napoleon gemusse ($8.50), julienne vegetables layered with layers of Swiss cheese and eggplant "pastry leaves" in a garlic cream sauce. Hecht in kapernsosse is pike sautéed in white wine and caper sauce ($9.50). The very interesting truthan pâté en croute ($8.50) is a pâté of turkey, vegetables, bacon, and herbs wrapped in red cabbage and puff pastry and served with red pepper coulis. Or, stick with some old favorites—gemusse goulash ($7.25), a vegetarian goulash over noodles, or chicken and dumplings in mustard sauce ($7.55). Leave room for a trip to the pastry cases at the end of your meal.

Closed Mondays. Brunch. Patio. Full bar featuring German and Austrian beers and lime rickeys (in season). Live opera and show tunes on Tuesday and Thursdays, and occasional special performances on weekends.

Bistro 1800 & My Bar

1800 Sherman, Evanston, (847) 492-3450

The easiest way to locate this hard-to-find bistro serving German and continental foods is to take advantage of the restaurant's free-parking-after-6:00 P.M. offer. If you can't find the lot, located behind an office building and across from Evanston favorite Buffalo Joe's, you'll never find the restaurant, which cannot be directly accessed from Sherman Avenue. Once you've found the place, enjoy German entrées that range from German sausages with homemade sauerkraut and potatoes ($6.95) to smoked pork chop kassler ($9.95). The menu offers wine recommendations with each entrée (a lot of gewürztraminer and riesling). You can enjoy your meal with live music, more oriented toward jazz than oompah. (Formerly Kaffehaus 1800.)

Open daily. Full bar.

Lutz Continental Café & Pastry

2458 West Montrose, (773) 478-7785

Around since 1948, Lutz boasts one of the city's ultimate "secret gardens," an astroturfed, tree-lined patio out back complete with a pool and fountain gurgling away amidst umbrella-shaded tables that may be the peaceful getaway you need after one too many steins. A sophisticated contrast to some of

Chicago's other open air celebrations taking place in beer gardens and tents, Lutz's serves Viennese and southern German specialties including homemade soups, chicken and fish, crêpes and quiche, salads, open-faced sandwiches, and some very serious tortes, all priced $3 to $12. Selections from the fatherland include liver pâté ($5.75), herring topf (herring with sour cream, apples, and boiled potatoes, $9.40), veal served in a pastry shell ($9.95), konigsberger klopse (meatballs in wine sauce, $9.75), relished salmon ($10.95), and konigens pastete (the queen's plate, $9.40). Top off your meal with a Viennese coffee and a multilayer, cream-filled, artery-clogging, eye-pleasing, tummy-busting delight—maybe a nice big baumkuchen with whipped cream?

Closed Sundays. Full bar.

The Berghoff

17 West Adams, (312) 427-3170

Over 100 years old with its own street fair every September, the Berghoff is arguably the best-known German establishment in the city. In spite of its downtown location, the restaurant still has reasonably priced entrées, including sauerbraten and chicken schnitzel (both $8.25). Those who want to economize can eat a hand-carved sandwich in the adjoining café while standing and draining either the Berghoff's home brew or a draft root beer.

Open daily. Full bar.

Editor's Note: For more on German bakeries and delicatessens, see "Taste of Lincoln Avenue."

Given the price of meals in some of the city's more popular German restaurants, it might be worth looking into some take-out/do-your-own spots:

quick bites

Lincoln Market

4661 North Lincoln, (773) 561-4570

Stocking German meats and food products from Poland, Hungary, and Yugoslavia, Lincoln Market is well known for its beerwurst and sausages, which are prepared in-house by master European butchers. Lincoln Market also specializes in more unusual cuts of meats, including spring lambs and young pigs.

Inge's Delicatessen

4724 North Lincoln, (773) 561-8386

Thirty years in Lincoln Square, Inge's specializes in imported German, Austrian, Croatian, Dutch, Danish, and French gourmet foods and specialty items. A wide selection of homemade sausages, cosmetics, and beer steins is available.

Enisa's Pastry Shop and Café

4701-03 North Lincoln, (773) 271-7017

Bakery in the front, café in the rear. Plenty of sweet and gooey cakes, imported truffles, and tortes in both front and back.

Open daily.

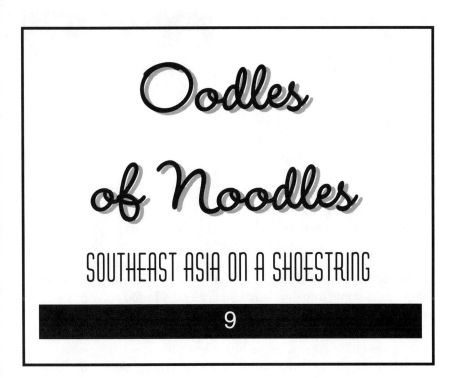

Oodles of Noodles

SOUTHEAST ASIA ON A SHOESTRING

9

Let's dispel a few myths. They don't all look alike, and they don't all taste alike. In spite of the recent trend to combine dishes and flavors for a menu of "Asian fusion," there are a lot of distinct differences among Asian cuisines. Thai and Vietnamese dishes can be as far away from sushi and chow mein as a burrito is from a spring roll. At first glance, there may be some surface similarities, but your first bite should firmly inform you that you're not in Kansas—or Canton—any more, Toto.

Southeast Asian cuisines, particularly the noodle dishes that are the anchor options on many of the proliferating fusion menus, can also be a bargain compared to their North Asian cousins. Frankly, it can be a lot easier to find budget pad Thai than tempura. A steady diet of Thai or Vietnamese carryout can really help save your baht.

Rockin' Ramen . . . The Chinese and Japanese have a history of noodle-making that goes back to 3,000 B.C., which they later exported to their Asian neighbors. Once considered peasant food, noodles are now mainstream dining, and noodle vendors are as much a part of the streets of Thailand, India, China, Japan, and other Asian countries as hot dog vendors are at a baseball game. Noodles in Asia are typically long and thin because of their associations with longevity—Asians have traditionally served noodles at birthday celebrations, left uncut to ensure long life.

> "Creative cooking when you can only afford 10-for-a-dollar pasta."
>
> —*101 Ways to Make Ramen Noodles,* **Toni Patrick**

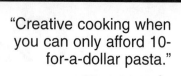

In contrast to the West, Asian cultures commonly use flours other than wheat to make their noodles. Cellophane noodles, those noodles you often see fried into "bird's nests," are made from mung beans, which were originally grown in India. Rice noodles are the foundation of many Asian dishes, and soba noodles made from buckwheat are a staple in many Japanese dishes. In India, you can find vendors in almost every city selling spicy fried noodles made half of garbanzo flour and half of chili powder, often eaten between bites of fresh green chili peppers. Some like it hot.

Thai one on . . . Cheap and noodles are synonymous with Thai and Vietnamese food. Chicago's first Thai restaurant opened some twenty years ago, and today, there are more than one hundred in the city and more than two hundred in the Chicago area—a surprising figure since Thais represent Chicago's smallest Asian group with a population of less than five thousand in the metro area. Chicago's Vietnamese population, one of Chicago's newest immigrant groups and more concentrated than the Thai, can be found primarily in Uptown around Argyle Street, once known as "New Chinatown" but now probably more appropriately termed "Little Saigon." Whether you run to your neighborhood corner storefront or hop the El uptown to the Lawrence stop, get out and Thai some Southeast Asian fare. You wouldn't want to miss Saigon, right?

Penny's Noodle Shop

3400 North Sheffield, (773) 281-8222
950 West Diversey, (773) 281-8448

Both Penny's locations are small and always packed, so be prepared to wait if you want to eat on-site. Just open one of those cold beers you brought, settle in, and join the crowd. Pennies from heaven—this remains the franchise concept for the nineties and beyond. What can you say about a place that consistently delivers a tasty meal for under $6 to packed houses and always serves with a smile? Both the wedge-shaped original location and the newer, spacious Diversey address are cozy and clean, appealing to scores of less adventurous eaters; the staff is freshly scrubbed, and all sport nifty mustard-colored polo shirts. Won ton soup, won ton with noodles (my personal favorite), Vietnamese spring rolls, pad Thai, udon noodles in dashi broth, all expertly tweaked for the palate of the Lincoln Park yuppie are best enjoyed at the counter, because who wants to stand around waiting for a table?

Open daily. BYOB. Sheffield location has sidewalk seating.

Hi Ricky Asian Noodle Shop & Satay Bar

1852 West North, (773) 276-8300
3737 North Southport, (773) 388-0000
941 West Randolph, (312) 491-9100

Cloning that successful Penny's formula, Hi Ricky is a bright and loft-like storefront that serves a variety of Asian cuisines at practically native prices, with nothing priced above $7.45 (those are the "with shrimp" dishes) and most entrées being priced $5.95 to $6.95. The noodles from the wok, tossed noodles, rice, soup, and curry dishes feature representatives from all of the Asian tigers—China, Thailand, Vietnam, Singapore, Malaysia, Indonesia, and even Burma. The Vietnamese bun thit ($6.95)—thin rice noodles, crispy spring roll, sliced grilled beef, crushed peanuts, mint, cilantro, and sprouts in a mild spicy sauce—is particularly tasty, as is the Burmese fried rice ($5.95)—spicy curry fried rice with onion, garlic, a lot of lemongrass, and a choice of meat. Soothing jasmine tea washes everything down, and a double red cream sweetie can finish things off as dessert. Free happy hour munchies are served on Fridays and Saturdays from 5:00 P.M. to 7:00 P.M.

Open daily. Full bar.

Vietnam Little Home Restaurant

4654 North Damen, (773) 275-8360

Tucked away just south of the Ravenswood neighborhood, this two-room storefront with a bright yellow facade serves a wide variety of Vietnamese food (sixty-five dishes) almost all priced $5.10 and under. Dishes are delicately prepared with a homey touch, making Vietnam Little Home worth the trip off the Argyle Street beaten path. Fifteen different noodle dishes are available to choose from. Seafood dishes feature stuffed squid ($5.25) and clay pot stewed fish ($6.95). Interesting starters include crab meat soup with asparagus and Hanoi beef noodle soup.

Closed Mondays. BYOB.

Pacific Café

1619 North Damen, (773) PACIFIC

Located in a tiny, converted produce market, Pacific Café opened during Around the Coyote 1995, sold out everything in the restaurant, and hasn't looked back since. Pacific Café offers Thai, Japanese, and Vietnamese dishes. There's a full sushi menu, with some innovative options, along with representative appetizers from all three cuisines. A long list of noodle dishes are priced mostly at $7.25 and under. Thai entrées, primarily curries, are $6.95 and under. There are a half dozen Vietnamese entrées and many Japanese dishes, priced $5.95 to $10.50. The sushi and sashimi dinners are too expensive, so you have to order sushi by the piece. Food is served on brightly colored dishes marked by sprightly Pacific Rim designs. Service is extremely hospitable, but can be slow since the place only has one over worked sushi chef. During the holidays, the restaurant decorates its Christmas tree with plastic sushi and soy sauce packets, topping everything off with a tempura shrimp star.

Open daily.

Banana Leaf

3811 North Southport, (773) 853-8683

Where better to go if you think you live on the artistic edge than the ultrahip Music Box, with the most cutting-edge films north of the Fine Arts? Grab a bite before the flick just up the street at Banana Leaf, an Asian restaurant serving Chinese, Thai, and other Eastern-flavored noodle dishes, along with stir-fry rice dishes and soups. The "specialties of noodles" at $5.95 each are a good deal with the peanut curry noodles being particularly tasty. "Banana Dishes," or the special entrées, range from $5.95 to $8.25. Nice deck here, those few months of the year you can enjoy it.

Open daily. BYOB. Patio dining.

Asia Bowl

1001 West Webster, (773) 348-3060
3411 North Broadway, (773) 529-2600

More a carryout than a sit-down restaurant, the tiny Asia Bowl storefronts are decorated with vivid photographs of the owner's travels in Asia. The restaurants feature inexpensive Thai, Vietnamese, Japanese, and Chinese dishes with a focus on soups, noodles, and wraps. The California roll is a six-inch seaweed billy club stuffed with rice, avocado, and crab, and, at $5.25, nearly the most expensive item on the menu. Wraps—mushu vegetarian and chicken, Java BBQ chicken, and samurai salmon to name a few—are similarly hefty. Noodles and rice dishes offer the usual stir fry and peanut-ty suspects.

Open daily. No alcohol.

Pan Asia Café

3443 North Sheffield, (773) 880-0008

Billing itself as "chopstick cuisine" and operating on the theory of "don't they all seem alike anyway?," Pan Asia manages to combine a number of Asian cuisines, including Korean, Chinese, and Thai, into a cohesive menu.

The place has to be good since it's sitting in a location that's been the kiss of death to so many others.

Open daily. BYOB.

Sunshine Café

5449 North Clark, (773) 334-6214

Japanese noodles and homestyle cooking are featured at this one-room Andersonville storefront with an almost exclusively Japanese crowd. Noodle dishes are all priced $6 and under with sunshine ramen, Cha Siu-chicken, kamaboko (Japanese fishcake), egg, shrimp, nori (seaweed), and veggies being the only $6 dish. Nonnoodle dinners, priced at $8 and under, are also available and include teriyaki (steak, $8, chicken, $5.75), tempura ($7), and saba shioyaki, lightly broiled mackerel, for $7. Where else can you get Norwegian salmon, served teriyaki or shioyaki style, priced $7?

Closed Tuesdays. BYOB.

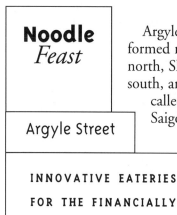

Noodle *Feast*

Argyle Street

INNOVATIVE EATERIES FOR THE FINANCIALLY FINICKY PALATE

Argyle Street, or more broadly, the area formed roughly by the square of Argyle to the north, Sheridan on the east, Lawrence to the south, and Broadway to the west has often been called "New Chinatown," although Little Saigon would probably be more appropriate. Even though some Chinese and other Asian establishments do exist, the area is primarily Vietnamese with a smattering of other Southeast Asian cultures thrown in. Two good Vietnamese options to check out are Hoang Mai and Song Huong. **Hoang Mai**, 5020 North Sheridan, (773) 561-3700, is a spanking-clean Vietnamese/Chinese storefront with 183 items on the menu priced $3.95 to $8.95. Roast quail, shrimp wrapped in sugar cane with vegetables, eel with coconut curry in a clay pot are all good bets. Traditional breakfast of steamed rice cakes with shrimp or pork fillings ($2.95) is an option if you're up early. Another storefront serving Vietnamese and Chinese, **Song Huong,** 5424 North Broadway, (773) 271-6702, also has an extensive menu with more than one hundred options, including coconut curries with frog legs or venison and stuffed Vietnamese pancakes. Finish it all off with a "sweetie," a kind of Vietnamese flurry made with mung beans, red beans, coconut milk, and crushed ice. Both Hoang Mai and Song Huong will set you back a "fork and knife."

Marked by a startling facade of turquoise and coral accompanied by two golden lions guarding the front door, **Nhu Hoa**, 1020 West Argyle, (773) 878-0618, Chicago's Laotian option, also serves Vietnamese and a couple of Cambodian dishes and will only cost you a "fork." Laotian dishes are similar to other Southeast Asian meals but are marked by the use of sticky rice and other culinary nuances. With more than two hundred options on the menu, there's a lot of opportunity to conduct your own taste test.

Culinary Colonial

Join the Wonton Club for a taste of pre-Boxer Rebellion

There were days when the sun never set on the British empire—and the colonies of the French, Spanish, and the rest of Western Europe. Days of glory and conquest that stretched from the Americas to the India and Indochina, past the dateline in the Far East. Even in the sunset years of colonial decay, there was still a feeling of faded grandeur that hung languidly over pale khaki- and linen-clad sahibs and their ladies as they sipped tea lazily in places like Rangoon, Saigon, and Shanghai and played lawn croquet at legendary establishments like Raffles, the Peninsula, and the Strand.

Slowly, and then in a wave of independence, the colonies slipped away, with the handing over of Hong Kong, gained over 100 years ago during the Opium Wars, shutting the door on the chapter of Western conquests. And, with an end to European geographic dominance has come a wave of Asian influence, a culinary conquest if the restaurant scene in Chicago is any sign of the times. In the past few years, the Asian tigers have roared into the mainstream of Chicago's gourmet landscape. Once relegated to ethnic neighborhoods and small storefronts, Pacific-influenced cuisine has sprung up on every corner at every price point. From the bright and perky Penny's and Hi Ricky's that have brought oodles of noodles for $5 a bowl to standing-room-only crowds to the Ben Paos and red lights that have made Asian-inspired dishes a passion for downtown gwailoh-gringos on their lunch breaks, Far East flavors are in.

One of the newest entrants to the "Asian fusion" food scene is the **Wonton Club**. The Wonton Club, which bills itself as a "sushi bar/noodle shop/saki lounge," stirs memories of former colonial grandeur while it cooks up a mixture of Asian-influenced dishes.

Lazily twisting ceiling fans push indolent breezes under the Wonton Club's drop bamboo ceilings. Celadon green walls, the color of a Ming vase, gleam softly against red, black, and copper accents. Largescale black and white photographs, portraits of small boys wearing Red Army caps and graceful kimonoed women, stare serenely at an Andy Warhol portrait of Mao.

The front of the club is dominated by a gleaming ebony sushi bar, while the back is exposed to an open kitchen, which produces artistically graceful preparations that repose tranquilly on blackcurved plates and wide-mouthed bowls. Smoking is discreetly tucked away in a mezzanine alcove that divides the restaurant in half. Cushioned booths flank the Club's interior and snuggle-ready pillows beckon diners. My coworkers, Paul and Alexa, adjusted the bolsters for office comrade-correctness, and we settled in for a voyage of culinary exploration.

A spatter of appetizers—steamed chicken wontons with ginger soy dipping sauce, tempura tuna sushi, fried crab and bean sprout spring rolls with toasted ginger, shrimp scallion satay with three pepper sauce, plum barbecued baby back ribs—perhaps combined with a few sushi selections, would have been enough for a meal. It was nice that the sushi card offered a whole section of vegetarian options.

Our waiter was right on target when he assured Alexa that her wide noodles with kung pao vegetables would be "hearty and robust," and, as promised, the coconut Thai noodles with shrimp were "rich and heavy and very coconut-ty." Debbie, our other companion, made a meal—and several since her original visit—of the cold Szechwan

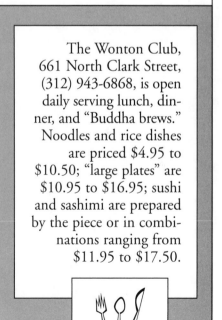

The Wonton Club, 661 North Clark Street, (312) 943-6868, is open daily serving lunch, dinner, and "Buddha brews." Noodles and rice dishes are priced \$4.95 to \$10.50; "large plates" are \$10.95 to \$16.95; sushi and sashimi are prepared by the piece or in combinations ranging from \$11.95 to \$17.50.

sesame noodles with cucumber and Chinatown vinaigrette. We tossed in the crackling calamari salad for some additional side greens.

We skipped the "interesting" vegetables, which as just a seasonal assortment sounded too dull to command valuable stomach space, and bypassed the rock shrimp and wok-seared ginger barbecued chicken fried rice dishes to make room for the "large plates." We wrestled with a choice between Lapsong suchon tea toasted salmon with mango miso, hoisen barbecued mahi mahi with rock shrimp fried rice, and Thai chili-spiked filet over wok-seared greens, and then settled for sharing a seafood hot pot with ginger lemongrass broth.

To our great dismay, the hot fudge dim sum, reputed to be a simmering hot pot of chocolate with tempura-clad bananas and mango morsels for dipping, was unavailable (and has also been unobtainable on subsequent trips), so we had to settle for green tea ice cream. Satisfied, we leaned back in the cushions and decided we were happy we chose to join the Club.

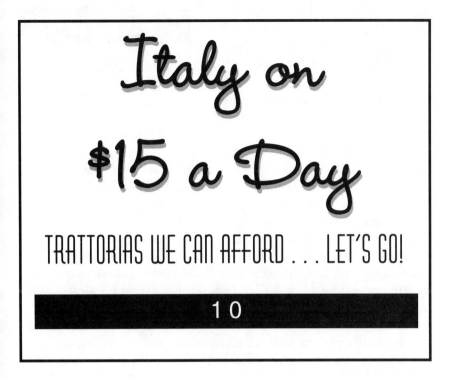

Italy on $15 a Day

TRATTORIAS WE CAN AFFORD . . . LET'S GO!

10

Contrary to popular belief, Marco Polo did not bring spaghetti back from China and then introduced pasta to Italy and the rest of Europe. The Western world has long had its own tradition of noodle making. The Tomba dei Rilievi, an Etruscan tomb in Italy dating from the fourth century B.C., was found to contain the rudimentary equipment for making pasta—the wooden board, the rolling pin, and the fluted cutting wheel—still used today in Romagna, Lazio, Abbruzzi, and other regions of Italy. Dry pasta is still made from water and hard durum wheat, the same wheat that was used to make pasta in ancient Roman times.

The famous Romans Horace (65–8 B.C.) and Cicero (106–43 B.C.) were both known to be fans of lagunam, the Latin term for lasagna. It is said that Cicero loved to eat thin strips of pasta, cooked in fat broth and garnished with cheese, pepper, saffron, and cinnamon. Italian history and pasta have been made together. The natives of Bologna (home of the sauce) invented tagliatelle, which was created to immortalize Lucrezia Borgia's long golden tresses. Today, pasta has become so ingrained in the Italian lifestyle that husbands phone home before leaving work and tell their wives, "Butta la pasta!" Literally, "Throw in the pasta!" In other words, "Hey, I'm on my way home, and dinner better be ready when I get there."

> "Everything you see I owe to spaghetti."
>
> —**Sophia Loren**

The wave of Southern Italians that emigrated to the United States beginning in the twenties established spaghetti as Americans' favorite pasta. Spaghetti was the dish Southern Italians thought of first; it was cheap, quick, and easy even for the most inexperienced cook to prepare.

During Prohibition, the only place where a glass of wine could be drunk legally was at Italian speakeasies, all of which served spaghetti. Pastas, spaghetti, and the some six hundred other noodle shapes remain popular—in fact, Italian endures as the most popular ethnic food in the country. The average American now eats nearly twenty pounds of pasta every year. Pasta is not only a complex carbohydrate that supplies six of the eight essential amino acids; but also, eating it also releases serotonin, a chemical in the brain that tells your body to feel relaxed and calm. Now that's what you call using your noodle.

Editor's Note: Price ratings in this chapter are typically based on the prices for pasta dishes, not for *secondi*—meat, chicken, fish, and seafood entrées.

Pompei Little Italy

2955 North Sheffield, (773) 325-1900

The north branch of a Taylor Street institution established in 1909, Pompei Little Italy is a cafeteria-style Italian eatery that serves handmade pasta, handmade pizza, and Pompei "strudels." Pasta ($4.95–$7.95) is made daily and includes spaghetti with homemade meatballs and three kinds of ravioli—spicy sausage, herb chicken, and vegetarian. Eleven different versions of strudels, including the poor boy, turkey stuffing, and steak fajita, are served by the slice ($3.25–$3.50) or in small ($14–$15, serves 4–6) or large versions ($25–$29, serves 8–12). Nearly two dozen different pan or stuffed pizzas are served by the slice, half tray (serves 4–6), or full tray (serves 8–12). No surprise given the location, type of food, and prices, Pompei Little Italy attracts a young college crowd.

Open daily. No alcohol.

Pasta Fina

921 West Belmont, (773) 528-4499

A small storefront on Belmont, Pasta Fina is another one of those pick-your-sauce-and-match-it-with-a-pasta type of place. Pastas come in either cut, gnocchi (small potato dumplings), or stuffed versions. Sauces are available in a number of groupings:

Creamy alfredo, gorgonzola, and creamy pesto

Herb sauces pesto genovese, parmesan and olive oil, and tomato basil

Marinara and bolognese

Specials such as white clam, olive oil and veggies, and spinach carolina (my all-time favorite with pine nuts and anchovies—aaahh)

Prices vary by sauce and type of pasta, starting at $7.25 for cut pasta or gnocchi with one of the cream sauces or marinara (the equivalent with stuffed pasta is $7.95) and going up to $9.75 for the specials.

Open daily. BYOB.

Anna Maria's Pasteria

3953 North Broadway, (773) 929-6363

If you've never heard of Anna Maria's Pasteria, that tiny jewel of Lakeview eateries, stay ignorant—I already have to wait long enough to get a table here. Since this small, unpretentious storefront opened in 1989, crowds of BYOB–toting diners have been driving the prices steadily higher. The restaurant itself reflects its success. When it first opened, Anna Maria's was a tiny, nondescript storefront with unbeatable home-made pasta and the best tiramisu in town. The restaurant then expanded south into the space next door and added another dining room and bar. Since taking over the storefront to the north formerly occupied by a pawn shop, Anna Maria's has not only added a third room, but has also totally redecorated. It now has three fancy rooms that glow with warm golden walls accented with wine colored drapes and tablecloths. Few would expect to find this luxury at Irving Park and Broadway.

These days, Anna Maria's really only qualifies for a "fork and knife" if you stick to pasta dishes, which will cost you $7.75 to $10.95 for the nonseafood pastas. Specials are always excellent, and the rotola aurora (vegetarian rolled pasta with ricotta cheese and spinach in a creamy tomato sauce, $9.50) is a house highlight. By sticking with pasta, however, you would be missing out on the truly magnificent veal marsala (with salad and a side of pasta, $13.95). So do this: have one night's kind-of-not-cheap dinner at Anna Maria's and the next night economize two doors down at the Taco & Burrito House (3946 North Broadway). Eat cheap by amortizing your costs. If you're going to blow your budget anyway, start off with an appetizer of crostini, roasted Italian bread with fresh tomatoes, spices, and fresh mozzarella, but save enough room for dessert. This is a place that pays homage to espresso-dusted mascarpone cheese.

Open daily. Wine and beer.

Bar Louie

226 West Chicago, (312) 337-3313

Simply one of the best watering holes in the city, on nice days Bar Louie treats its patrons to sidewalk tables whose well-positioned view of picturesque Chicago Avenue running through the heart of River North is serenaded by the low hum of the Ravenswood El overhead. Aside from the scenery draw, Bar Louie has an abundant menu loaded with Italian pub selections, including pastas, pizzas, insalate (salads), antipasti (appetizers), and panini (sandwiches) all priced at $6.95 and under. Salads are meal-sized; the antipasto ($5.95) and the chicken and goat cheese salad ($6.50) are both highly recommended. Sandwiches should yield more than enough for now and later. Try the muffaletta—salami, smoked ham, and provolone with Sicilian olive mix ($4.95). Decorated with colorful tiles and bright murals, Bar Louie is a good place to relax in an atmosphere of soothing culture and fine Mediterranean food.

Open daily. Full bar.

Cucina Bella

543 West Diversey, (773) 868-1119

Locals rave about Cucina Bella's "authentic Italian comfort foods" and reasonable prices, but I rarely go there because you can't buy a parking spot in this neighborhood, and it's a real hike from the El. Although some are higher priced, plenty of pastas are available from $4.95 (the spaghetti simpatico) to $10.95. Among the secondi, only the pollo romano ($10.50) and the torta rustica ($9.50), a Tuscan-style pot pie with sausage, vegetables, and tomato cream sauce, are the right price. The place has its own cookbook, and for $35, you can sit in the kitchen and sample the whole menu.

Open daily. Full bar.

Mucho *Mange*

Taylor Street

INNOVATIVE EATERIES FOR THE FINANCIALLY FINICKY PALATE

Just south of the University of Illinois—Chicago's campus is Taylor Street, the heart of Chicago's Little Italy. Lining Taylor from Morgan to Ashland are numerous Italian eateries, most far more expensive than the neighborhood's location and general appearance merit. There are, however, some reasonable options (made even more inexpensive if you stick with pasta or chicken). Skip the long waits at the Rosebud, skip trendy Tuscany, skip the fake Roman ruins at Trattoria Roma Terza, and try some of the lesser-known places. Anchoring the neighborhood is **Tufano's**, The Vernon Park Tap, 1073 West Vernon Park Place, (312) 733-3393. For more than sixty years, diners have been heading for the room in back of the bar where the blackboard lists the daily selections, priced $6 to $12. Pastas are served with red or white sauce; meatballs and sausage are extra. There's a fish special on Fridays. Check out **Rosal's Cucina,** 1154 West Taylor, (312) 243-2357. Homemade pasta ranges from $5.95 to $9.50. Daily specials feature dishes such as spinach ravioli with gorgonzola ($8.95). **Gennaro's,** 1352 West Taylor, (312) 243-1035, where Mama Gennaro has been making homemade pasta for over 40 years, also has reasonable prices. If you're looking to downscale, try **Little Joe's Circle Lounge,** 1041 West Taylor, (312) 829-5888, where you can get spaghetti or mostaccioli with soup or salad for $5.75 and chase it down with a $3 pitcher of beer. Or, if you're only comfortable with the familiar, the newest **Leona's,** 1419 West Taylor, (312) 850-2222, is a cozy addition to the chain with an outdoor patio. If you just want to grab a quick meal, head for the intersection of Taylor and Aberdeen, 1100 West, where you can get a slice of pizza at **Little Gusto** or a sandwich at **Al's #1 Italian Beef,** 1079 West Taylor, (312) 226-4017—plenty of police cars in this parking lot. Finish off this succulent repast with a frozen lemonade across the street at **Mario's Italian Lemonade** (closed in the winter).

The Pasta Bowl

2434 North Clark, (773) 525-BOWL

A mini version of Pasta Palazzo, the Pasta Bowl serves fresh made pastas, panini sandwiches, and *bona vita* ("good life" food prepared without oil, butter, or cheese), all for $3.95 to $6.50. "B.V." dishes include bow ties with chicken and grilled veggies, spaghetti primavera, and linguine with bay scallops, all of which are in a marinara sauce. The fresh made pastas range from fettuccine alfredo to ravioli, tortellini, and gnocchi in a choice of sauce, including rosemary gorgonzola for those who like it rich at a cheap price.

Open daily. No alcohol.

Club Lago

331 West Superior, (312) 337-9444

Club Lago is where the Corleone family would eat if they lived in Chicago. An old-time Italian eatery and bar in the heart of chic River North, Club Lago's menu is the "full cucina Toscana." Entrées vary depending on the day (fish is only available on the weekends), but there's always a lot of red sauce.

Open daily. Full bar.

The Dancing Noodle

1954 Central, Evanston, (847) 475-1200
215 Skokie Valley, Highland Park, (847) 831-9555

The Dancing Noodle chain, which at one point had four or five restaurants, brought the mix-and-match pasta and sauce concept to the Northshore. You pick the type of pasta (angel hair, linguine, fettuccine, or cheese ravioli), the flavor of pasta (plain, spinach, basil, wheat), and the sauce. Prices, based on the type of sauce, range from $6.10 for veggie marinara to $7.10 for tarragon asparagus in white sauce, red snapper filet, or shrimp in heavy cream. All pasta selections include a salad and garlic bread.

Open daily. Wine and beer.

Torrefazione Italia

2200 North Lincoln, (773) 477-6833

To experience "the warmth of Italy" and Seattle's ultimate coffee, stop by Torrefazione Italia, a bright café reminiscent of the sunny terra-cotta patios that line the Italian coasts. Enjoy an Italian breakfast pastry with a cup of coffee that will make Starbucks' taste like that stuff you get free at the office.

Open daily. No alcohol.

Penne Wise

Find a fair deal on pasta

My best friend Susan once told me that the one kind of food she refuses to pay a lot of money to go out for is pasta, because it's the one dish she should be able to throw in a pot and boil up herself. Don't get me wrong, I love pasta, but my friend is right. Pasta should be a no-brainer. You pick either plain noodles—long and skinny or short and curly—or stuffed—a plump ravioli pillow or a chubby crescent of a tortellini or maybe even a buxom cigar of a cannelloni—toss it in a bubbling cauldron until pliable, and then swim it in a, preferably, cholesterol-rich cream sauce. What could be simpler? Unless you're incompetent and cook things to mush, there's no reason to pay $15.95 for a plate of farfalle pomodoro, high-priced speak for bowtie pasta with tomato sauce.

So, isn't it refreshing to find **Pasta Palazzo**? Finally, here's an Italian eatery that doesn't pretend to take us to the Tuscan countryside at downtown Rome prices. Pasta Palazzo doesn't even aspire to the pretenses that cloak the trattorias that populate our city. Billing itself as a "gourmet pasta diner," Pasta Palazzo is a change of pace that delivers hearty, tasty fare to satisfy your appetite while leaving you lira to spare.

A cozy slice of a restaurant at Armitage and Halsted between a vacant lot and a space reserved for Mexican-style tapas bars destined to go out of business, Pasta Palazzo skips the wine jugs and grape leaves that deck so many of the city's Italian establishments for lengthy tables that have that clean and lean look of Milan. Walls are illuminated with a bright mosaic of broken ceramic tile, and colorful pictures extend the impression of warmth where the Crayola-hued tiles leave off. The narrow interior is dominated by a counter that runs the length of the restaurant.

Now I am quite partial to counters, especially ones that have chairs with back rests. At the counter, you get to see what's going on, blend with the regulars, strike up a discussion with the stranger next to you. It's a comfort seat. At Pasta Palazzo, the counter treats you to all the usual counter benefits, along with the opportunity to observe short-order Italian. Who ever suspected chicken could be efficiently grilled up with sun-dried tomatoes, cream, and mushrooms like a slider waiting to be flipped on a bun? That haughty porcini mushrooms would consent to be shoved around by an industrial-strength spatula that's more often seen pushing chopped onions destined for the common Italian sausage? Or have we been fooled all along, and, in the depths of our city's most aristocratic Italian kitchens sporting pasta prices that are truly royal, is *sauté* really only French for *grill*?

Although prepared simply, Pasta Palazzo's dishes offer as much zest as any other local trattoria's. Pastas include handmade options (gnocchi, tortellini, and ravioli with a choice of sauces) and "healthy" alternatives prepared without oil, butter, or cheese. The conchigliette gorgonzola, small shells with spinach, gorgonzola cheese, tomato, and cream, is particularly good for those who don't care about their arteries. Although the various risottos served periodically as specials are tasty, they can be a little chewy, since it's tough to grill up a dish that's supposed to simmer endlessly. It's particularly refreshing to see polenta offered for a reasonable $5. A selection of panini—a.k.a. sandwiches—is also available, including "vegetariano 1" and "vegetariano 2."

So, next time your stomach's thinking you should treat yourself like Caesar, but your wallet's reality is Chef Boy-Ar-Dee, don't hesitate to think pasta. Pasta Palazzo.

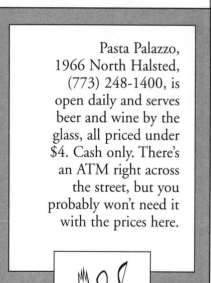

Pasta Palazzo, 1966 North Halsted, (773) 248-1400, is open daily and serves beer and wine by the glass, all priced under $4. Cash only. There's an ATM right across the street, but you probably won't need it with the prices here.

No Raw Deal

SUSHI SAVINGS

11

"I'd like to be . . . under the sea . . . in an octopus's garden . . . in the shade . . ." In Japan, sushi is everyday food. You can find it everywhere, even in fast-food establishments and saran-wrapped in the refrigerated section of convenience stores. In Chicago, you can find an abundance of sushi—particularly cheap sushi—in Lakeview between Belmont and Addison. Peppering Clark Street are numerous storefronts with sushi bars and sit-down tables that will satisfy your yen for bargain-priced varieties of seaweeded, rice-balled sushi delights.

Sounds kind of fishy to me. Sushi, which has more than 1,000 years of history and tradition behind it, was developed by the Japanese who, using salt and rice to preserve varieties of fish, pressed the fish into thin layers until it fermented. But sushi has evolved beyond just fish to encompass a wide variety of seafoods and vegetables. If the thought of raw fish doesn't float your boat, there are plenty of options available in potentially more palatable shrimp, crab, and other crustaceans. The ubiquitous California roll is, frankly, fishless. Or, you may opt to go the straight vegetarian route and order the common kappa maki (cucumber roll) or various other vegetable-only sushis.

You don't have to be a sushi tzu (sushi expert) to know your way around the bar. Here are some sushi sayings that'll help even a novice order from the itamae-san (sushi chef) with the assurance of a veteran.

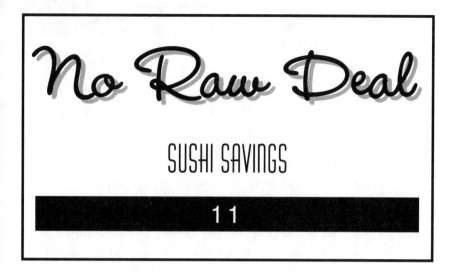

There are several common forms of sushi. Nigiri sushi are oblong bars of vinegared rice (shari) topped with a dab of wasabi (green horseradish) and a slice of fish or seafood. Maki are long, rolled tubes of rice and filling cut into several pieces. Temaki are handrolls that look like cone-shaped seaweed bouquets.

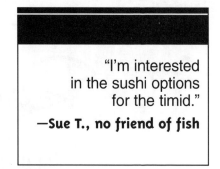

> "I'm interested in the sushi options for the timid."
>
> **—Sue T., no friend of fish**

Your sushi is usually accompanied by several condiments. Gari is the pickled ginger that cleanses your palate between varieties. Wasabi is the green horseradish that masks the fishy taste by temporarily paralyzing your palate. Murasaki is the soy sauce you use for dipping. Agari is the steaming green tea that's drunk in great quantities to refresh the palate and rinse away fish fats that stay on the tongue.

Many restaurants offer a moriawase plate, or a mixed menu of sushi, which is a very economical way to try a number of sushi pieces. Sushi commonly found in this combination includes kappa and tekka maki (cucumber and tuna rolls), maguro (tuna), sake (salmon), hamachi (yellowtail), ebi (shrimp), saba (mackerel), tako (octopus), tamago (egg), and uni (sea urchin).

You don't have to be able to maneuver the ohaji (chopsticks) to eat this sometimes slippery dish. Sushi is finger food. Just pick the piece up, flip it over, dip it in the soy sauce fish side down, and put it in your mouth so that the fish hits your taste buds. Irrasshai! (Welcome to the sushi bar.)

Nakayoshi

919 West Belmont, (773) 929-9333

This no-nonsense storefront has the menu on the wall and dented tin pots of steaming green tea on the tables. For sushi, you can select from (A) the eight-piece Nakayoshi special seafood or (B) the nine-piece mixed maki and inari (vinegared rice wrapped in fried bean curd) both for $7.50. Examples of both these options are available in plastic and displayed in the glass case at the front counter. Sushi is also available à la carte, although this is not stated on the bulletin board on the wall. In addition, tuna or mixed sashimi is available for only

$8.50. Other non-sushi meals, most for under $6, are also available. This place is really tiny, and if you happen to sit down at the one big table, you may end up eating with some strangers.

Open daily. No alcohol.

Shiroi Hana

3242 North Clark, (773) 477-1652

Nohana

3136 North Broadway, (773) 528-1902

Incredibly popular and crowded at all times, these two related restaurants set the standard for value sushi. Not only do the 'Hanas have the best sushi prices in town, but both serve very fresh fish—the proprietor was in the wholesale fish business. Both restaurants have similar menus. Both offer a sushi deluxe special of nine pieces and one maki roll for $7.95 (Shiroi Hana's is available daily, Nohana's only Monday through Thursday). Nohana also has a "Nohana's Choice" for $6.95; Shiroi Hana has a "sushi regular," six pieces and one roll for $6.50. Both restaurants offer excellent "dinner box" combinations that allow you to sample tempura or teriyaki (beef, chicken, or tuna) with one California roll, three additional pieces of sushi (tuna, salmon, and shrimp), suomono (seafood and cucumber with vinegar sauce), and soup. Combinations range from $8.75 to $9.25. If you're hanging out around lunch time, you can get a great deal on a "lunch box" at either restaurant—a choice of chicken or tuna teriyaki, fish cutlets, or tempura, accompanied by a California roll, tekka maki (tuna roll), soup, and salad. All lunch boxes range from $5.95 to $6.95.

Both open daily. Full bars.

Tokyo Marina

5058-60 North Clark, (773) 878-2900

Looking much like it spent its former life as a Roy Rogers, Tokyo Marina brings quality sushi to the

Andersonville area in spite of its low-budget, fast-food decor. Tokyo Marina offers its own interesting twists on the sushi theme designed to appeal to the locals, including Windy City maki-battered nori maki deep-fried with flounder/hirame, cucumber, avocado, and Japanese mayo ($5.75)—and sloppy Tokyo Marinara maki with a fried shrimp tucked inside ($5.75). All dinners start with a free appetizer, and a standard eight-piece sushi combo is $10. An extensive menu offers a good choice of tempura dishes, casseroles, donburi (bowl dishes), and udon (noodle dishes) generally priced between $6 and $8. Wash it all down with Japanese beer on draft or in the bottle. If you're with a partner and budget's not an issue, try the Tokyo Marinara Love Boat, at $35.50, "a dining pleasure designed for two."

Open daily. Wine and beer.

Sanko's

3485 North Clark, (773) 528-1930

If you can't stand the crowds at Matsuya a couple doors south, head up the street to Sanko. A thin series of rooms, Sanko lures in Cub fans looking for exotic adventure with its weekend karaoke in the back room. Yes, every Thursday and Friday night, you can belt out "Sanko's pop hits" from 9:00 P.M. to 1:00 A.M., Muzak at its best. If you need to build up energy for singing, you can order from a large selection of sushi that graciously categorizes offerings for the sushi novice: raw, boiled or broiled; vegetable; makimono (rolled and cut); nigiri (seafood on hand-pressed sushi roll)—you won't get lost here. As with other local Japanese restaurants, Sanko has sushi specials with local appeal. Here, it's the Cub maki (broiled salmon, cream cheese, scallion, and avocado, $5.25). Sanko also serves one of the most expensive maki rolls around, the spider, an eight-piece roll of fried soft shell crab, cucumber, scallion, and masago, $9.75.

Open daily. Full bar.

Akasaka Japanese Restaurant

5978 North Lincoln, (773) 989-1115

No storefront here, Akasaka, located on the northern section of Lincoln Avenue in the land of small motels with neon "Sleep Cheap!" signs from the 1950s, is a full-blown restaurant with plenty of blond wood and screens to make it an appealing option to the no-frills storefronts on Clark. The sushi here is excellent—large, tender slices spilling over supporting rice balls with, whoa now, noticeable amounts of wasabi to make things memorable. This sushi, however, is really not cheap chow (the cheapest sushi combo is $10.95) unless you order à la carte, come for lunch, or get lucky. To get lucky, stop by after 11.30 A.M., sit at what is, hopefully, the empty sushi bar, and make friends with the itamae-san, the sushi chef. Order the $6.95 lunch special, but ask if you can substitute a different maki roll for the boring kappa maki (cucumber roll). If the chef's in a good mood and it's particularly slow, you'll probably get both rolls—six extra pieces of sushi! And, if the chef's in a really congenial mood, he's going to whip you up a hand roll (probably tuna with skin), hand you that little goody gratis, and tell you it's the special of the day. Once you've eaten all that, plus the three or so free appetizers that come with every meal, washed it all down with the tasty nutty, green tea, you'll have really made the most of the drive (and the bill was only $7.60). Try this strategy yourself.

Open daily. Full bar.

Kotobuki

5547 North Clark, (773) 275-6588

Like Akasaka, Kotobuki is pricier with more elaborate food than the standard Wrigleyville cheap sushi. This storefront located on the northern edge of Andersonville stands out with its aesthetically pleasing and innovative presentation. An excellent example is the futomaki, or big roll. Kotobuki's version of this sushi bar mainstay is an eight-piece, spinach-stuffed roll with a sweet walnut sauce ($6.95). More than enough for a meal. The interesting bargain here is the $17 "temaki for 2," a platter with all the fixin's for two adventurous diners to roll their own handrolls. For dessert, in addition to the standard green tea ice cream, Kotobuki also offers ginger and red bean ice cream.

Closed Monday. Full bar.

quick bites

Matsuya

3469 North Clark, (773) 248-2677

Matsuya has long set the standard in Lakeview for good, cheap Japanese cuisine. This popular two-room storefront always has a wait to sit down. A large selection of rolled makimono and molded, Osaka-style oshi-sushi is supplemented with a variety of cone-shaped temaki handrolls. Sushi combos start at $7.75 for the temaki assortment. Ginger ice cream is sometimes available.

Open daily. Full bar.

New Tokyo

3139 North Broadway, (773) 248-1193

Three different combos are priced $9.95 and under, and all of the other entrées are $6.95 and under and served with rice and salad. This small corner Lakeview storefront is one of the city's Japanese values with its "authentic Japanese char-broiled teriyaki at fast-food prices!"

Open daily. No alcohol.

Kyoto Japanese Restaurant

2534 North Lincoln, (773) 477-2788

For DePaul yuppies who don't mind spending a lot of money on sushi, Kyoto is a convenient option just up the street from the Biograph Theater. The cheapest combo here is $9.95 for only six pieces and one roll. If you're not going to venture north of Wrightwood, you might want to stick with the donburi (rice bowls) or udon (noodles) here, all priced at $6.95 and under.

Closed Monday. Full bar.

quick bites

Star Market

3349 North Clark, (773) 482-0599

One of the largest Japanese grocery stores in the city, this is the place to buy supplies for your own personal sushi bar. One refrigerator case is stuffed with varieties of seaweed; another is filled with tuna, eel, and other fish, much of which is flown in fresh twice a week. Grab a screen and give it a roll.

Closed Sunday.

Editor's Note: This chapter's price ratings were based on the whole menu, not just the sushi selections. I encourage you to mix and match sushi with other menu options.

Sushi Banshee

Dive into the raw fish rolls at Tomodachi

Do you ever have a yen for raw fish? Weekly, if not more often, do you get the urge to swim with the sharks and gobble up salmon, mackerel, and shrimp and other chilled and sliced water creatures mounted on oblong beds of rice?

When the siren call of Charlie the Tuna becomes impossible to ignore, I head to Lakeview. Located just south of Wrigley Field, one of Chicago's bastions of Americana, is Chicago's sushi strip. Baseball, apple pie, and raw fish are celebrated liberally by the Japanese storefronts that pepper the blocks of Clark Street between Belmont and Addison. Now joining strip anchors—double-storefront Matsuya and Shiroi Hana, king (or emporer, if you prefer) of budget sushi with the $7.95 sushi deluxe (recently raised from $6.95)—is Tomodachi, a recent addition to the neighborhood.

Although a smaller space than some of its neighbors, **Tomodachi, Japanese Cuisine**, makes an impact with a splashy interior. Giant paintings of kimono-clad, top-knotted natives that are a cross between Kabuki and Roy Lichtenstein gaze benignly at patrons snarfing maki rolls and experiencing the joys of soy. Peter Max-ish splashes of Crayola-bright psychedelic swirls cover the hardwood floor. A spacious gray and white counter with red trim offers patrons up-close-and-personal access to both the sushi chefs and a small hibachi grill where the cook regularly performs his own version of *Stomp* with assorted stir-fry equipment and Ginsu knives (this is a "smoking" area). Meanwhile, the sounds of perky oldies rock in the background.

Sushi, from sliced maki rolls to individual pieces, or nigiri, is bodaciously big and fresh. Slabs of glistening fish flesh nestle around plump rice balls while chunks of seafood poke out coyly from rolls of seaweed and vegetables. The standard sushi combination ($7.99) offers only seven individual pieces in combination with the kappa maki and California rolls—in comparison to Shiroi Hana's nine. But, as my dining companion pointed out on a sheer weight comparison, the Tomodachi offering tips

Tomodachi Japanese Cuisine, 3468 N. Clark, (773) 296-0857, fax (773) 296-0858, is open seven days a week and BYOB. Four tiny parking spaces are available in the alley behind the restaurant and shared with the Thai place next door.

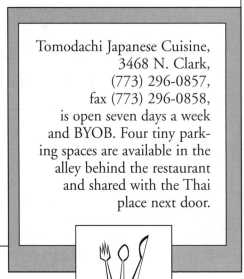

the scales and wins by about a kilo. A good selection of other sushi combinations is available. The Popeye ($6.25) is an interesting combination of a spicy spinach maki roll and four cooked mussels on the half shell in an egg and, apparently, mayonnaise sauce. The Tokyo Rok combo ($7.50) offers tobiko nigiri (flying fish egg), unagi roll, and a California roll. Unagi, which is eel, is known to build stamina and should be eaten during the hottest days of summer to avoid exhaustion and anytime as an aphrodisiac.

The menu, amusingly decorated with drawings of rambunctious pigs that bear a strong resemblance to energetic sumo wrestlers belly-flopping against each other, offers a variety of cooked dishes in addition to the sushi selections. Various hibachi grilled dinners range from $8.50 to $12.50 and are accompanied by the aforementioned percussion performance at no extra charge. Donburis (rice dishes) and noodles are a mere $4.50, while tempura with a choice of either sushi or sashimi is $9.50. If you find yourself really to be no fan of fish after all, plenty of vegetarian options are available. Tomodachi is open for lunch and serves a good variety of hibachi choices priced $4.50to $6.95.

Tomodachi, which means "friend" in Japanese, lives up to its name. Service is prompt and smiling, and diners are greeted with a full-throated "Irashaimase," or "welcome," as they walk through the door—or, if you've already established yourself as a regular, shouts of "Hey, Mike!"

Here's a Pita Advice . . .

12

Dolmeh about it. The Middle East, that small sandy stretch on the eastern shores of the Mediterranean gave rise to three of the world's major religions and, subsequently, a reason for endless office parties in December. Think about what civilization has gained from the Middle East: a lot of religions (Christianity, Judaism, and Islam), a lot of books (*The Source*, *Exodus*), a lot of movies (*The Ten Commandments*, *Ben-Hur*, *Lawrence of Arabia*), and a lot of food.

Oh, I'm hooked on a phyllo . . . and feta and fava and falafel. Due to close proximity and climactic similarities, Middle Eastern and Mediterranean cuisines share a variety of common flavors and ingredients, including olives, chickpeas, eggplant, spinach, bulgur, rice, feta cheese, yogurt, and lamb. Derivations of dishes that originated in the Middle East reach west all the way to the Iberian Peninsula and beyond to the American heartland.

Rock the Casbah. Whether you're up in Andersonville or in the Orthodox Jewish neighborhood at California and Devon or right down on Michigan, if shawirma is your karma, you're probably no more than a couple blocks from a fresh stuffed pita. So get out there and start sampling—there's ample opportunity to eat your fala-fill!

Hummus A Little Tune . . .

Cheap Chow Chicago's Guide to 1,001 Middle Eastern Delights

> "It is dull, Son of Adam, to drink without eating," said the Queen pleasantly. "What would you like best to eat?"
>
> "Turkish Delight, please, your Majesty," said Edmund.
>
> —***The Lion, the Witch, and the Wardrobe,* C. S. Lewis**

Overture

Baba Ghanoush a classic pita spread. Flame-roasted eggplant, ground and mixed with tahini sauce and spices
Hummus Cooked and mashed chickpeas mixed with tahini sauce and spices. A staple in coffeehouses all over Chicago
Moroccan Eggplant Sautéed eggplant slices and chopped onions marinated in a spicy tomato sauce
Tabouleh "salad" of chopped parsley, bulgur, diced tomatoes, onions, lemon juice, and olive oil

Intermezzo

Dolmeh "stuffed food," usually grape leaves, eggplant, zucchini, or peppers stuffed with rice, lentils, spicy meat, and so on
Falafel the national sandwich of Israel and New York City, ground chickpeas and spices rolled into balls and deep-fried
Kibbeh mixture of ground lamb, cracked wheat, and herbs
Moussaka casserole made with layers of potato, eggplant, zucchini, cheese, and egg custard topping; spiced lamb or beef is optional
Souvlaki and Gyros Greek shish kebab and Greek cheesesteak (How do you pronounce *gyros*?)
Shawirma Middle Eastern gyros made with lamb or chicken
Tsaztziki yogurt sauce to spread on everything

Finale

Baklava Scheherazade's favorite, 1,001 calories worth of layers of phyllo dough, honey, and nuts

Reza's

5255 North Clark, (773) 561-1898

432 West Ontario, (312) 664-4500

Reza's is the grande dame of Chicago's Middle Eastern restaurants. A huge, airy, multi-story establishment in Andersonville, Reza's has acquired a well-earned reputation for good food at a good value, although prices have increased steadily in the past few years. As Reza's popularity has climbed, so have its prices, but it's still a great budget option, just pushing the "fork and knife" rating limit. All dinners are multicourse, including a radish and feta appetizer plate, lentil soup, and an entrée. Don't order an appetizer here unless you're really a pig. Regardless, you probably won't make it through dessert. Best bet is to squeeze in a sweet, sludgy Turkish coffee. Be sure to try Reza's special chicken, a marinated chicken kebab on dill rice ($7.95), and the stuffed grape leaves (with meat or vegetarian, $7.95). The vegetarian sampler ($9.95) is worth stopping by for weekly. If you're there on a lucky night, you'll be able to buy a lovely rose from the flower lady who circulates through the tables. Reza's other location is at River North at the old Sieben's Brewery location. But keep in mind that it was some of the waiters at the original Andersonville location who were included in *Chicago* magazine's article "25 Sexiest People in Chicago."

Open daily. Full bar. The River North location has sidewalk seating.

Hashalom

2905 West Devon, (773) 465-5675

You know a place must have something going for it when it's a cold, rainy Sunday night, and it's still SRO–packed. Well, Hashalom offers both price and taste to the hungry crowds that pass up the surrounding Indian restaurants to enjoy Israeli and Moroccan specialties at rock-bottom prices. You'll work hard here to get the bill into double digits, and before you do, after numerous courses, you may simply run out of room. Try the Israeli combination plate (small $4, large $7.50), offering hummus, baba ghanoush, falafel, "Israeli salad," warm pita, and handsdown, the best Moroccan eggplant in the city. The specialty of the house is bourekas, triangles of phyllo dough filled with a choice of feta and onions, feta and spinach, potatoes and onions, or ground beef and pine nuts. $4 gets you two bourekas served with sliced tomatoes, tahini sauce, and a sliced brown egg.

Open Monday through Friday. BYOB.

Uncle Tutunji's

615 Wells, (312) 751-9600

Mag Mile lunchers mourned the move of this storefront to River North after Uncle's landlord raised the rent at the ritzy, close-to-Michigan-Avenue location. At its new location, Uncle Tutunji has become a real sit-down, almost fancy restaurant with the same great food and prices it had as a counter grill. The Uncle still has the best hummus in town, along with tasty shish taouk (chicken kabobs, $9.95) and domeh (stuffed grape leaves, $7.95), as well as its ever-popular falafel sandwiches ($5).

Closed Sunday.

Cousins

2854 North Broadway, (773) 880-0063
5203 North Clark, (773) 334-4553

Originally just a small sit-down storefront, Cousins has since expanded to two fancy locations decorated with rugs and pillows and featuring reliably good "Turkish dining with a vegetarian flair." Cousins offers a wide range of affordable options and a changing list of seasonal specialties. Half of the menu is vegan, except for the use of feta cheese, which can be omitted. Eight different kinds of kebabs and six different types of couscous, ranging from vegetable ($7.95) and portabella à la Mediterranean ($8.95 with portabella mushrooms, banana peppers, potatoes, sun-dried tomatoes, and shallots sautéed in a tomato sauce) to shrimp ($10.75), are available. Try Eggplant Imam Bayeldi—in Turkish, "The Imam fainted"—roasted eggplants stuffed with tomatoes, green peppers, onions, garlic, and pine nuts, $7.95. Or, if you can't decide, try one of the many combination plates (available for appetizers) of couscous, dolmeh, kababs, and other Mediterranean specialties. All meals are served with warm pita and chay (Turkish tea).

Open daily, BYOB.

Old Jerusalem

1411 N. Wells, (773) 944-0459

After being in business for twenty years, these people know what they're doing. Old Jerusalem serves some of the most reasonably priced Lebanese and Middle Eastern food in town, and always with friendly, smiling help. Sandwiches, priced $3.25 to $4.25, are big enough for a meal. Entrées ($7.00–$8.95) are huge, mounded platters served with salad and bread. At $8.95, Old Jerusalem's combo plate of shawirma, kefta kabob, shish kabob, rice pilaf, salad, and bread, is one of the best-priced grazing opportunities in town.

Open daily. BYOB.

Casbah Café

3151 North Broadway, (773) 935-3339

A small Lakeview storefront that's more of a carryout than a sit-down restaurant, Casbah's menu is 70 percent vegetarian and offers a wide range of entrées priced mostly at $9.95 and under, which include soup or salad. At $8.95, the Moroccan lamb, chicken, or the Tangier (veal stew) couscous is one of the best deals in town. Lamb Marrakesh, lamb stewed with onions, raisins, almonds, and herbs, is also a great option ($7.95). The combination plate ($7.50) is a great opportunity to graze through yalanci sarma (vine leaves stuffed with rice, pine nuts, and currants), neevick (seasoned spinach and chick-peas), hummus, beans plaki (white beans simmered with carrots in olive oil), and falafel.

Open daily. BYOB.

Kan Zaman

5204 North Clark, (773) 506-0191

A relative new comer on the Andersonville scene, Kan Zaman offers comfortable pillow seating up front and a huge menu (70 percent veggie) of extremely flavorful Mediterranean food served in enormous helpings. The lamb couscous ($8.95) is about the best anywhere.

Desert Treat

1125 West Belmont, (773) 871-1696

More than just the sassy neon palm tree and desert dunes over the front door make this storefront special. Entrées—more of the sandwich types such as shawirma and kabobs—are all priced $7.95 and under and include pita and soup or Desert Treat salad.

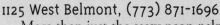

quick bites

Jerusalem Pastries

3105 West Devon, (773) 262-0558

One of the many Middle Eastern bakeries lining Devon, Jerusalem Pastries bakes over a half dozen phyllo, honey, and nut combinations that ooze sweetly in large shallow pans.

Andie's

5253 North Clark, (773) 784-8616
1467 West Montrose, (773) 348-0654

The original location is right next door to Reza's. Reputed to have the best falafel in the city. Entrées are priced $4.95 to $6.95.

A la Kazaam

Get stuffed like a grape leaf at A La Turka

Turkey has been a global hot spot since civilization's earliest days. Much of Mesopotamia covered what is now Turkey. Many of Homer's heroes lived on Turkey's shores in the lost city of Troy or other fabled places. Alexander the Great marched through what is now Turkey to conquer the world on a path that later became Marco Polo's Silk Road.

With one foot in Europe and the other in Asia and historically standing over all the trade between, Turkey has had an impact on the Old World since ancient times. Now that influence has reached the New World—west to the Western Hemisphere to the Midwest to a rapidly regentrifying and recivilizing strip of Lincoln Avenue.

A La Turka Turkish Kitchen opened on a stretch of Lincoln once known for hollow, abandoned department stores, now home to pricey, rehabbed lofts. As they enter the seemingly modest storefront from the street, those walking through the door enter a lush interior with a ceiling draped liked a tent and terra-cotta daubed walls. Turkish-style seating on cushions at low tables is mixed with standard Western options. Intimate conclaves of businesspeople with dark hair and desert countenances huddle in conversation over steaming glass thimbles full of strong coffee or tea.

A La Turka's menu touts distinctive Turkish cooking as one of the world's three great cuisines. I've always thought most Mediterranean cuisine to be the same, just often spelled differently. Hummus, pita, dolmeh—it all looks the same, tastes the same, just is presented with a different combination of vowels and consonants depending on if you're eating in Greece versus Morocco versus Persia or Iran or Istanbul or Constantinople. At A La Turka, however, it's clear that a kebap is not just a kebap.

The menu is extensive and loaded with tasty, tangy options

for both the carnivore and the vegetarian. The best plan that will allow you to taste with abundance without ending up stuffed liked a vegetable yourself is to order a couple appetizers and then split an entrée. Good cold starters include lebni, a yogurt spread mixed with walnuts, garlic, and mint that you can spread on the homemade flat round bread served with every meal, and dolma, cold grape leaves draped in yogurt and stuffed with rice, pine nuts, onions, parsley, and currants. Imam Bayeldi, pan-fried eggplant stuffed with onions, tomatoes, green pepper, and onions, is also a good bet.

Hot appetizers to try include mucver, zucchini pancakes served artfully with dill and feta cheese. The adventurous should try arnavut cigeri, pan-fried calve's liver and potatoes served with onions, tomatoes, and parsley. Yayla yogurt soup with rice and mint or mercimek red lentil soup with bulgur rice, parsley, onions, peppers, and mint are filling but light with a minty flavor.

A long list of entrées is available, and if you can't make up your mind, split the karisik izgara with a friend. This mixed grill will give you and a companion a trip around the menu with an assortment of chicken, beef, and lamb kebabs, baby lamb chops, and doner (gyro) all arranged in a tower dedicated to the unrestrained meat eater. For a lighter option, there are a number of vegetable, fish, and seafood options, including four kinds of dolma—zucchini, tomatoes, grape leaves, or bell peppers stuffed with ground beef, onions, parsley, and rice and dressed in yogurt and toma-

A La Turka Turkish Kitchen, 3134 North Lincoln, (773) 935-6447, is open daily. Entrées range in price from $8 to $15. Alcohol is served.

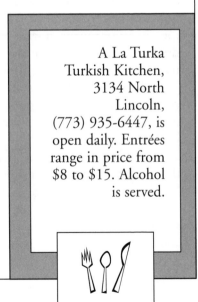

to sauce. There are also six different kinds of karadeniz pide, a kind of Turkish pizza made from homemade bread shaped like a flat lemon and topped with a choice of ground beef, feta cheese and parsely, mixed vegetables, pastrami, beef sausage, or Turkish kashar cheese.

Desserts include the fabled Turkish Delight (that sugary, gelatinous fruity treat otherwise known as lokum), baklava, and a huge helping of sutlac, a creamy rice pudding with a sweet, cinnamony skin on top served in a small ceramic kettle. Wash it all down with sips of Turkish coffee or tea, served in tiny glasses so hot there should be a temperature warning for those who grab below the rim.

Service on a slow night is almost too attentive, like the flight attendant who wakes you on a plane to ask if you're hungry. On a busy night, the kitchen is still learning how to keep up. So if you're visiting on a weekend, grab a pillow and relax.

Decent American Values

13

You say potato, I say potahto. You might question the concept of "American food." After all, as a nation of immigrants, many of the dishes we enjoy today sailed to our shores from faraway lands. But keep in mind, when the Pilgrims partied with their Native American neighbors, they feasted on indigenous food products found readily in the wilds of North America—turkeys, corn, squash, cranberries, and maple syrup. Many of these foods, including the lowly potato, were carried back to the old country and became staples in foreign diets.

You call it maize, we call it corn. As settlers spread in all directions to fulfill manifest destiny, distinct regional cuisines began to spring up. Some, like Southern cookin', were influenced by local conditions. In the South's temperate climate, gardens flourished and foods such as sweet potatoes, rice, okra, collards, pecans, peanuts, black-eyed peas, and watermelon became meal mainstays. The warm weather also created a taste preference for spicier and sweeter foods. In other regions, such as the Southwest, settlers borrowed from their new neighbors, synthesized flavors, and developed their own distinctive fare. Additional emigration to our shores continued to infuse local cooking with foreign flavors and brought new menus. Driven by economic and social change, migrations within our country's boundaries spread regional specialties to other areas—witness soul food's northward journey from the plantations of the South to the urban kitchens of the North.

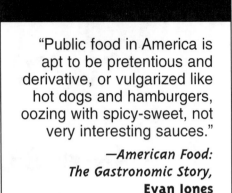

> "Public food in America is apt to be pretentious and derivative, or vulgarized like hot dogs and hamburgers, oozing with spicy-sweet, not very interesting sauces."
>
> —*American Food: The Gastronomic Story,* **Evan Jones**

So, in this most patriotic of times, as we contemplate our freedoms and privileges as citizens of the U. S. of A.—our contract with America—exercise your culinary rights and sample some of the unique American dishes that truly make this the land of the beautiful. Yes, dig into that turkey and gravy, wrestle down some ribs, savor some fresh salmon, kick back, tune in 'da game, and enjoy a Coke, some Fritos, Twinkies, nachos with Cheese Whiz, Oreos, and other American specialties.

And, don't forget to vote.

Editor's Note: This chapter is dedicated to the gone-but-not-forgotten Dixie-Que, the joint that brought that Southern truck-stop style to Chicago. Remember those blues jams in the parking lot? Was it the location that finally did the DQ in?

Wishbone Restaurant

1800 West Grand, (312) 829-3597
1001 West Washington, (312) 850-BONE

How many restaurants in Chicago do you know that actually serve that Southern classic Hoppin' John? How many Chicagoans even know what Hoppin' John is? How many care? Well, Wishbone is an establishment that will give you reason to find out. Originally a single trendy bistro in an "artistic" neighborhood, Wishbone offers a variety of American regional, mainly Southern, specialties. From standard stuff served with a gourmet twist, such as baked bone-in-ham (served with a corn muffin and two sides, $6.25) and crab cakes with black beans ($7.25), to dishes not often found north of the Mason-Dixon line, such as chicken and shrimp étouffée ($8.75) and North Carolina bean cakes ($7.25), Wishbone offers reasonably priced entrées that stay reasonably priced even when accompanied by a number of sides. If you're a vegetarian, be sure to try the corn cakes (served with red pepper sauce and slaw, $4.95) or one of the other numerous meatless options. (By the way, Hoppin' John is black-eyed peas served on rice with cheddar cheese, scallions, and tomato.)

Both Wishbones open daily. Wishbone on Grand is BYOB. Wishbone on Washington doesn't serve dinner on Sundays and Mondays.

Dixie Kitchen & Bait Shop

5225 South Harper, (773)363-4943

If it were found in Lincoln Park, it would be just another Bub City knockoff, maybe a Stanley's, and there'd be a big sports bar up front to ruin the place. But, the Hyde Park location adds flavor that the Dixie Kitchen & Bait Shop tries to stay true to. Yeah, it's got that truck-stop, gas station "Bubba" decor with all the kitschy memorabilia on the walls, but the menu takes you back to the real thing. Fried green tomatoes ($3.75) and oyster po' boys with rémoulade ($7.95) are tasty fixin's. The catfish fillet ($9.95) is also a good bet and a good deal. Avoid the jambalaya ($7.95), just not a great dish. Hot cornmeal johnnycakes start each meal instead of a basket of bread. Wash it all down with a Blackened Voodoo beer. "Do Dixie!"

Open daily. Blackened Voodoo beer.

Brother Jimmy's

2909 North Sheffield, (773) 528-0888

Brother Jimmy's is an establishment that hasn't figured out whether it's a restaurant with a hoppin' bar or a bar that just happens to serve food. That's too bad, since the cuisine here is abundant and relatively tasty. The prevailing theme is North Carolina barbecue, and if you can ignore the occasional prancing idiot standing on the bar throwing out free pig T-shirts, you'll enjoy the various sandwiches and dinners. Ribs are of the larger, meatier St. Louis style instead of baby backs and come in "Southern style" (smoked and spicy), "Northern style" (sweet and tender), and "Dry Rub" (hot and spicy and not very good). Barbecue side sauces come in "West Carolina–style" (thick and tangy) and "East Carolina–style" (thin and vinegary). Avoid the rib tips ($5.50) which are only Dry Rub. The pulled pork sandwich ($7.25) is a good bet, as are the succulent fried chicken livers (content yourself with the appetizer size for $3.95, served with a huge mound of mashed potatoes). As always, the mashed potatoes are the definitive measure of a place like this. Brother Jimmy's potatoes, although properly lumpy, are a bit too peppered. They are, however, served in massive quantities, which is always admirable. A free side of coleslaw is also served to each diner upon seating. Read the free "bar-be-que guide," published by the North Carolina Pork Producers Association and available at the hostess desk while you're waiting for your order.

Open daily. Really full bar. Good happy hour. All you can eat Sundays. Kids under 12 eat free. Music on the weekends.

Stanley's Kitchen & Tap

1970 North Lincoln, (773) 842-0007

Situated in the old Papa Milano's "big fork" location, Stanley's has a spacious front bar packed with patrons who have shifted across the street from the excitement of Gamekeeper's and a back dining room reminiscent of a Carolina truck stop. Given the annoying sports bar atmosphere up front and the almost too perfect, down-home 1950s decor (complete with red-and-white checkered tablecloths accented by an ant motif), was already tempted to give Stanley's the forks down. But then, I ordered. Stanley's dishes up huge, whopping portions of tasty slabs of meatloaf, tubs of Southern-style spaghetti, and creamy chicken shortcake (an updated potpie) for $6.95 and under. All "suppers" come with a choice of sides, including mashed potatoes and gravy, French fries, wet fries, coleslaw, buttered corn, mac and cheese, or

Southern spaghetti. Loosen your waistband and dig in.

Open daily. Full bar.

Margie's Candies

1960 North Western, (773) 384-1035

What could be more American than an old-fashioned candy shop lit up by the name over the door in four-foot high orange and pink neon script that dishes up sundaes made with homemade hot fudge and homemade, 18 percent butterfat ice cream? Margie's Candies has been serving up homemade candy and ice cream for more than seventy-five years and is still going strong. Margie herself sat behind the register for years, and although she passed away recently having lived well past ninety, her legacy lives on. Wander in anytime between 9:00 A.M. and midnight, pass the display cases of rock candy and truffles, and grab a booth ornamented with an out-of-order jukebox containing some of the 1970s greatest hits. Then, dig into one of Margie's specialties, such as a "Turtle Tummy Buster" or an "Eiffel Tower." If you're extra hungry, start off with a shake ($3.25) and some solid comfort food, like a "solid sirloin of beef," served with a cup of the soup of the day ($5.50).

Margie's is open daily until midnight. No alcohol.

The Zephyr

1777 West Wilson, (773) 728-6070

For a Northside ice cream option, try the zephyr, with its signature fried ice cream or, if you're with a friend, the "War of the Worlds"—ten scoops with four toppings. Sidewalk seating, serenaded by the click-clack of the Ravenswood El, is available in the summer.

Open Sunday through Thursday until midnight, Friday and Saturday until 1:00 A.M.

N. N. Smokehouse

1465 West Irving Park, (773) TNT-4700

At the front of N.N. Smokehouse, the former Nida's, you run into a large steel contraption labeled "Southern

Pride" that's smoking away. Try a "smoked" sandwich, a choice of brisket, turkey, or pulled Memphis pork ($5.85). The deluxe (add $1.50) comes with coleslaw and French fries, skin still on and the size of small Havana cigars, or barbecue beans. Rib tips with all the trimmings are $7.50. Daily specials are also a good way to go, on those days they are available:

Tuesday Caribbean Night—jerk chicken with black beans, rice, and plantains ($8.25)

Wednesday Southern Soul Food—half chicken or rib tips, black-eyed peas, sweet potatoes, greens and cornbread ($8.25)

Thursday BBQ Beef Ribs—All You Can Eat ($8.95)

Sunday sliced turkey platter, mashed potatoes, gravy, veggies, and cranberries ($8.99)

Whole smoked chickens are $7.95. N. N.'s chef, formerly of Ditka's, also serves up some Filipino selections, including excellent pancit noodles ($7.79), in honor of his wife. Wash it all down with a root beer, blue raspberry, black cherry, ginger beer champagne kola, or a ting.

Open daily. BYOB.

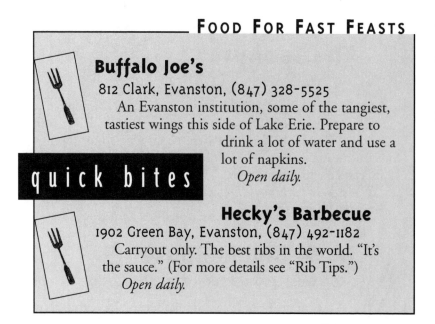

Food For Fast Feasts

Buffalo Joe's

812 Clark, Evanston, (847) 328-5525

An Evanston institution, some of the tangiest, tastiest wings this side of Lake Erie. Prepare to drink a lot of water and use a lot of napkins.

Open daily.

Hecky's Barbecue

1902 Green Bay, Evanston, (847) 492-1182

Carryout only. The best ribs in the world. "It's the sauce." (For more details see "Rib Tips.")

Open daily.

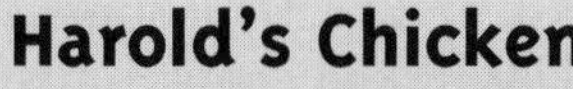

Harold's Chicken

7310 South Halsted, (773) 723-9006
Other multiple locations

quick bites

What Hecky's is to the Northshore and ribs, Harold's is to the Southside and chicken. Another take-out mecca that Chicagoans flock to from the far corners to carry out wings, nuggets, and fried okra.

Open daily.

Soul Asylum

Head south for home cookin'

It's been said that Chicago really is a city of neighborhoods—a vast mosaic of separate enclaves, each with its own history, personality, and particular landmarks and institutions—individual entities that originated most often as ethnic settlements or as gleams in the eyes of ambitious land developers. We become very comfortable in our own neighborhoods with the "everyone knows your name" notion. We've got our local haunts, the grocery store and cleaner, the corner bar, the coffee shop where they know you want a tall double shot half decaf skim latte before you order. We become complacent. Sometimes it's hard to leave home.

I regularly leave the comfort of my own ward to get something interesting to eat. There just aren't many opportunities for culinary excitement on my block. Sometimes, I head northeast to Argyle Street for a little Southeast Asian. Or maybe northwest for some scorching hot Indian. And occasionally, I head south to Pilsen or Little Village for a serious margarita. I've even zipped down to Marquette Park and back for some Lithuanian. And once in a while, I get lucky and go enjoy some real soul-food.

The South Side offers the city's best soul food. Other than dishes like johnnycakes (cornmeal bread with pork cracklings), traditional Southern soul food has been termed the only true American cuisine. Cajun and Creole arguably borrow too heavily from French and Spanish culinary traditions. (And last time I checked, no one had classified the Big Mac as a gustatory accomplishment.) But outside of a rare slab of stupor-inducing baby backs, I rarely eat soul food. Some things are hard to get in my neighborhood. Good deli. Or real damn-the-diet, let-down-your-hair, loosen-your-waistband soul food.

So, it didn't take much prodding to join the crowd when one of my friends organized a group dinner at **Gladys' Luncheonette**. Gladys Holcomb started cooking in Memphis in the late 1930s. She relocated to Chicago and opened her luncheonette in 1945, where she's been dishing up plates of solid soul food ever since. Not the pseudo-Southern that most plastic, truckstop wannabe eateries downtown and in Lincoln Park serve to North Siders and tourists. Gladys cooks up the kind of deep-fried, "smothered" dishes that make you tired and happy to just think about it. Guilty pleasures. Cholesterol-laden, artery-expanding, heart-stopping comfort food.

A modest place, almost half of Gladys' is taken up by the U-shaped counters that run the length of the restaurant in the smoking section, which is separated from nonsmoking by a white lattice wall divider between back-

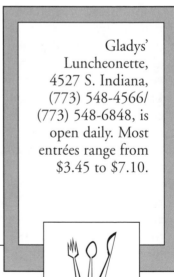

Gladys' Luncheonette, 4527 S. Indiana, (773) 548-4566/ (773) 548-6848, is open daily. Most entrées range from $3.45 to $7.10.

to-back green plastic booths. Black and white pictures of prominent African Americans—Martin Luther King Jr., Malcolm X, Harold Washington—decorate the walls. Besides the booths, large tables for six and eight offer ample accommodations for serious eaters.

The focus here is on food. Smothered or fried chicken, offered in white or dark meat. Breaded, fried catfish or perch. T-bones and pork chops. Hash and rice, corned beef and cabbage, ham hocks and northern beans, oxtails and potatoes. Meals start off with homemade biscuits and are accompanied by fresh baked corn muffins. Sides are a highlight, and most entrées come with two, with a choice of collard greens with a smoky pork flavor, squash, fried corn, or assorted other greens and roots. Save room for dessert. Homemade sweet potato pie or peach or apple cobbler, syrupy sweet fruit with a rich pastry roof. Or maybe some lemon icebox pie or bread pudding. Wash it all down with ice tea, lemonade, or a strawberry pop. When was the last time you had a strawberry pop?

My friend Brent tucked into a Cornish hen with homemade dressing while he smugly told us he had given up red meat, conveniently ignoring the baby pool of gravy his half a hen was back stroking through. Jay, born on the Mason Dixon line, thought he had been transported back to his old Kentucky home and dove into his smothered fried chicken. Smacking his lips, he insisted on meeting Gladys.

Gladys turned out to be a lovely, tiny sparrow of a woman. As she saw to our comfort, she told us she still gets up at 5:00 A.M. every day to come to the restaurant. She ascertained that our waitress, who had been wheeling large carts of food to our table for the past hour, had been taking good care of us. Periodically during our discussion, Gladys would poke Alexa, who was packing up leftovers for a week, and ask her if she had gotten enough to eat.

The six of us wrestled over the bill, which was less than $50. Content, we sleepily made our way home, back to our own neighborhoods. So satisfied, it was almost a shame to begin the process of digestion.

One Mag Meal

REST, RESPITE, AND REFRESHMENT AFTER ALL THAT SHOPPING

14

Shop till you drop . . . You've waded through the crowds at Crate & Barrel looking for that functional but oh-so-attractive gift. You've just done it with a swarm of tourists at Nike Town. You've combed through the racks at the season's last Field Days, and you've used up all the free coupons you were sent when you signed up for a new Bloomingdale's charge card. Your personal debt level has ballooned to startling levels, you're juggling so many packages you'll need at least two cabs to get home, and your dogs are barking. Time to take a break.

But wait—you've already made two trips to the cash station, and your wallet's empty again. Your cards are charged up to the limit. Can you even afford a cup of coffee—or will even that have to wait until your next credit card grace period?

You just need to know where to go. You don't have to limit yourself to McDonalds, nor do you have to settle for a cafeteria tray at the food court in the basement of Marshall Field's. Yes, a little knowledge will get you a tasty, filling meal served in a relaxing and attractive ambiance where someone else clears the dishes for less than the price of a pair of cashmere socks at J. Crew, a turtleneck at the Gap, or even a good-sized box of Frangos. My mama told me, I'd better shop around . . .

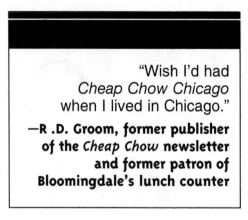

"Wish I'd had *Cheap Chow Chicago* when I lived in Chicago."

—R .D. Groom, former publisher of the *Cheap Chow* newsletter and former patron of Bloomingdale's lunch counter

The Ivy at the Oak Tree

900 North Michigan, (312) 751-1988

Once a nondescript coffee shop on the corner of State and Oak, the new Oak Tree has spiffed up both its image and its prices since it moved into the old Carnegie Deli space on the sixth floor of 900 North Michigan. With its harvest-y decor, autumn colors, and grapevines twisted around any available post or pole, the Oak Tree supports the oh-so-chic atmosphere of the mall it calls home while still offering a large selection of tasty dishes with generous portions. Some two dozen different salads, both green and garden salads (What's the difference? Garden salads aren't necessarily green-based, aha.), are priced for the most part between $7.25 to $8.25. Kind of pricey for lunch but not bad for dinner, for which they are more than ample. The "Blue Plate Specials", particularly the turkey burritos ($7.50), are highly recommended. In a tribute to its predecessor, a number of sandwiches under the "Carnegie Deli Favorite" label are available and range from $7.75 to $8.25.

Open daily. Wine and beer.

foodlife

Water Tower Place, (312) 335-3663

Leave it to the people at Lettuce Entertain You to come up with a politically correct food court for the 1990s—a kinder, gentler, and definitely tastier food court. Enter and pick up your f* card, your foodcard. You then wander through the fantasy land of the various food stations, where you charge the items you choose to your f* card. At the end of your dining experience, you cash out all your charges and settle your "account." A wide variety of snazzy food stations are available, including pizza, pasta, Mexican, Asian, salads, desserts, rotisserie chicken, Mother Earth Grains, the Roadside Hamburger Stand, the Miracle Juice Bar (gigantic bags of carrots waiting to be pureed), and the inevitable coffee stand, the Sacred Grounds Espresso Bar. My favorites include the chicken Cobb salad that's loaded with stuff ($5.75) and the mondo berry smoothie ($3.25). The emphasis at many of the stations is on build-your-own. Food is tasty, presentation is slick, and the prices are actually right. foodlife now even has a carryout store with prepackaged options, some build your own "bars," a lot of samples, and prices that are half off on prepared foods before closing. It's worth the trip over just to snag a few tastes of this and that. Maybe you should try opening an account here.

Open daily. Wine and beer.

Zodiac Room at Neiman Marcus

737 North Michigan, (312) 642-5900

Does the thought of eating at Neiman Marcus conjure up images of elegantly dressed little old ladies sipping tea with lemon while they nibble on small tuna salad sandwiches? Well, that's certainly an option at the Zodiac Room, although the tuna salad can come in the form of a very tasty sandwich on a croissant with pecans and water chestnuts ($7.95). Plenty of other designer sandwiches and salads grace the menu, along with some more elaborate entrées that are almost all too expensive—try the pepper jack quesadilla ($8.95) or the orange soufflè served with the "signature" chicken salad, fresh fruit, and banana spice bread ($10). Seasonal soups come with popovers and the "signature" strawberry butter.

Open daily except Sunday, 11:00 A.M.–4:00 P.M No alcohol.

Café Escada

840 North Michigan, (312) 915-0500

If you can afford to shop at Plaza Escada, why are you reading this? Anyway, if you've just purchased a couple of designer froufrous and you need to take a load off, trot up to Café Escada on the fourth floor to the only somewhat affordably priced selections in the building. Baguette sandwiches and salads are all $9.50 and under. The veggie frittata is an expensive but tasty egg at $8.50. Roast beef with red peppers and horseradish sauce or the chicken Caesar salad are hearty enough to restore your shopping vigor (both $9.50).

Open daily 11:30 A.M.–3:00 P.M. Champagne and wine.

Service Deli

215 East Chestnut, (312) 787-4525

If you're out to shop until you drop, this is the place to stuff down a big old deli sandwich when you need sustenance to go on (who cares about fat at this point). Conveniently located just down the street from Water Tower and in close proximity to 900 North Michigan, the Service Deli is found by going in the back alley, past the dumpsters, and in the service entrance of one of those vintage Streeterville high-rises. Deli sandwiches the size and quality of which are rarely seen in this town run $4.95 and under. Try one of the twenty special sandwiches, one of the eight tortilla wraps, or just build your own. Three kinds of homemade soups are available daily.

Closed Sundays. Saturdays only open from 11:00 A.M. to 4:00 P.M.

Chalfins

200 East Chestnut, Lower Level, (312) 943-0034

Billing itself as a "real" New York–style deli, complete with "properly insulting" waitstaff, Chalfins boasts the best pastrami and corned beef sandwiches in the city, "flavorfully marbled with a bit of fat" and served with New York mustard. All your deli favorites are here, including smoked fish platters served with a bagel and fixings and priced $7.50 for smoked chub and up to $10.95 for baked salmon. Sandwiches run $3.25 to $6.95. Breakfast, including matzo brie and chicken livers and onions omelets, is served all day. The menu gives you a complete glossary of Yiddish terms, so you'll feel more ethnic. Wash it all down with a Dr. Brown's.

Open daily from 7:30 A.M. to 8:00 P.M. (Mondays only to 3:00 P.M.)

The Signature Room on the Ninety-Fifth

Hancock Building, 875 North Michigan, (312) 787-9596

A room with a view, the $8.95 pig-out lunch buffet, loaded with hot and cold stuff, makes this one of the Mag Mile's hidden gems. All the other items on the lunch menu—sandwiches, salads, pastas—are a great deal at $7.25 and under but pretty pedestrian, so stick with the buffet. (Hey, the waiter picked out the fettuccini with smoked chicken and broccoli floretes in a parmesan cheese sauce, $6.95, as the best pasta on the menu; it was a huge serving, but so bland, I was not inclined to take the leftovers. That never happens with me.) You can't afford dinner here, so live it up with at noon.

Serving lunch Monday through Saturday, 11:00 A.M.–2:00 P.M.

India House

247 East Ontario, 2nd Floor, (312) 280-4934/4910

One of Devon's best Indian options has joined the Michigan Avenue shopping crowd. India House with its

$7.95 all-you-can-eat lunch buffet complete with a steaming plate of fragrant tandoori chicken delivered to your own table offers an exotic option for those who've really worked up an appetite. Besides its extensive and fresh buffet, India House is known for its tawa and kadhai dishes. A tawa is an iron plate used to cook meats and breads over hot coals. The kadhai is an iron wok usually used to cook mug (chicken) and goths (meat) with chilis and tomatoes with fenugreek and coriander over hot coals. India House uses both pieces of cookware to prepare a variety of interesting dishes, all priced $9.25 and under.

Open daily. Full bar.

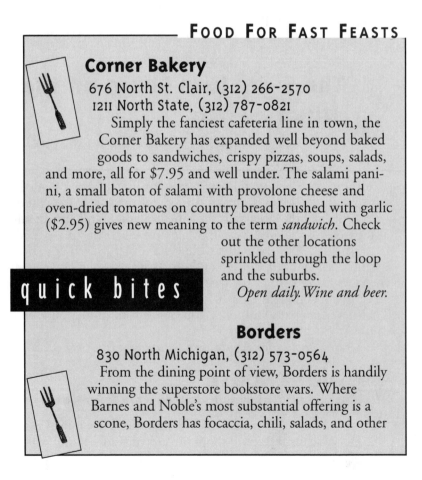

Food For Fast Feasts

quick bites

Corner Bakery

676 North St. Clair, (312) 266-2570
1211 North State, (312) 787-0821

Simply the fanciest cafeteria line in town, the Corner Bakery has expanded well beyond baked goods to sandwiches, crispy pizzas, soups, salads, and more, all for $7.95 and well under. The salami panini, a small baton of salami with provolone cheese and oven-dried tomatoes on country bread brushed with garlic ($2.95) gives new meaning to the term *sandwich*. Check out the other locations sprinkled through the loop and the suburbs.

Open daily. Wine and beer.

Borders

830 North Michigan, (312) 573-0564

From the dining point of view, Borders is handily winning the superstore bookstore wars. Where Barnes and Noble's most substantial offering is a scone, Borders has focaccia, chili, salads, and other

light bites in addition to the obligatory coffeehouse pastries. Borders has a large dining area where you might actually get a seat (if they administer their periodic PA announcements asking those who are just camping out and not eating to vacate their seats).
Open daily during the bookstore's regular hours.

Flapjaw's Saloon

22 East Pearson, (312) 642-4848
This is a rustic grill and sandwich spot for a plain good ole sandwich or burger that doesn't strain the wallet. Fries are available in both whole and half baskets—which is great. Don't you hate paying for what you're not going to eat?
Open daily. Sidewalk seating in nice weather.

quick bites

Ghirardelli Chocolate Shop & Soda Fountain

830 North Michigan, (312) 337-9330
For those who need to tie on a sugar buzz to keep going, Ghirardelli has the options. Serving only ice cream and chocolate, not so much as a burger here, decadence doesn't come cheap. Standard, but "world famous," sundaes start at $5.95. "As famous as the Golden Gate and as thick as any San Francisco fog."
Open daily.

Unleaded

Fill up on petroleum products at Diesel Café

I was a child of the sixties, but didn't really begin to hit my fashion stride until the seventies. My formative adolescent years were guided by the likes of the Brady girls. If Marsha wore polyester bellbottoms, I did too. Crushed vinyl side-zipper gogo boots, slippery turquoise and brown striped pointy-collared shirts, halter tops—I'm not sure I remember Jan sporting a halter—but I did, and she probably had one too.

Then one day, I discovered natural fibers. Cotton, wool, and linen. Fabrics that breathe and that don't melt in the dryer. Fabrics that wrinkle and crease, allowing for the snobbism that you display when everyone knows you spent a lot of money on 100 percent natural to wear pants that look like you slept in them. Looking back at my orange wide-legged hip huggers and cork platform sandals, I can't believe the fashion "don'ts" I committed in my early years.

So imagine my dismay after nearly two decades of corrective action on my closet to see fashions that had been put in a time capsule and that should have stayed there being resurrected. Various flimsy petroleum-based body coverings storming back with a vengeance. Worn initially by those who didn't have to wear them the first time, but then gradually seeping their way back into the wardrobes of those who should know better.

After nearly two years, I've accepted polyester as back. Who's to say that resurrected saran wrap coverings of today aren't an improvement over the multilayer black bag look I sported through much of the eighties? To be ugly is often to be stylish, although I try to restrain my extreme ugly fashionableness to shoes with the thought that I'm better off not making any trendy statements around my face or hips.

The intersection of Rush and Walton has become a real

destination point for those stocking up on the petroleum products. Urban Outfitters is a mecca for those who want to look like they shop at the Salvation Army but want to pay more. Since Urban Outfitters doesn't seem to carry larger than a size seven, those who need more coverage can buzz into Bloomingdale's across the street. Or, if you're really fashion-forward and can slide into form-fitting latex even after a light bite, Diesel might be the place for you.

Diesel, which has built itself up on the ashes of the former Boogie's, not only offers some of the most expensive and ugliest—and therefore most stylish—fashion items in town, but also boasts the **Diesel Café**, designed to assuage the hungers brought on by the rigors of shopping. In pleasant weather, the outdoor seating at the Diesel Café, which marches north on Rush, is one of the best sidewalk seats in town. Just make sure you sit as close to the hostess stand as possible, since the level of service correlates inversely with the distance of your seat from the servers' entrance. But don't be in a hurry here anyway. This is a prime spot to see and be seen, while being shaded by some generous umbrella coverage and being framed by a backdrop of some fascinating fashion dioramas in the windows behind the patio.

For those days when alfresco eating is not an option, the Diesel Café moves indoors and upstairs to a space that's a cross between a department store lunch counter and the Brady's rec room. Comfortable chairs span a long counter, while booths offer additional space. Family room seating is arranged around an aged TV that

Diesel Café, 923 North Rush Street, (312) 255-9256, is open daily for brunch, lunch, and dinner. Alcohol is served. Entree prices range from $4.75 to $8.75.

doesn't look to have cable access, board games are available, and a mini pool table offers additional entertainment for the young and the restless. A curious note, the Café's logo, an aggressive teapot eating a fork full of pasta surrounded by the tag line "un piacere di ristorante!" that I was told means "the pleasure of the restaurant," is plastered everywhere.

In keeping with the current fashion theme that requires those revealing various pierced body parts to be lean and mean, the Diesel Café offers mainly light meals including sandwiches, salads, pizzas, pastas, and the ubiquitous wraps. The theme here is Italian. Sandwiches, or "panini," come in either full size, with options like a tasty grilled vegetable and smoked gouda or a warm salami and fontinella cheese, or "tramezzini," defined as "northern Italian sandwich halves" and available in prosciutto ham with artichokes, mozzarella and tomato, or tuna salad with mixed greens. If you prefer pizza, "pizzette" slices are served in several flavors. Pastas include a cold marinated penne with mozzarella and tomatoes, a spicier penne al'arrabbiata in a red sauce, and a wild mushroom fettuccine.

Salads are meal-sized. The sun-dried vinaigrette is nearly too rich with almost too many dried tomatoes, olives, and chunks of feta. Wraps deviate from the Italian theme with an Athenian herbed chicken wrapped around feta, sun-dried tomatoes, and olives and also an Asian five spice chicken combined with marinated tofu, vegetables and five spice mayo.

Prices are as light as the entrées themselves, leaving you more room in your budget and in your waistband to accommodate those low-rise lycra hip-huggers that you thought you would never wear again.

Pass the Buck

Bucktown Bistros, Wicker Park Watering Holes, and Other Westside Stories

15

For some of you, the ever-gentrifying Clybourn corridor once defined your range. Yes, if you were a wildebeest and Lincoln Park a game preserve, the Webster Place Theater would have marked the edge of your territory clearly. You roamed with the herd, and why would you venture off to some unknown watering hole westward ho?

Time passes, and things change. Now, the hippest stop on the CTA is at Damen, Milwaukee, and North. What's this city coming to when any average Lincoln Park yuppie can be found sipping a cold draft on the roof at Danny's? When J. Crew–clad hordes mob the Riptide after midnight? When Around the Coyote can market itself like the Taste?

Michigan Avenue is for tourists. Lincoln Park has degenerated into postcollegiate sports bars and plastic trattorias. Today's eaters with attitude, the beautiful people—the "in" crowd, are doing Damen. Once the stomping grounds of starving artists, the area's resident tattoos and body piercings mingle increasingly with yuppies and suburbanites as the cutting edge of nightlife, both for music and dining, has moved to 2000 West. From Webster south to Division, Damen Avenue is packed with culinary trendsetters feeding on Italian, Mexican, French, South American, various Asian, and solid Polish cuisine.

> "Wanted: Urban pioneers to venture west of Western!"
>
> **—Advertisement for Rosa's, a blues club**

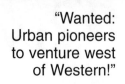

These days, if you yearn to be a leader instead of just somewhere back in the pack, you need to venture out to neighborhoods like Wicker Park, Bucktown, East Village, and Ukrainian Village where new, trendy, and somewhat pricey restaurants are just busting out all over. These once fabled, once edgy Westside neighborhoods are now invaded nightly by the mainstream crowds that have discovered those neighborhoods' abundance of eating options that can be explored at all hours. These neighborhoods pulse with that special eclectic ambiance once found in River North before Lettuce restaurants conquered the area. So head west to find your manifest destiny or just a good meal.

The Babaluci

2152 North Damen, (773) 486-5300

Go one door north of the trés cher Café du Midi and its sparkly patio, and you'll find Babaluci, a dark "Italian modern" eatery at the top tip of Bucktown and another neighborhood mainstay. Babaluci is a cautious "fork and knife"—stick with one of the excellent pasta dishes, which all range from $7 to $8 (most entrées are too expensive). Try the spicy spaghetti al puntanesta with red and black olives, capers, anchovies, and eggplant ($7.75) or the tricolor rotini ($7.50). A couple of the entrées are affordable, including the chicken vesuvio ($9) and grilled Italian sausages with homemade polenta ($8). Don't order an appetizer; you'll be taking home extras with just a main dish. There's live music upstairs on the weekends.

Open daily. Full bar. Piano bar.

Frida's

2143 North Damen, (773) 489-3463

Bucktown's Frida's fulfills the theory that if you offer reasonably priced, tasty, and somewhat creative entrées—and you build a parking lot—*they will come*. Frida's, with its facade modeled after Frida Kahlo's home, the Blue House, is an eclectic Mexican restaurant that specializes in interesting sauces. Start your meal with an appetizer of chalupas, a Mexican pastry shell filled with shredded chicken and topped with Colija cheese ($3). Then move on to the entrées (priced $7.95 and up), maybe pollo asada con crema de nueces, roasted chicken with a pecan sauce ($8.95); or, you may want to try the half slab with adobe pepper barbecue sauce ($8.95). Lomo de cerdo, pork tenderloin with cilantro cream sauce, is $9.95. All entrées are served with a choice of cilantro or tomato rice. Enjoy your meal and, perhaps, a couple of margaritas in an ambiance enhanced by various paintings of the restaurant's patron saint, Frida Kahlo, one of Mexico's artistic giants, she of the single eyebrow.

Open daily. Full bar. Parking.

Northside Tavern & Grill

1635 North Damen, (773) 384-3555

A former auto parts store, the Northside, Bucktown's established anchor, is packed 365 days a year. The draw is the spacious patio, which is now a year-round option since the owner gave in to the allure of profit and eliminated the boccie ball court to make room for more indoor/outdoor space. Helpings are big, the waitstaff is cute, and the service is generally spotty. But hey, this is the kind of place where you want to hang out for the night anyway. You can park your motorcycle in front (squeeze it into the row of Harleys obscuring the sidewalk diners' view and thumb your nose at the crowds at the Mad Bar across the street), and relax with a blue margarita or a large vodka and lemonade while you wait for your pasta special (different each night but usually includes sun-dried tomatoes, for around $8). In addition to the daily pastas, a full page of specials is available each day including soup, salad, and pizzas. Special entrées may include jerk chicken or a grilled porkchop (around $8) or broiled fish (varies, but usually around $10). Burgers are huge, and salads are big enough for two. Brunch is another good meal here, with most options running $5.95. Try to ignore the cheesy, giant neon drink sculpture that illuminates Damen Avenue and would probably be more appropriate at the Big Nasty on Lincoln.

Open daily. Full bar. Brunch. Patio. Bar menu available to 1:00 A.M.

Leo's Lunchroom

1809 West Division, (773) 276-6509

Leo's by day: a dingy dive with fewer than a half dozen tables, a lengthy counter, and no air-conditioning offering pretty standard diner fare. Leo's by night: still rather seedy, but serving up a multiethnic array of appetizers and entrées, ranging from soba noodles ($3.75), wild mushroom risotto ($4.25), and sesame chicken wings ($3.50), to chicken tagine with couscous ($7.25), sea scallops with achiote sauce ($9), and chicken with Thai red curry and yams ($7). Dinners come with a salad. Alcohol is BYOB (no corking fee) and will be served to you in plastic teacups. Street parking is plentiful here. An after-dark piece of advice: Division is one of those streets that has yet to acquire the glitzy veneer of the rest of Wicker Park and Bucktown.

Open daily. BYOB. Patio.

Twilight

1924 West Division, (773) 862-8757

Twilight illustrates what cheap chow is all about—taste for less. The diner offers exciting food—grilled mahi with cranberry-pomegranate relish or chicken breast sautéed with chorizo, poblana, and orange, and grilled potato mole—for exciting prices—$8.50 and $7.95 for the previously cited dishes. Appetizers and soups will put you over budget, but it's worth paying the price for the roasted sweet potato and garlic soup ($3.75) or the Thai red coconut curry soup with lemon grass, Napa cabbage, baby corn, and toasted sesame seeds ($4.25). The menu changes at whim, but usually includes catfish and a pasta. Like Leo's Lunchroom across the street, Twilight's low-budget decor—a long Formica counter, diner-style table and chairs—is comfortable but rather ramshackle like the neighborhood itself.

Open daily. BYOB. Brunch on weekends.

Bite

1039 North Western, (773) 395-BITE

So you indulged at Twilight on the seedy edge of Wicker Park, and you thought you just couldn't get any hipper. But if you journey around the block, just southwest to the Ukrainian Village into an even more geographically undesirable neighborhood (GUD), paradoxically making a location far cooler, you can dine at that one-word gustatory delight Bite. Adjoining the Empty Bottle (a music locale that is, again, hipper than its near neighbor the Double Door, by virtue of GUD) and sporting bright yellow wall tiles decorated with smiling lips rolled back from clenched teeth, Bite is a storefront with character and really good food at the right price. Sandwiches and pastas are $2.50 to $5.95, but the real draw here is the nightly dinner specials. Seemingly a regular, the Indian sampler with eggplant and vegetable curry ($7) is an artistic version of what's offered up at California and Devon. Chicken with cilantro sauce, rice, and grilled potatoes ($7), leg of lamb with red pepper sauce and ratatouille ($9), and miso-marinated shark with rice, sprouts, spinach, and cucumbers ($8) all receive two forks up. Added value: Once you've snarfed down one of Diane Radford's homemade desserts, you can roll yourself next door to the Empty Bottle for some cutting-edge music and a game of pool, saving yourself some cab fare!

Open daily. Alcohol can be purchased at the Empty Bottle. Breakfast.

Privata Café

1957 West Chicago, (773) 850-4720

Privata Café brought inexpensive gourmet meals to the Ukrainian Village that focus on "Italian with a touch of Mexican." Privata's extensive list of creative pasta sauces includes mole verde, chipolte black bean pesto, jalapeno cream, and tomatillo alfredo, all priced $8 and under. The Privata burritos ($4.50–$5.00) are other good options and are available with grilled chicken, steak, homemade sausage, morcilla, or grilled zucchini with four cheeses. Since the entrées are so inexpensive, you may be able to splurge on one of Privata's artistic appetizers, maybe the Mexicali ravioli, two pasta pillows stuffed with chicken pate nestled on a bed of creamy red sauce, or the tangy grilled octopus with plantains, olive sauce, and couscous.

Open daily. BYOB.

La Pasadita

1140 North Ashland, (773) 278-2130

Run for the border for less than four bucks. The bulletin board offers two basic dishes—steak burritos ($3.24) and steak tacos ($1.46). Order with all the fixin's, and you'll get cheese, cilantro, and green salsa with an edge. If steak tacos are too tame for you, try the barbacoa (soft beef), lengua (tongue), or sesos (brains). These variations on the taco theme can also be had for $1.46.

quick bites

Open daily and late.

The Map Room

1949 North Hoyne, (773) 252-7636

The Map Room is a bar that sponsors a free, international night buffets every Tuesday night that highlights a different country's cuisine with food provided by a local restaurant. Can't beat that. Get there early; food goes fast. Check out the schedule for upcoming tastings at their web site www.maproom.com. The bar also hosts Saturday beer schools with lectures from local brewers.

Free food Tuesdays only. Open by 7.30 A.M. Monday through Saturday with newspapers, Torrefazione coffee, and microbrewed Tazo tea.

Cloud Nine

Rediscover a neighborhood joint with a silver lining

Hey, hey, you, you—if you typically push the culinary cutting edge by standing in line at one of the ultra chic establishments that populate Wicker Park's six corner intersection at Damen, Milwaukee and North, you may have overlooked the **Silver Cloud**. Although located on that hip strip of Damen Avenue, the Silver Cloud keeps to its quiet neighborhood self while establishments a few doors down attract long lines of those hoping to see and be seen.

The Silver Cloud opened in a space previously occupied by a Mexican karaoke bar. On the surface a traditional Chicago bar with glass blocks in lieu of any windows, the cozy confines directly contrast with the dark, smoky interiors of outwardly similar corner establishments. Inside is a snug albeit dimly lit room with comfy booths, a long bar, and patrons ranging from neighborhood regulars to an occasional policeofficer taking a break next to a sporadic poseur who drifted a few doors too far north (more often when the sidewalk tables are out during nice weather). This is the kind of place regulars talk about with a proprietary air versus the sense of unfulfilled aspiration expressed after a visit to some of the other eateries in the area.

The restaurant debuted ahead of the recent gastronomic back-to-basics wave, and the guiding principle was to offer food like Mom would make if she was still getting paid. Like its cozy, comfortable interior, the Silver Cloud continues to serve cozy, comfort food. Small bites and sandwiches are available, along with full-blown entrées, or "good eats" that come with soup or salad, and a selection of pastas. Grandma's meatloaf, served with mashed potatoes, green beans, and Bell's amber ale gravy; and pot roast, "cooked till it's fallin' apart" and served with roast potatoes, carrots, and beans are both good traditional values.

Such standbys populate the menu but in a spiffed-up state, like the pan-fried catfish with a cornmeal crust and roumalade sauce or the grilled chicken breast served over black beans with steamed vegetables and pico di gallo. Of the pastas, the krazy noodle carbonara, thick, wavy noodles in a heavy carbonara sauce with peas and prosciutto, stands out, spreading a warm, lethargic glow as you loosen your belt and relax.

"Every day special stuff" highlights the menu. Tuesday's shepherd's pie is a deep, bubbly rendition of the original with generous layers of savory ground meet, mashed potatoes, and cheese on top. Thursday's chicken marsala with capellini is a plentiful dish of chicken breasts on a fluffy bed of pasta dressed with a tangy mushroom sauce.

Friday and Saturday are chef's choice, but don't worry, it's going to be good. Sunday is Jeffersons' Sunday after-church, mom-style roast.

When you find yourself hungry and heading down Damen and don't want to have to feel beautiful, when you just want to sit down instead of standing around for an indeterminate amount of time watching select lucky others eat—forget trendy, forget sponge-painted. Get off the treadmill of chasing what's new and go for what's good.

Think about casual, think about comfort, think about the girl next door. Think about the Silver Cloud.

The Silver Cloud is located at 1700 North Damen, (773) 489-6212. Open daily, lunch Tuesday through Friday. Brunch on weekends. Entrées range from \$6 to \$11. Sidewalk seating is available on nice days. Cigar and pipe smoking is allowed only after 10:00 P.M. and those silly clove cigarettes, never.

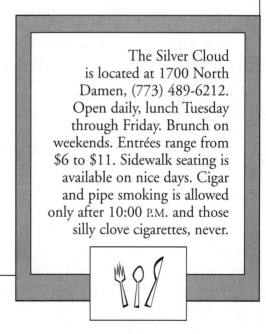

Counter Props

Find table-free dining that stands tall

When I was little, I used to go visit my grandparents. Pittsburgh, where they lived, was one of those cities that still had a viable downtown. As a treat, I'd get to spend a day with my grandmother. We'd take the bus downtown. Sometimes we'd go to the beauty parlor, and she'd get her hair done. We'd go shopping—I think the local department store was called Kaufman's or something like that. And then, tired from exploring the wonders of downtown Pittsburgh, we'd go to a lunch counter for something to eat.

Good lunch counters are hard to find these days. Woolworth's use to have them. I think Chock Full 'O Nuts is still around in New York City, but they're tough to find in Chicago. The good ones, the ones with a counter running around the whole place. Many didn't even have tables. Everyone just sat at the counter, enjoyed his or her meal while sitting next to a stranger, and finished it off with a piece of warm fruit pie à la mode.

Well, I miss my grandmother and I miss those counters. That's why I like Hilary's, a throwback to the real thing.

Located not quite far enough west to be hip Wicker Park or far enough south to be up-and-coming Noble Square, **Hilary's Urban Eatery** (HUE) reposes modestly on a stark strip of Division in the shadow of the Kennedy Expressway. In nice weather, HUE livens up its barren surroundings with impromptu sidewalk garden dining. When it's chillier, diners can enter the double wood doors with their etched decorative glass at the storefront and enjoy the cozy confines.

Two small tables sit in the windows flanking the entrance, but it's the counters that dominate the room. The main counter, with its comfy bright red upholstered seats and stone mosaic top that matches the restaurant's floor, winds around the serving area. A second counter flanks the west wall, ready to catch an overflow of eaters. Mason jars of jellybeans are spaced intermittently between sugar dispensers whose contents are speckled with colored crystals along the counter. The interior's details are completed with a tin-plate ceiling painted a plush pink. An antique baby carriage hangs from the ceiling over a TV that runs constantly with no sound. Various knickknacks and pictures, including one of a more famous Hilary, comfortably clutter the shelves over the espresso maker and throughout the interior. A recently opened back room offers more table seating in a parlor atmosphere.

Instead of the little blue-haired ladies that might have been found having a cup of coffee and a tuna sandwich at the counters of the past, many of HUE's regulars reflect the surrounding neighborhood—scruffily hip, assorted piercings in overly pale skin crowned with mops of unnaturally streaked hair. Much of the staff reflects the flavor of the patrons but is unfailingly friendly.

Although many of the menu options have been updated from diner days, they still maintain the warmth of comfort food. Breakfast is served all day. A fluffy tower of pancakes, the "pan special," redefines the term "stack of flapjacks" and is served in regular, blueberry, or banana oat bran. Huevos rancheros are mounded generously onto plates. The rib eye steak and eggs, served all day, at $7.25 is one of the most expensive items . A side of grits is optional.

Fat sandwiches are

Hilary's Urban Eatery, 1500 West Division, (773) 235-4327, is open seven days a week at 7 :00 A.M. Monday through Wednesday, Hilary's closes at 9:00 P.M., Thursday through Saturday at 10:00 P.M., and Sundays at 5:00 P.M. Dishes are all under $7.75.

served with fresh slaw and fries. Chubby piles of barbecued beef and grilled chicken breasts. Entrées range from the traditional to the healthy. A standout is the salmon cakes studded with nubbins of corn and red pepper and served with homemade Louis sauce and a side order of rice and beans or homemade macaroni and cheese. Steak fajitas are plentiful enough that you'll probably have to ask for extra tortillas. Lasagna comes in two flavors: veggie with ricotta and feta cheese or spinach and herbed goat cheese. Other pastas and homemade pizzas with an assortment of toppings are available. The catfish, baked or fried, quesadillas, and chicken parmigiana are also good bets. Wash it all down with a cold drink served in a mason jar or a cup of coffee, steaming in a mismatched cup. And then there's dessert. Flaky homemade fruit pies—always cherry and apple and sometimes others—and what every counter must serve, rice pudding. Also New York–style cheesecake and sour cream chocolate cake. Special treats that you remember from when you were young. Go experience them again at Hilary's Urban Eatery.

Taste of Lincoln Avenue

16

With warm weather and the change of seasons comes that uniquely Chicago rite of summer the Taste Festival. Many city dwellers have learned to avoid the Taste, that multiday eating orgy that long ago ceased to be cheap chow. One of the many smaller versions, however, located smack-dab on top of one of the city's worst intersections at Lincoln, Fullerton, and Halsted offers a pleasant option to celebrate summer with the obligatory greasy assortment of entrées cradled in paper trays, washed down with numerous sixteen-ounce, hops-based beverages.

Lincoln Avenue is steeped in the kind of tradition that entitles it to throw a "taste" type of party regularly. Once an old Indian and fur trapper trail leading to the Green Bay and Fox River portages, Little Fort Road had become by the mid–nineteenth century the main drag through the village of Lakeview and was flanked by the farms of settlers from Germany and Luxembourg. These Germanic farms made their mark early on the area's palates, feeding both nearby Chicago and the Budlong sauerkraut-pickle works. The village of Lakeview was particularly attractive to ethnic Germans due to village officials' tolerant attitude toward social drinking. The biergartens of "Chicagoburg" flourished thanks to the Saloon Keeper's Society, which was organized to "protect and demand their common interests by all lawful means and measures." By 1889, the village of Lakeview had been annexed by the city of Chicago, and improvements in public transportation encouraged settlement of areas to the north and west. German families moved out from Lakeview to what became the posh suburb of Ravenswood and the more modest Lincoln Square area at Lincoln, Western, and Lawrence. Brauhauses, delicatessens, and pumpernickel bakeries continued to pop up farther and farther north to feed this movement.

> "Ich bin ein Berliner."
> (I am a doughnut.)
>
> **—JFK's famous expression of appreciation for German pastry**

Today, a trip up Lincoln Avenue is a study in Chicago's ever-changing demographic profile. The southern tip of Lincoln now runs through Old Town and DePaul, the city's gems of urban renewal. The former 'burgs of Lakeview, the historic German neighborhoods, have become increasingly Hispanic while, at the same time, are coming under the real estate pressures of regentrification. Further north, the Lincoln Square area has retained its Germanic atmosphere while acquiring various Eastern European and Greek elements. North of Lawrence, the flavor becomes distinctly Korean, with the north Lincoln Avenue stores and restaurants reflecting that trend.

Change, of course, brings opportunity—here culinary. Explore Lincoln Avenue. Just for the taste of it.

Pasta Cucina

2461 Lincoln, (773) 248-8200

Once the Dancing Noodles Café, Pasta Cucina retains the Dancing Noodles' concept—mix and match your sauce to your pasta flavor to your pasta shape. Flavors include spinach, egg, or a daily special, which can be as exotic as basil and tomato rotini or garlic and thyme shells (both $8.95). Shapes include angel hair, linguine, or fettuccine. Sauces range from $7.95 for vegetable marinara to $8.95 for the highly recommended sun-dried tomato with basil cream sauce. If you're not in the mood for pasta (why are you here?), a small number of nonnoodle house specials are available, including a Caesar salad ($6.50) and rosemary chicken aglio e olio (chicken tenders, rosemary, roasted garlic, sun-dried tomatoes, and olive oil, $9.25). Pasta Cucina is close to the Biograph, so you can grab a bite before you grab a flick. If the place is crowded, eat at the bar. Weather permitting, a good patio option is available.

Open daily. Full bar. Patio dining.

Gin Go Gae

5433 North Lincoln, (773) 334-3895

A huge selection of complimentary sides (standard at good Korean restaurants) offsets the somewhat high prices at one of Chicago's best Korean establishments. Entrées are grouped into charcoal broiled, stir-fried, and "very traditional." Try the bulgogi and the galbi, very tasty and tender Korean barbecue both priced under $11 for either beef or pork. (For more details on Korean dining see "Seoul Food: Bi-Bim-Bopping Through Chicago's Korean Barbecues.")

Open daily.

J. T. Collin's Pub

3358 North Paulina, (773) 327-7467

(Technically not on Lincoln, but close enough.)

The old Torchlight Cafe, a rehabbed Rexall drug store, evolved one giant step higher into J. T.'s, almost the perfect neighborhood watering hole. A wedge-shaped, single-room bar with two sides made up of floor-to-ceiling windows, J. T.'s is a light, friendly spot where even a woman alone can feel comfortable stopping off for a drink on her way home from the Paulina El stop. Food is also lighter and a step above standard bar fare. The flat bread with Italian chicken sausage, shredded parmesan, spinach, gorgonzola, and tomatoes, served with a salad ($5.75) is more than enough for a meal. Sandwiches, at $5.75 and under, are all a good deal and all served with fries. Choose from among the stuffed gorgonzola burger, the spicy chicken burger, grilled chicken with chipotle mayo, or the andouille sausage poor boy. If you want to get fancy, there are four entrées—a half roasted marinated chicken ($6.75), chicken with fettuccine and veggies in olive oil and garlic ($7.50), angel hair pasta with chicken sausage, goat cheese, and marinara ($6), and filet mignon kabobs served on pita ($7.25). This is the kind of place where everyone knows your name. (Well, at least they all know mine.)

Open daily. Full bar. Brunch on weekends.

The Flying Chicken

3811 North Lincoln, (773) 477-1090/1099

The Flying Chicken serves chicken—some of the best mesquite roasted chicken around—supposedly produced from an old family recipe, starting at $7.99 for a whole chicken. A quarter chicken, your choice of light or dark, with rice and potatoes is only $3.99 (half a chicken is $5.49). The chicken platter includes a quarter chicken, chicken soup, rice, beans, salad, and potatoes for $7.99. The menu is in Spanish, and the place is always packed with patrons who speak it. You'll know the place by the humorous logo of a wily, skinny rooster chasing a hen that hangs over the door.

Closed Tuesdays. BYOB.

Daily Bar & Grill

4560 North Lincoln, (773) 561-6198

A wedge-shaped neighborhood joint harking back to a time when movies were black and white and dining was accompanied by soothing, live music, the Daily Bar & Grill offers a comfortable atmosphere where patrons enjoy reasonably priced, jazzed-up dishes such as traditional comfort foods like veal meatloaf or pork cutlet "hot plates" with mashed potatoes and gravy (both $9.95) and grilled portabella mushroom and grilled calamari "small plates" ($5.95). Fish dishes change daily, and seasonal specials are also often available, with the chicken brats being a big hit during Oktoberfest. Entrées have begun to inch up on the expensive side, but sandwiches are always a good option

($5.95–$7.50). Meals begin with a traditional crock of cheese spread served with a basket of rolls and updated flat bread. Breakfast is available on the weekends. Stop in for a bite at the Daily Bar & Grill after a bargain movie up the street at the Davis Theater ($4 tickets, $2 on Sundays) to enjoy an evening of well-priced entertainment.

Open daily. Full bar. Brunch on weekends. Patio dining.

Chicago Brauhaus

4732 North Lincoln, (773) 784-4444

The Chicago Brauhaus, a Lincoln Square landmark, lets you celebrate Oktoberfest year-round. A traditional German oompah band rocks here nightly, cranking out your favorite Bavarian drinking tunes and occasionally slowing it down with a little "Edelweiss." Like a Munich beer hall, this is a big place; don't let them seat you too far away from the action on the packed parquet dance floor. While most of the dinners are too expensive, except for koenigsberger klopse (meatballs in caper sauce) and Bavarian leberkaese à la Holstein (German fried potatoes, red cabbage, soup or salad) both priced at $9.95, various sausages, served in pairs with a choice of potatoes, sauerkraut, or red cabbage ($5.75–$5.95) will get you in the spirit. Liver dumplings and stuffed cabbage are available in bulk for carryout. Every year, the Chicago Brauhaus throws an Oktoberfest in its rear parking lot starting the last weekend of September, a kickoff marked by the Von Steuben parade, and continuing through mid-October.

Closed Tuesdays. Full bar. Nightly music.

Eatin' *Large*

Lincoln Avenue

INNOVATIVE EATERIES FOR THE FINANCIALLY FINICKY PALATE

Lincoln Avenue is also known for its breakfast options, its delicatessens, and bakeries. Here's a quick look at some of the best:

Breakfast Joints The intersection of Lincoln, Wellington, and Southport is not only the home of St. Alphonsus, the church that was the center of the Lakeview German community in the late nineteenth century, but is also one of the premier 24-hour dining spots in the city. Flanked by the **Golden Apple** (2971, gigantic breakfast burritos) on one corner and the **S & G** (3000, creative assortment of egg casseroles) on the other, this intersection attracts breakfast aficionados, policemen, and sailors on leave at all hours. Other fine breakfast spots on Lincoln are the **Cozy Café** (2819, ham hash on the patio in the summer), **Salt & Pepper Diner** (2575, the original), and **Clark's** (2441, try the Northshore potatoes), which is also open late for those who've got the munchies after a show at the Lounge Axe. (For more details on breakfast spots, see "Early to Rise")

Delicatessens You can save a lot of money and still eat exotic specialties if you carry out from one of these establishments. **Paulina Market** (3501), is an old-time meat market where the line is bodies deep for fresh cuts and other gourmet goodies. Heading north toward Lincoln Square, try the **European Sausage House** (4361), which advertises whole pigs available. (For more details on delicatessens see "Oktoberfeast, Ja!")

Bakeries For over 75 years, **Dinkel's** (3329) has served up breads, cakes, and decorated frosted cookies commemorating holidays, seasons, the Bears, and the Cubs to the locals. This stretch of Lincoln was recently renamed after Dinkel's founder. Take a number and get in line here. **North Star Bakery** (4545) sells only bread, including real German kommisbrot, bauernbrot, and pumpernickel. For another bakery that also offers a light bite, try the **European Pastry Shop** (4701).

Trusty Italian

Da Nicola—always in fashion

Somewhere in your wardrobe, there's probably a frequently forgotten favorite shirt, sweater, or pair of jeans that you've had for years. Occasionally, you rediscover this garment and put it on. Once you check it out again, you realize just how great it looks, no matter what you wear with it. Unlike most things you buy that lose their allure by the third wearing, you can reaffirm to yourself how happy you are to own this item every time you put it on. And then for ultimate fulfillment, you go out in your old standby. You think you look great, then somebody says to you, "Hey, I love that sweater. You look amazing. Thirty pounds lighter. Your hair has bounce and body, and your eyes are intense and sparkling. Is that a new sweater?" I think of **Da Nicola** much as I think of my favorite trusty sweater. It's been around for years, and sometimes I even forget it's there. But every time I go back and rediscover the restaurant, I'm glad I did. The food is always bravissimo, no matter what I order.

Da Nicola has been serving fine Italian food for some seven years from its Lincoln Avenue location. While the restaurant, with its Mediterranean facade of stucco and tile located next to a cavernous army-navy surplus store, has survived the empty-storefront stage Lincoln went through and is now set to take advantage of the area's regentrification, it remains a throwback to the gracious old-world family-operated restaurants that seem to have gotten lost as trattorias and bistros have popped up all over the city. It's dark and cozy with accents of leather and brass. The service is friendly, competent, and attentive. It's quiet, except on weekends when a keyboardist entertains with lounge lizard music. The food is reasonably priced, and servings are generous. And although this is a comfortable family place, it's no Chef Boy-Ar-Dee, Leona's, or the plain Jane girl-next-door.

There are a lot of special touches at Da Nicola. For example, they make their own mozzarella—grow it themselves in what must be a huge mozzarella garden back in the kitchen. When was the last time you tried to wrap your teeth around bruschetta with homemade cheese? When was the last time you had the opportunity to order bruschetta in three different flavors—tomato, basil, and mozzarella; artichoke hearts and romano cheese; or tomatoes, basil, and garlic? Do you even know what bruschetta is? Maybe you should go find out.

Salads are big enough for a meal and can be ordered with organically grown greens. When you ask for a Caesar with anchovies, you get some serious filets.

Da Nicola, 3114 North Lincoln, (773) 935-8000, is open daily for lunch and dinner. Most pastas are under $10. Entrées, which are accompanied by a side of pasta and vegetable, are priced $8.95 to $14.95.

Soups come in either "bowls" or "large." All meals start off with fresh—baked, warm focaccia bread that's studded with tomatoes or onions and dipped in X.V. (extra virgin) olive oil.

Care needs to be taken so you don't get too full on the starters. Leave room to enjoy dinner-yours and anyone else's whom you're eating with. At least four or five specials are offered daily, including a risotto, a meat, and usually some fish or seafood. Delicacies like mixed seafood grill, featuring prawns on the half shell and silver dollar–sized scallops in a red wine sauce on a bed of potatoes and eggplant. Or a tangy chicken risotto with sun-dried tomatoes, capers, and porcini mushrooms.

If you bypass the daily specials for the regular menu, you won't be disappointed with the everyday options. Twenty-six different pasta dishes are offered, with nine of them being vegetarian including grilled vegetable ravioli, fettuccine Napoletano (homemade spinach noodles tossed with roasted eggplant, spinach, porcini mushrooms, garlic and X.V. olive oil), and spaghetti "fantasy" (tomatoes, peas, red onion, mushrooms, black olives, garlic, and X.V. olive oil).

If you're a pasta carnivore, you can choose from three different raviolis (salmon-stuffed with baby shrimp in cream sauce, porcini mushroom in red wine and cream sauce, or veal in tomato cream sauce with peas, mushrooms, and prosciutto), two varieties of tortellini in either vodka sauce or cream sauce, lasagnas, linguinis, fettuccinis, fusillis, farfalles, gnocchi—oodles of various noodles.

Full entrées, *secondi*, are served with a side of pasta and vegetables. Various chicken and seafood dishes, including the signature shrimp and scallops Nicola in a saffron cream sauce, are a good bet. Five different veal variations available daily are also a menu highlight.

There's an old Italian saying that the best restaurant is at home. I'm pretty familiar with what my own kitchen can do, though. I'd rather rediscover and be surprised by Da Nicola's any day.

Simplon Irresistible

Take a culinary ride on the Orient Express

> "And now let us make the fantasy more fantastic," said Poirot cheerfully. "Last night on the train, there were two mysterious strangers . . ."
>
> —*Murder on the Orient Express,* **Agatha Christie**

La Belle Epoque, days of wine and roses and Art Deco, of crowned and uncrowned heads, of adventurers and femmes fatales, of "spies, murders and lovers" riding luxury trains that journeyed from the Mongolian Steppes to London Bridge. Gleaming blue and gold "Wagon-Lits" that crossed the boundaries of Europe, the Middle East, and Asia under the names Train Bleu, Golden Arrow, Transsiberian, and the Orient Express.

Founded in 1884 and known for its gold logo of two lions holding an intertwined *WL*, the Compagnie Internationale des Wagons-Lits et des Grands Express Europeans offered sophisticated travelers a luxurious environment that mixed adventure with technological performance. Wagons-Lits express sleeper trains crossed the Eastern Hemisphere carrying the brass of the continents, including Margaretha Zelle MacLeod, known better as Mata Hari, who earned frequent traveler status during World War I as she cruised the Orient Express in her attempts to spy for the Germans on the Allied officers aboard.

The Wagons-Lits trains reached their sumptuous zenith in the Roaring Twenties. World War II, which wiped many of the countries from the map that once played host to the Orient

Express and its sister trains, also marked the decline of the era's luxury rail travel.

Today, the Orient Express has been revived with journeys on its traditional route from Zurich to Istanbul. But you don't have to fly all the way to the Continent to experience the mystique of the legendary express train. Non! You can take our fair city's own less than sumptuous Brown Line to Lincoln Square, where you can reexperience a forgotten era at **Simplon Orient Express**.

Decorated like the inside of one of the luxury sleeper cars of its namesake, Simplon Orient Express specializes in traditional dishes from the countries the train once steamed through on its way from the capitals of Europe to the mysteries of the Near East. You can eat your way through an entire continent from the comfort of one time zone.

Starting in France with veal cordon bleu, you, the culinary traveler can work your way—menu in hand—east through Switzerland for chicken sauté in wine sauce with a stop for holstein schnitzel in Germany (a country a little off the train's original route unless you're counting the entire region originally encompassed by the Germanic Holy Roman Empire). Then you're off to Austria for wiener schnitzel, and you continue south to Italy for spaghetti Milanese. A zig and a zag back takes you through Hungary (veal goulash), Romania (meat à la Romanian), and Serbia (numerous options). A side trip to Greece for royal moussaka, and then you're back on track through Bulgaria (natur schnitzel) for your final destination Istanbul, Turkey for a finale of sarma (rolled sour cab-

Simplon Orient Express, 4520 North Lincoln Avenue, (773) 275-5522/ (773) 275-0033, is open Monday through Saturday until 2:00 A.M., Sundays from noon until midnight. Live music includes strolling violins and an accordion.

bage leaves filled with veal, beef, and rice— "the most popular dish.")

It's clear from the menu that the real specialty at Simplon Orient Express is Serbian cuisine. We're told, "Serbian cuisine enjoys an exquisite reputation among European connoisseurs of cooking. Try it and convince yourself." Simplon Orient Express has got a number of carnivorous options to taste test, including a succulent dish of cevapcici, the ground veal and beef pieces common in a number of Eastern European cuisines, raznjici (pork tenderloin shish kebab), bele vesalice (grilled pork loin), pljeskavica (ground round steak), muckalica (a spicy gourment dish with a pork tenderloin base), and veal shank.

For those who like to experiment, there's a combination dish of cevapcici and raznjici. And, for those who want to go over the top, there's the family-style dinner for two or more that includes the combination's two entrées in addition to royal moussaka, vegetable, potato, dessert, and coffee. After eating all that, you'll want to make your way to your berth to lie down.

All dinners include appetizers and soup, which are an additional highlight. Soup is usually a choice of chicken or veal, and appetizers are a combination of chopped chicken liverers, a hard-boiled egg in a tart mayo dressing, and kajmak, a fermented "milk-bread spread" garnished with an olive that originates from the Caucasus. Delicious, in spite of what you may think it sounds like.

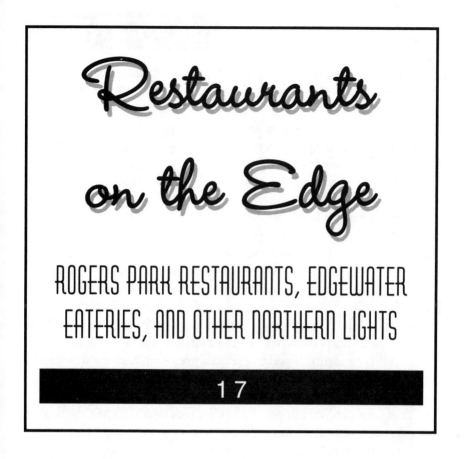

Restaurants on the Edge

ROGERS PARK RESTAURANTS, EDGEWATER EATERIES, AND OTHER NORTHERN LIGHTS

17

Who are the people in your neighborhood? Well, if your neighborhood is on Chicago's northern border—Rogers Park, Edgewater, Albany Park, the Northwest Side—your neighbors probably reflect the mixture of ethnic groups and cultures that come together to form the mini United Nations found just south of Howard Street and the Evanston city line. Africans, Koreans, Thais, Chinese, Vietnamese, Indians, Pakistanis, Lebanese, Orthodox Jews, Filipinos, Native American Indians, Greeks, Germans, Swedes, Norwegians, and various Hispanic groups—the list goes on and on—live in separate enclaves anchored on streets or around intersections or simply all mixed up with each other.

Chicago's Northside took off in 1907 with the extension of the El from Wilson north to Evanston on the Howard Line and the opening of the Ravenswood Line north from Lawrence. Edgewater, with its most recognizable landmark being the pink, rococo Edgewater Beach Hotel, was a community of Prairie School–influenced mansions and luxury high-rise co-ops. Streets planned by developer John Cochran were named after stops along the Pennsylvania Railroad's mainline out of Philadelphia—Bryn Mawr, Berwyn, Ardmore. Although the eastern edge of Edgewater on the lakeshore retains its exclusiveness, much of the rest of that neighborhood, along with the other northern enclaves, reflects the words of Studs Terkel, who described Uptown as the "United Nations of the have-nots." Many of the original ethnic groups, mainly European, around whom these communities developed have moved on and left these streets to thosewho arived later off the boats. Some flavor of the earlier residents, however, inevitably remains, and the sights and smells of Europe mix with those of Asia, Africa, and Latin America.

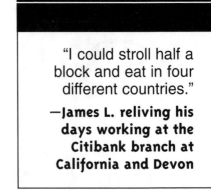

> "I could stroll half a block and eat in four different countries."
>
> **—James L. reliving his days working at the Citibank branch at California and Devon**

From the 1960s-style high-rises on the lakeshore to the suburban-like bungalows of West Rogers Park, Chicago's northern neighborhoods offer a variety of options in eating experiences as well. Beginning in the southeast corner of this area in Uptown's Argyle Street neighborhood, diners can graze through Vietnamese and Chinese dim sum that's served daily. Head slightly northwest and find the Scandinavian and Middle Eastern options of Andersonville. Slide up the lakeshore, and you can kick back among Afro Caribbean eateries or hang out in one of the many coffeehouses that dot the area around Loyola University. Turn west from the lake, and you'll graze through the Indian and Pakistani restaurants and Jewish delis of West Ridge and Devon. The Northwest side has the bar options—that would be sushi bars—along with other Japanese offerings. Moving south again, you'll end up in the Seoul of Chicago amongst the Korean storefronts of Albany Park. Head back to the lake, but before you finish, stop in Lincoln Square to drink at a year-round Oktoberfest. Around the world in 80 blocks. You don't need a passport, but you should be hungry when you go.

Anna Held Fountain Café

5557 North Sheridan, (773) 561-1941

Looming over the northern stretches of Lake Shore Drive is one of the Northside's most recognizable architectural artifacts, the powder-room pink Edgewater Beach Hotel. And, occupying the northwest corner of this monument to earlier times is the Anna Held Fountain Café, a combined soda fountain and flower shop that makes you believe time can stand still. Sandwiched among the flora is an old-fashioned counter where sodas, sundaes, muffins, and other desserts can be savored under black-and-white photos of old Chicago. Overflowing cupboards and drawers offer a variety of knick-knacks, children's toys, and books. Artsy T-shirts and shelf-stable gourmet food items can be found amongst the beribboned straw hats and stuffed animals. Anna Held is just like a visit to grandma's, when she'd let you discover the treasures of her attic and then, when you were tired, stuff you full of sweets (you were probably too young then to finish it off with a cappuccino).

Open daily. No alcohol.

The Dellwood Pickle

1475 West Balmoral, (773) 221-7728

Andersonville's Dellwood Pickle is like stepping into someone's 1960-ish Formica kitchen. The Dellwood Pickle has apparently gone through a few reincarnations in the kitchen, and the current life it's living is a good value for some tasty food. Sandwiches, including a po' boy sliced pot roast sandwich, are all $6.25 or under and served with a side. Entrées—peanut or cranberry chicken, spicy New Orleans shepherd pie, and tomato basil ravioli, among others—are all $8.25 and under. Seafood options—blackened catfish, salmon, or tuna or grilled soy salmon—are $9.25 to $9.95. Mix-and-match pastas and sauces are the centerpiece of the menu, and a tortellini special ($9) changes daily. Try the tortellini with the broccoli walnut sauce, a cream sauce with broccoli and seasoned with walnut pesto. After dinner (we don't want to rush you, but the place is small), you can relax in the back room, a room particularly reminiscent of someone's 1960-ish family room.

Closed Monday. BYOB.

Moody's Pub

5910 North Broadway, (773) 275-2696

Even when summer is over, it's never too late to appreciate a really good garden. And, Moody's has got one. Seating one hundred and fifty under the shade of maples and surrounded by clinging vines and burbling fountains, Moody's is an urban oasis on north Broadway. According to management, the garden has been the scene of numerous engagements and even a few weddings. When the weather turns nasty, you can move inside to the intimate atmosphere of the pub, graced by flames from the fireplace and numerous candles. Winter, spring, summer, or fall, it's always the season for the Moodyburger ($5.25). Voted "best burger" by all three of our city's premier newspapers (*Chicago Tribune*, *Chicago Sun-Times*, and *Reader*), the Moodyburger is one-half pound slab of premium beef sporting an 80/20 meat-fat ratio to minimize the grease without sacrificing flavor. A platter of beer-battered onion rings are the right side ($2.75). All entrées and sandwiches run $3.25 to $6.25, and cholesterol-free cooking oil and fat-free salad dressing are used year-round. Not issues you're usually concerned about when you're slurping down some wings at the local sports bar, right? Free parking next door, large-screen TV inside, Moody Brews, Moody Moonshine, and Summer Sippers, along with Sangria by the glass or pitcher, are all available. The final plus rendering Moody's unavoidably appealing is the presence of discount coupons that appear every Friday in the *Reader*, *Chicago Tribune*, and *Chicago Sun-Times* for half-price entrées. Kitchen's open until 1:00 A.M., so you've got plenty of time to get uptown to the grill.

Open daily and late. Full bar. Patio dining. Free parking.

Mei Shung Chinese Restaurant

5511 North Broadway, (773) 728-5778

Having lived on the East Coast and in San Francisco, I've never been a big fan of much of the Chinese food served in Chicago, and I almost never go to Chinatown. On the other hand, I have discovered a couple good Chinese options in New Chinatown around Argyle Street and elsewhere on the Northside. Mei Shung in Edgewater is one of those finds. The restaurant has a huge menu, but you can skip all the tasty Mandarin options and head right to the Taiwanese menu with its narly eighty alternatives. Seafood and fish dishes, including mussels with sweet basil in a brown sauce ($8.95) and silver side fish with leaf mustard ($7.95) are excellent. There are also some interesting options like two-designed sea slugs ($12.95) and hot three strips, pork, dried beancurd, bamboo, and chili strips in a special sauce ($7.95). If you can't make up your mind, pick from any of the specials posted daily on the wall.

Open daily. Full bar.

Capt'n Nemo's Subs & Soups

7367 North Clark, (773) 227-6366

"The last good deal in great eating" and one of the city's most creative sandwich shops, Nemo's heaps meats, cheeses, eggs, and vegetables onto French bread and serves up huge, club-like meals. Free samples of Mrs. Nemo's homemade soup are offered to you before you order, and soup is sold by the cup or the gallon ($9, take-out only). Take-out sandwiches are available in lengths from two to six feet (a foot serves six to eight). Nemo's also has branches at Ashland and Addison and downtown on Wacker if it's hard for you to get up to Rogers Park.

Open daily. No alcohol.

El Dinamico Dallas

1545 West Howard, (773) 465-3320

Rogers Park and Edgewater are home to much of Chicago's Afro Caribbean community, and a number of restaurants in the area cater to those tropical tastes. El Dinamico Dallas is a small, greenery-filled storefront on the Evanston border serving Jamaican, Cuban, and Haitian specialties. Entrées start at $6.50 and include griot (Haitian pork), chilindron de chivo (goat meat stewed in beer and wine with green olives, capers, and onions), lambi (conch in spicy tomato-wine sauce), congri (Cuban-style rice and beans), and various jerk or curried options, including goat. An all-you-can-eat buffet is available Fridays and Saturdays. Tropical shakes are a highlight and can be made from papaya, passion fruit, mamey, guanabana, tamarindo, mango, and other fruits. (See "Out of Africa" for more African and Caribbean options.)

Closed Tuesday. BYOB.

A & T Restaurant

7036 North Clark, (773) 274-0036

This low-key diner in Rogers Park is breakfast heaven for the devotees who flock here for the giant omelets served all day. Fluffy cholesterol pillows built from three extra-large eggs ($3.75–$4.65, cooked in 100 percent virgin olive oil imported from Greece add $.40), omelets come not only with veggie fillings, but also with fruit options of banana, peach, or apple. Cheese blintzes with homemade fruit toppings ($3.15–$4.15) are a good bet if you're not an egg fan.

Open daily. No alcohol.

Affy Tapple

7110 North Clark, (773) 338-1100

Chicago's candy apple factory offers bargain prices on factory seconds—undersized apples, those that were unevenly coated, or with broken sticks. Get up there in time for Halloween.

Closed Sundays.

Ennui Café

6981 North Sheridan, (773) 973-2233

Are you surprised to find great coffeehouses in close proximity to a major urban university? Loyola's Ennui, serving up sweet pastries and hot coffee, is best known for its steaming neon coffee cup in the window. Another northern coffee classic is **Don's Coffee Club** on 1439 West Jarvis; it's open late, and Don himself will serve you desserts on "real" china. Check out Don's annual Prom Night in September.

Open daily, no alcohol.

Great Seas Chinese Restaurant

3254 West Lawrence, (773) 478-9129

A Chinese restaurant in the heart of Koreatown specializing in Mandarin, Hunanese, and Szechuan regional cuisines, the pride of Great Seas is its deep-fried barbecued chicken wings (and legs and other parts, $7.95). Coated in a spicy-sweet sauce and heaped on platters, the wings are worth the drive northwest just to gnaw on one of these.

Open daily. Full bar.

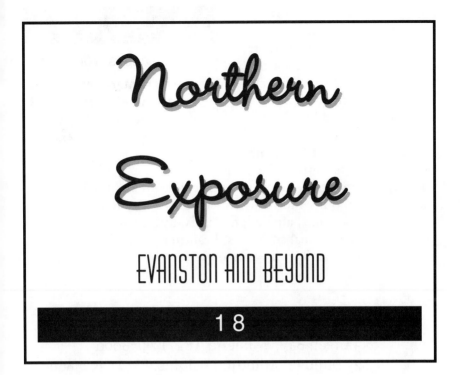

Northern Exposure

EVANSTON AND BEYOND

18

Do you need to make a quick getaway? What's wrong? Still catching up on bills? Can't afford that little pick-me-up ski vacation or a rejuvenating jaunt to Mexico? Feeling stuck with no way out? Well, it doesn't have to be that way. In fact, just a hop, skip, and a jump away is a beautiful lakefront community offering spectacular views of the water, abundant trails and paths to hike or cross-country ski, tobogganing, downhill skiing, exclusive shopping, and numerous cozy establishments where a comforting hot meal can be savored with a refreshing drink. One catch—don't count on that drink being fermentation-based, because the bucolic community we're talking about is Evanston, the Northshore's outer frontier, the academic jewel of the Northside, 847 heaven for real estate investors, and the historic home of the Ladies' Temperance Union.

History aside, things have loosened up a lot in Evanston. Although Evanston's still influenced by its patron and the founder and first president of Northwestern University, John Evans, who established a four-mile alcohol-free corridor around the University, absolute temperance is now a thing of the past. There now exists a selection of restaurants besides the dining room at the Orrington Hotel that serve alcohol as an accompaniment to their menus. In addition, Evanston and its Northshore neighbors now sustain a number of restaurants that bridge the culinary and monetary gap between McDonalds and the four-star Trio. From rib joints and cushy coffee shops—very few "bare bones"–type hangouts, after all, this is Evanston, not Madison—to perky bistros and casual sit-downs, Evanston and its Northshore neighbors offer a variety of eating opportunities that won't tax the wallet.

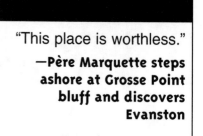

"This place is worthless."

—Père Marquette steps ashore at Grosse Point bluff and discovers Evanston

Walker Brothers

153 Green Bay, Wilmette, (847) 251-6000
825 Dundee, Arlington Heights, (847) 392-6600
1615 Waukegan, Glenview, (847) 724-0220
620 Central, Highland Park, (847) 432-0660
200 Marriott, Lincolnshire, (847) 634-2220

A spiffed-up IHOP, for 36 years the Walker Brothers on Green Bay has been serving breakfast selections all day to the patient crowds of patrons who park it in the Walker Bros. front lobby for up to two hours on weekend mornings for the pleasure of digging into some hefty stacks of batter-based, syrup-laden, whipped cream–garnished pancake, waffle, and French toast tasties. Most of the pancakes run $2.95 to $5.00. Classic pancake dishes include Swedish, chocolate chippies, and Georgia pecan. There are six different kinds of "crêpe pancakes" (Do Northsiders not recognize a crêpe as a pancake?) and five different types of Belgian waffles. Specialties include apple pancakes ($6.25) and German pancakes ($6.75). While you're waiting for your order, take time to admire the stained glass windows that surround the dining areas, which, along with the food, truly distinguish Walker Brothers from the run-of-the-mill pancake house. In case you've run dry on things to do while waiting to eat, the history of the stained glass is detailed on the back of the menu.

Note, the Glenview and Arlington Heights locations carry through on the oak, brass, and stained glass look, while the Lincolnshire restaurant maintains "the oak appearance but added an English country theme." Both Lincolnshire and Highland Park have expanded menus with salads and sandwiches.

Open daily. No alcohol.

Blind Faith Café

525 Dempster, Evanston, (847) 328-6876

3300 North Lincoln, Chicago (773) 871-3820

Staid Evanston's answer to the "granola" element every college town claims, the Blind Faith Café is one of the few restaurants in Evanston that both manages to span the gap between McDonalds and the former multistar Café Province stay in business. Now a big enterprise, the Blind Faith Café has expanded its concept of a healthy lifestyle to encompass two sit-down restaurants—one recently opened in Lakeview, a self-service café and a catering service. The original is not as fancy nor as good as its city cousin, but the prices are slightly cheaper and the service far better. "Favorites" are $6.95 to $9.50 and range from the barbecue seitan sandwich to the macrobiotic plate, which is supposed to resemble the traditional Japanese diet by combining whole grains with land and sea vegetables and eliminating fat, meaning you can actually enjoy a plate of brown rice topped with shiitake mushroom sauce, vegetable and bean of the day, steamed kale vinaigrette, sea vegetable, cup of miso soup, and a pickle (probably not dill). Light entrées including pastas, healthy Mexican (such as bean tostadas and chili enchiladas) and various combinations of seitan, tofu, and tempeh range from $8.50 to $10.50. Breakfast is served every day until 2:00 P.M. Scads of Northshorers are keeping the faith. Maybe you should check it out.

Open daily. Wine and beer.

Lulu's

626 Davis, Evanston (847) 869-4343
1333 East 57th, Chicago (773) 288-2988

With its bright decor and no-frills style, the original Lulu's is the Penny's of the Northshore. Lulu's takes Penny's a step further in creativity, though, and serves a selection of "fusion Asian," including dumplings and other "small eats," soups, salads, and stir-fries. Dim sum is a big hit here, especially on Mondays from 5:30 to 9:00 P.M. and Sundays when it's $10.95 all-you-can-eat between 11:30 and 3:00 P.M. Try the blue mussels steamed in an iron pot in broth flavored with chilis, ginger, garlic, and cilantro ($4.95). Or, spear a dumpling filled with pork and scallions ($4.15). Entrées are priced $6.50 to $7.25 and play on a range of Japanese, Chinese, Thai, and Vietnamese themes. Noodles are big and can be found in both soups and salads. The Vietnamese rice noodle salad topped with grilled beef and a spring roll is a big hit ($6.75) as are other entrées such as jumbo shrimp and mixed veggies with Thai panang coconut curry and rice ($7.25). In white bread Evanston, Lulu's is the place that has "dim sum and then sum." Note, Lulu's now has a Hyde Park location too.

Open daily. Beer, wine, and sake.

Buffalo Joe's Original Restaurant

812 Clark, Evanston, (847) 328-5525

Buffalo Joe's Seafood

2000 Green Bay, Evanston, (847) 868-5400

Listen to a story about a man named Joe . . . Buffalo Joe's is one of the Northshore's most successful franchises. Founded by former Buffalo resident, Joe Prudden, who created his own sauce recipe and pioneered wings in the Chicago area, Buffalo Joe's has gone on to expand into three sauces (tasty mild, powerful spicy, and suicide) and multiple locations. Buffalo Joe's Original Restaurant is a cafeteria-style restaurant that still hums daily with students and other wing devotees from near and far looking to put some spice into their lives. The second location, Buffalo Joe's Seafood, is almost exclusively carryout, with a couple of stools at the counter if you want to munch on-site. The seafood place has some excellent homemade gumbo, hot and spicy and starting at $1.59 for a bowl, ranging up to $12:00 for a gallon. The full pound of jumbo shrimp for $7.99, although not spicy, is a great deal.

Both Joe's open daily. No alcohol.

Roxy Café

626 Church, Evanston, (847) 864-6540

Roxy Café has replaced the old J. B. Winberie's and its cheese fondue with a very reasonably priced and attractive Italian-American bistro serving a variety of thin-crust pizzas and salads. Roxy also has entrées, but they're generally too expensive for us.) Roxy recently brought in a new chef from the Culinary School of Kendall College. Pizzas and the calzone of the day are priced $5.95 to $6.95. Meal-sized salads range from $5.50 to $10.00 for the shrimp Ceasar. Pastas are $5.95 to $8.95 and include a tasty seafood linguine and an Italian sausage lasagna.

Open daily. Full bar.

Noyes Street Café

828 Noyes, Evanston, (847) 475-8683

Located up the street from the Noyes El stop, Noyes Street Café, along with Roxy Café, have managed to fill a gaping hole in Evanston's eating options by providing creative dining at prices reasonable even for students (OK, a special night out for students). There's nothing like being able to enjoy linguine with garlic, olive oil, sun-dried tomatoes, and roasted pine nuts or a pesto fettuccine with garlic bread and a salad for $10.05 (most places force you to order the extras separately, setting you back again the price of an entrée). A number of chicken dishes are also priced at $10.05. A large variety of sandwiches, burgers, and meal-sized salads ranges from $3.60 to $8.05.

Open daily. Wine and beer.

Gary Barnett's

1710 Orrington, Evanston, (847) 864-6700

The Orrington Hotel has gone wild with the rest of Evanston and, handing over its entire dining room, has put its faith in Gary Barnett sticking around for the long-term and fulfilling the terms of his contract. Gary Barnett's, "where the season never ends," is full of purple people eaters munching burgers (all $5 to $6), Big Ten chicken sandwiches ($5.96), and Gary's favorite Santa Fe chicken sandwich ($6.46). Most of the entrées are too expensive, but those who feel the need to bulk up can afford the half slab of ribs ($9.77).

Open daily. Full bar.

Other Northshore establishments, some of which I may have written about in other chapters, that you may want to check out include **Hecky's** (the best ribs in town), **Lindo Mexico** (sister to the Lincoln Avenue spot), **The Flat Top Grill** (make your own stir fry from the people on North Avenue) and the **Dancing Noodle Cafés** found in various locations running up the lakeshore.

Food For Fast Feasts

quick bites

Cross Rhodes

913 Chicago, Evanston, (847) 475-4475

Forget the Athenian Room, forget Greek Town. If you're looking for tasty, cheap Greek food, this is the place to go. The Greek salad here, at $3.50, a full meal, is simply the best—millions have been consumed by legions of Northwestern females. The vegetarian salad ($4.60) dressed with copious amounts of large, greasy Greek fries, is also great. The half Greek chicken, with white wine sauce or barbecue sauce (both $7.35), is also a good option.

Open daily. Wine and beer.

quick bites

Café Express

615 Dempster, Evanston, (847) 864-1868

Evanston's enduring coffeehouse, a bustling hot spot when a Chicago-based Starbucks was just a twinkle in the eye of a savvy investor, Café Express and its spartan menu and interior steams ahead ignoring growing competition. About as radical as Evanston gets, you can get a croissant or bagel sandwich here while you read your subversive Northwestern student literature. Desserts are under $2.50, a deal for this kind of place!

Open daily. No alcohol. Sidewalk seating. Live jazz Sunday afternoons.

Dave's Italian Kitchen

906 Church, Evanston, (847) 864-6000

The traditional bastion of cheap chow on the Northshore, Dave's is always packed with students who are out for something "nice" and hordes of other devotees. Long one of the only places in town where you could get a decent, homemade meal for under $6 that didn't feature a Big Mac, Dave's and its adequate Italian food remain a fixture for cheap eating in this town.

Open daily. Full bar.

Merle's #1 Barbecue

1727 Benson, Evanston, (847) 475-7766

Nothing personal to Merle's, but if you're in Evanston and craving some baby backs, I can't believe you wouldn't be up the street at Hecky's, unless you need a sit-down place. If you need it "for here," Merle's will do the trick, especially the half slab of St. Louis ribs ($7.95). Merle's serves carryout by the pound or slab, but for that, you should definitely be at Hecky's.

Open daily. Full bar.

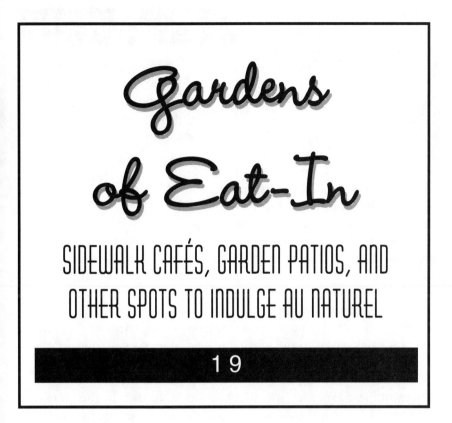

Gardens of Eat-In

SIDEWALK CAFÉS, GARDEN PATIOS, AND OTHER SPOTS TO INDULGE AU NATUREL

19

Tran•scen•den•tal•ism (tran-sen-den-t'l-izm) n.: A nineteenth-century intellectual movement that assumed the imminent presence of God within both man and nature and elevated the powers of intuition over logic and reasoning. Characterized by the writings of many American authors of the era celebrating nature and a raw, open new continent.

We have a long history of communing with nature, from the founding of our country and the subsequent push westward through the wilderness to fulfill manifest destiny, to the nineteenth century when Thoreau shucked the shackles of civilized constraints to retreat to the pond, to this century's periodic resurrections of Woodstock. Today, those of us who cannot satisfy our latent primal urges to chuck it all and go back to the bush have to find substitutes in the urban jungle that release the tensions built up driving the information highway into cyberspace.

> "Give me books, fruit, French wine and fine weather, and a little music out of doors, played by someone I do not know."
>
> **—Letter to Fanny Keats, John Keats**

Come pleasant weather—in Chicago, defined as any moderately sunny day where there's no snow on the ground, generally found only between the months of May and October—a primitive drum starts to beat in the blood of our urban fellow residents, driving them to fulfill their basic instincts to strip down and bare pasty, winterized bodies to the elements to absorb the life-renewing rays and balmy breezes. As spring moves into summer, the denizens of our city are driven by an increasingly frantic need just to be outdoors, with each day passing meaning one more day of fair weather over, one day closer to the inevitable cold, one less day to just do it.

Coupled with this need to heed nature's call while the great outdoors can still be enjoyed without a parka comes the urge to fulfill the most basic impulses, including eating, of course. To the average citizen of Chicago, there's nothing grander than a picnic by the lake, a dog in the bleachers, or a leisurely afternoon in a beer garden quaffing some cold ones while nibbling on some wings. Yes, Adam and Eve may have lost out on Eden, but at least their descendants discovered patio dining.

At the first sign of warm weather, savvy restaurants and bars all over Chicago liberate their plastic furniture from storage. Many commandeer an adjacent piece of public walkway and, violà, instant sidewalk café. But, if you're interested in a real place to dine, you're searching for one of those rarer establishments that offer an authentic patio or porch—some separate dining area that no one is going to walk his or her dog through as you dabble in your calamari and an iced latte.

Since the summer's too short to waste time debating patio vs. sidewalk vs. possibly your own back yard, here's a range of outdoor eateries to satisfy your needs, from simple to formal. And, being very sun sensitive, they're ranked by that all important exposure factor:

SPF 2 a sidewalk café or other open place that's going to leave you vulnerable to not only the dangerous rays of the sun, but also the potential mishaps of bikers, roller bladers, and other passing bodies that may hurtle through your dining space without regard to your delicate digestive requirements

SPF 8 a separate deck or patio space that's been built to detach the diner from the hurley-burley of the sidewalk, but does not necessarily provide the patron with any more serenity or view than that found at the makeshift sidewalk SPF 2 café

SPF 15 a separate, enclosed patio often found at the back of the restaurant that graciously shields the patron from the potentially grim realities of the city seen from the front of the restaurant. The ultimate SPF 15 includes trees, well-groomed gardens to perfume the air, and a bubbling fountain, preferably with tasteful statuary

Whatever your idea of the perfect outdoor dining experience, you can find it in Chicago. They're all open for business—whether it's lunch at high noon or dinner during some enchanted evening. So, get out of here.

Resi's Bierstube

2034 West Irving Park, (773) 472-1749

Resi's Bierstube, a cozy year-round Oktoberfest celebration tucked away in an old Northside neighborhood, nudges out Moody's Pub (see "Restaurants on the Edge") for best beer garden. Moody's has an expansive, tree-studded patio graced with two fountains that seat 150 and the half-pound Moody burger, but Resi's urban oasis wins on breadth of menu, both for food and drink. Hefty entrées usually served with two sides can be enjoyed for around $7.50 to $8.95 (except for the five types of schnitzels, which are slightly more pricey). Various sausages, no less than six kinds of wursts—bratwurst (both regular and Sheboygan-style), smoked thuringer, knackwurst, wieners, and liver and blood sausage—range from $4.75 à la carte to $8.50 with sauerkraut and other fixin's. Hackepeter, a German steak tartare ($6.50), is available on the weekends. There are over 130 beers to choose from, including over two dozen weissbiers and seventy bottled imports—all of which can be enjoyed within the snug confines of its tree-shaded, flower-studded back patio. Lift a stein served to you by your Frau waitress, who has probably been with the establishment for about twenty years, to share your good cheer with a stranger with whom you may also have to share your picnic table if the place gets packed. (For more details on Resi's see "Oktoberfeast, Ja.")

SPF 15. Open daily. Full bar.

Dao Thai Restaurant and Noodle Palace

230 East Ohio, (312) 337-0000

Outside of its loft space, Dao Thai is the proud owner of one of the finest dining patios in the 312 area code. A second-floor wood platform that's sheltered from the traffic on Ohio, the Dao's deck transports diners from the hustle and bustle of Streeterville to a tranquil dining experience punctuated by excellent spring rolls and pretty good ginger chicken ($5.75). The menu is pretty standard Thai, with standouts being beef with basil leaves ($4.95) and bamee and barbecued pork soup ($5.50). Specials include lots of currys. It's a treat just to come here to get out of your office and hang out on the patio, sipping an iced coffee.

SPF 15. Open daily. Full bar.

Village Tap

2055 West Roscoe, (773) 883-0817

The Village Tap is, hands down, one of the best garden/food values for the money in town. A classic neighborhood bar with a lot of gleaming, dark wood and an extensive drink list, the Village Tap also has the kind of cozy garden you can hang out in all night as long as you respect the sensibilities of the neighbors (actually, my neighbors, as the Village Tap is practically an extension of my kitchen). The food is highlighted by entrées that are mainly $7.95 and under and served quickly with minimum fuss. The vegetarian burrito ($5), a weighty tortilla cylinder stuffed with beans, cheese, sprouts, broccoli, and other healthy stuff, is served with a side of chips and salsa and is highly recommended. The falafel and hummus plate ($5.50) is also a good choice and usually yields another meal for later. Burgers, salads, and a couple of different grilled chicken breast sandwiches are also a good bet.

SPF 15. Open daily. Full bar.

Corosh

1072 North Milwaukee, (773) 235-0600

A surprisingly attractive restaurant and bar with an Italian emphasis, this East Village establishment is worth the trip just for the atmosphere. The loft-like feel is reinforced by brick walls and handcrafted hardwood floors and a polished wood bar. A tree-lined brick patio, complete with pink marble-topped tables and bullet-proof glass, camouflaged by trees, sits calmly outside. Salads, including the Caesar combo ($8.50), are extremely well endowed. Entrées are really too expensive, but almost all of the pastas are good options. The fettuccine alfredo comes with a choice of vegetables, chicken, shrimp, or straight-up cheese ($8.50–$11.95). The fusili Corosh, spiral pasta with sausage, peppers, escarole, and cannelini beans in a light tomato touch is also a good choice.

SPF 15. Open daily. Kitchen open until midnight. Patio.

The Riverside Deli

1656 West Courtland, (773) 278-DELI

The Riverside Deli is a hidden Bucktown gem, probably discovered only if you take the Armitage bus or you live down there (in which case, you've probably kept it a secret). Old-time decor with old-time prices, Riverside has a menu of items all under $5, with deluxe sandwiches running under $4. All of these delicacies can be savored on a shady, elevated wood deck tucked away on the north side of the restaurant. Here, an all-you-can-eat, $8.95 Sunday brunch is a winner with sideboards groaning under the weight of cereals, breads, fruit, cold salads, and hot entrées that range from pancakes and eggs benedict to cheese blintzes with fruit to fried tamales. To do this brunch justice, you should plan to relax a good part of your early Sunday here.

SPF 15. Open daily. All-you-can-eat brunch.

Bar San Miguel

3313 North Clark, (773) 871-0896

An attractive bar specializing in "traditional border food," Bar San Miguel is inevitably overshadowed by its trendy next-door neighbor Mia Francesca. No problem, the hordes can wait in line next door, while you sip sangria in the shady arbor of Bar San Miguel's back patio. Enjoy a balmy summer evening by munching a molieta, a Mexican pizza ($5.75–$6.50, try the four cheese with toasted almonds and capers), under the trailing grapevine. Other light meals include enchiladas ($6.50–$7.75) and sandwiches ($6.50–$7.50). If you need something more substantial, order from a number of platos de casa, including roasted pork with black bean sherry sauce ($9.75), chicken breasts stuffed with three cheeses, poblano peppers, and garlic in a caper cilantro sauce ($10.50), and fajitas ($9.95–$11.95).

SPF 15. Open daily, full bar.

Southport City Saloon

2548 North Southport, (773) 975-6110

Southport City Saloon is a gem of a watering hole with one of the most picturesque patios in the city. The broad limbs of a tree shooting up through the bar shade diners lazing at finished wood tables. On brisk days, the outdoor fireplace throws off warmth to the more determined outdoor eaters. Although most entrées, except the half slab of ribs ($10.50) and the barbecue chicken ($11.25), will put you over the "fork and knife" limit, a large selection of sandwiches, salads, and burgers is available, most for between $6.95 and $10.25. Among the entrées, the daily Blue Plate Special is a deal. Different every night, the Blue Plate is a full-course meal priced $8.95 before 7:00 P.M. and $10.95 after 7:00 P.M.

SPF 15. Open daily. Full bar.

Black Cat Chicago

2856 North Southport, (773) 404-4800

If you like the patio at Southport City Saloon, go up the street a bit and try its sister restaurant Black Cat Chicago. Specializing in "country Italian," Black Cat has the same type of porch as Southport City Saloon, with the only difference being an awning instead of the natural tree umbrella. The awning, however, allows diners to eat outside rain or shine. Sandwiches, including a New York strip steak, are $8.95. Pastas, priced $9.50 to $10.95, are a good option. Try the portabella capecci with mushrooms sautéed in white wine, garlic, and basil or the artichoke fusilli with goat cheese and mushrooms in a marinara sauce.
SPF 15. Open daily. Full bar.

Tilli's

1952 North Halsted, (773) 325-0044

Opened by a three siblings who grew up in their father's suburban Italian restaurant, Tilli's is a year-round garden in a former garden center. One of the sisters was the head chef at Tucci Milan, so the menu has a good number of Italian options, but the menu is really global with Asian soups and salads, Middle Eastern appetizers, and good old American entrées joining the pastas and pizzas ($3.25–$8), Entrées are served with a side and include "top secret" barbecue chicken ($7.95), many-herbed chicken breast ($8.95), and the gorgonzola pork chop ($10.95). For those of you who get tired of wandering the world gastronomically, there's the big @#!!! Burger for $6.95.
SPF 15. Open daily, full bar.

La Novita

1232 West Belmont, (773) 404-8888

Inside, La Novita, a modest little establishment in

West Lakeview, looks like a country inn with its brick fireplace; outside, the restaurant has a spacious deck that allows diners to enjoy the view of traffic on West Belmont Avenue. La Novita offers excellent trattoria food at, generally, lower-than-usual trattoria prices. As with most trattoria-type restaurants, if you stick with the pasta and chicken dishes, you can stick with your budget. Very appetizing risotto contadina (with mixed vegetables) is only $9.50, an extremely modest bill by risotto standards. Various other pastas, including daily specials, range from $7.50 to $9.75. Interesting pizzas, such as the smoked salmon, mozzarella, and tomato, are available for $6.50 to $8.50. Our waitress couldn't pronounce the names of dishes correctly, but do you really have to be a linguist to enjoy a sublime farfalle dello chef with a cold Moretti under the stars on a balmy summer night? (That's bowtie pasta with sun-dried tomatoes and mushrooms, $8.95, with a cold Italian beer, if you really do need to know. Capisco?)

SPF 8. Full bar. Open every day except Monday.

Pontiac Café

1531 North Damen, (773) 252-7767

A converted fruit stand, this Wicker Park sandwich place comes into its own when summer comes and it throws open its storefront to the elements. A spacious patio fronting the café allows diners to relax on Damen Avenue and sip fruit smoothies and slushes, which are served by the glass or by the pitcher ($7.50 for slushes and $9.50 for smoothies). Dining options are primarily sandwiches, with a couple salads thrown in. Ten kinds of subs—from old standards such as ham on rye to new age cool breezes such as smoked turkey, mozzarella, alfalfa sprouts, cucumber, oil, and balsamic vinegar—are served in eight-inch ($4.50) and twelve-inch ($6.50) versions. Add $1 for "double stuff" combos of two meats. Similarly, nine kinds of panini are served in the same sizes for the same prices. Try the olive panini with calamata olives, artichokes, orange zest, and olive oil. Seven different combinations of stuffed tomato focaccia, including one with artichokes, red pepper, and provolone, are $4.75 each.

SPF 8. No alcohol. Open daily.

Justin's

3358 North Southport, (773) 929-4844

Justin's is more than just a neighborhood sports bar with a dozen TVs and three satellite dishes that can hone in on "a field hockey game in Morocco at the drop of a hat." Justin's spacious, tree-studded beer garden, ornamented by a table and chairs on the roof, serves generous portions of your standard bar food for very reasonable prices, along with thirteen "pretty decent" beers on tap. Nothing trendy, no Ice or Zima here.

quick bites

SPF 15. Open daily.

Moody's Pub

5910 North Broadway, (773) 275-2696

Moody's, one of this town's classic pubs, has a tree-shaded patio that seats 150. Diners are serenaded by two fountains underneath a canopy of leafy branches. Moody's flash is in the flora, not the food, which is hearty pub fare. (More on Moody's in "Restaurants on the Edge.")

SPF 15. Open daily serving until 1:00 A.M., full bar.

Lutz Continental Café & Pastry

2458 West Montrose, (773) 478-7785

Around since 1948, Lutz's boasts a tiny walled garden out back, complete with greenery and a small fountain, bubbling away among the umbrella-shaded tables. The menu has some heavy, traditional Austrian selections, light meals including crêpes and sandwiches, along with some very serious tortes. (For more details see "Oktoberfeast, Ja!")

SPF 15. Closed Sundays.

McKlintock Court Garden Restaurant (The Art Institute)

110 South Michigan,
(312) 443-3508 [summer]
(312) 443-3530 [other seasons]

After Hours Jazz Tuesday summer evenings from 4:00 to 7:30 P.M. offers an opportunity to let music wash over you while your senses are lulled by the gurgling of the courtyard fountain and the various drinks and tidbits you must consume to cover your $7 minimum. The museum is free on Tuesday, so it all washes out. Although sandwiches and salads are all under $10, entrées are too expensive for you and me. (See also "Diversionary Dining.")

quick bites

SPF 15. Open May through September.

Sheffield's Wine and Beer Garden

3258 North Sheffield, (773) 281-4989

It doesn't get much cheaper than this! Sheffield's defines the meaning of BYOB—bring your own beef. Tucked off of Sheffield behind a picket fence is one of Lakeview's best-liked bars and beer gardens, complete with grills so that you can do your own. What you save on dinner, you'll probably drink away here, so don't feel too fiscally smug.

SPF 15. Open daily. Open late.

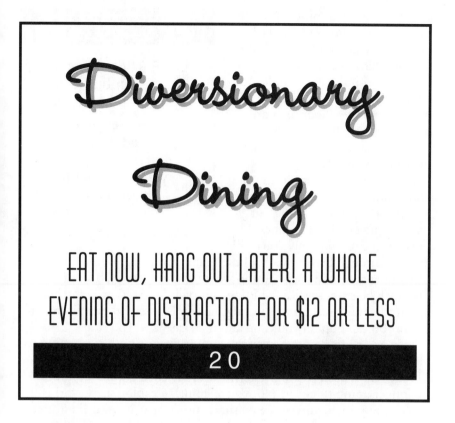

Diversionary Dining

EAT NOW, HANG OUT LATER! A WHOLE EVENING OF DISTRACTION FOR $12 OR LESS

20

What good is sitting alone in your room? Come hear the music play . . . So, what do you want to do tonight? These days, is your definition of "dinner and a show" take-out and a rental from Blockbuster? Was your cousin's wedding the last time you dined and danced—or was it your high school prom? Do the words *On Broadway* conjure up images of a big-ticket production at the Auditorium Theater or just that classic George Benson album stuffed in the back of your closet? Can you spell p-o-t-a-t-o, as in couch?

Sociologists have declared that the two biggest issues negatively affecting relationships are not enough quality time together and channel surfing. Both of these evils can be drastically alleviated by just getting out and having a good time. So, what's stopping you? Are you simply lacking in the *I*s—imagination and income?

Imagination, creativity, spontaneity—some of us are more bodaciously gifted than others; for those of you who are sadly lacking in those areas, you can shore up your deficiencies, make friends, and influence people. Yes, with a little direction, you may not become the life of the party, but at least you'll know where it is. And, even better, you'll be able to afford to go to it.

> "3 B & V beats sittin' on your butt gettin' fat at home."
>
> **—Chicago *Reader* advertisement, describing "3 things you might not have known about the Brew & View."**

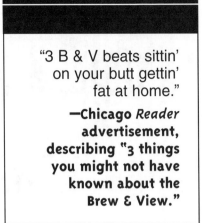

Just say no! No more sitting at home, only referencing your weekly copy of the *Reader* to dig out the ever-present Tsang Chinese carryout menu. No, now you'll be flipping through Section 2, "Culture Club," to check out the current scheduling at several local theatres where you can also grab a tasty meal. Or, you'll be enthusiastically hitting "Hitsville" in Section 3, catching up on the music scene and spotting the bands at several establishments where you can bop till you drop and then eat when you stop.

Hey, your life is gonna change! Laundry is just no longer going to be a satisfying way to spend your Saturday night. That old line "Things have been so crazy lately, I really needed a quiet evening" is no longer going to cut it. No, you're going to explore new worlds. You're going to acquire some cultural enrichment in your life (or at the very least, a T-shirt from the show—overpriced event T-shirts are not included in *Cheap Chow Chicago* pricing). And, making it even better, you're going to do it all, and you're not going to be hungry!

So, read on and get out. Just do it. Be young. No more excuses—save those for your boss.

Mud Bug

901 West Weed, (312) 787-9600

Open 8:00 A.M. until 2:00 A.M. with over 100 televisions most of which are focused on live thoroughbred and harness racing from tracks across the country, a teletheatre, sports bar, and access to the Illinois Lottery, Mud Bug is your conveniently located offtrack betting resource. The place has two eating options, a cafeteria line and a sit-down restaurant, both of which have essentially the same pub grub type food with some emphasis on the Cajun. (Mud Bug is a legend about a Louisiana thoroughbred who was slower than a "mud bug" until a miracle happened, and the horse became faster than any other four-legged critter around.) Ordering in the restaurant will cost you $1 per item more than the cafeteria line (plus tip, of course). Nightly specials include:

Sunday Italian Combo ($5.95) or BBQ roast beef ($4.95)
Monday meat loaf ($5.95) or chili dogs ($4.95)
Tuesday chicken stir fry ($6.95)
Wednesday teriyaki chicken ($6.95) or meatball sandwich ($4.95)
Thursday beef shish kebab ($6.95) or chili dog ($4.95)
Friday fish and chips ($6.95) or macaroni and cheese ($4.95)
Saturday roast beef with mashed potatoes ($6.95) or tuna melt ($5.95)

Races run after 2:00 P.M. and can be prewagered with results and cashing available the following day.

Open daily. Full bar.

Chicago Brauhaus

4732 North Lincoln, (773) 784-4444

Are you ever in the mood to just dance, dance, dance? Well, if you want to get out and try some dancing that's not, say, strictly ballroom, check out either the Chicago Brauhaus or Tania's.

The Chicago Brauhaus (for more details see "Taste of Lincoln Avenue"), the established German restaurant and nightclub anchor in Lincoln Square, offers a reasonably priced menu of assorted wursts, schnitzels, and other German delicacies that can be danced off six nights a week to the energetic strains of the Chicago Brauhaus Band. Patrons are not shy here. Requests and singing along are encouraged in addition to dancing.

Open daily. Full bar.

Tania's

2659 North Milwaukee, (773) 235-7120

If you feel like rhumba-ing late into the night to the strains of salsa and merengue, try Tania's (for more details see "Late for Dinner"). Tania's specializes in Cuban tapas ($1.80–$9.00), and the kitchen is open until 2:00 A.M. There is a dress code—no jeans or sneakers; shiny suits or tight skirts and high heels preferred.

Open daily. Full bar.

Big Shoulders Café (Chicago Historical Society)

1601 North Clark, (312) 587-7766

If you've been absorbing enough culture to work up an appetite, you don't have to settle for the museum cafeteria (depending on the museum you're at). The Big Shoulders Café at the Chicago Historical Society, named in tribute to Carl Sandburg, is a greenhouse-y café serving healthy American fare including Sheboygan bratwursts, wild rice cakes with wild mushroom sauce, and jalapeño corn bread, all for under $10. In nice weather, the outdoor café encourages dogs, and profits from the "bowser bistro biscuit menu" go to the Anti-Cruelty Society.

Open daily for lunch from 11:30 A.M. to 3:00 P.M. and Sundays for brunch. Full bar.

M Café (Museum of Comtemporary Art)

220 East Chicago, (312) 280-2660

The M Café, a collaboration between Trio restaurant owner Adaniya and Blue Plate Catering, bills itself as "a contemporary fusion café featuring an eclectic menu of global cuisine." Its sleek, stainless steel surroundings offer a view of the lake beyond the its back patio and gardens. Soups, sushi, spring rolls, sandwiches, pastas, pizzas, and stir frys are all for $6.95 and under.

Open every day except Mondays until 5:00 P.M.

McKlintock Court Garden Restaurant (The Art Institute)

110 South Michigan, (312) 443-3508 (summer) (312) 443-3530 (other seasons)

McKlintock Court Garden Restaurant at the Art Institute offers outdoor dining by the courtyard fountain during nice weather, along with After Hours Jazz on Tuesday evenings from 4:30 to 7:00 P.M. ($7 minimum). Sandwiches and salads are all under $10, with the most expensive being the lamb nicoise salad at $9.95. All the entrées, though, will put you over the limit.

Open daily, Memorial Day through September, from 11:00 A.M. to 3:30 P.M. (seating only until 2:30 P.M. Tuesdays). Full bar.

Bocaditos (Brookfield Zoo)

8400 West 31st, Brookfield, (708) 485-0263

If you find yourself ready for your own feeding time during a visit to the wild kingdom, try Bocaditos, Brookfield Zoo's first full-service restaurant. Meaning "little bites," Bocaditos, which is found in the South American exhibit, serves a variety of hot and cold tapas, most of which are priced well under $5. Options include the ubiquitous baked goat cheese in tomato sauce, shrimp fritters, a "sandwich" of fried Chilean sea bass with red peppers sprinkled with lime juice, and cold plates like alcachofas (a blend of artichoke hearts, black olives, and roasted peppers), black bean and corn salad, and three kinds of traditional Peruvian potato dishes.

Open daily for lunch. Children's menu; serves South American beers and Chilean wines.

Soundings Restaurant (Shedd Aquarium)

1200 South Lake Shore, (312) 986-2286

The Shedd lets you check out the marine life and then

continue to admire the marina and the city's skyline from its Soundings Restaurant. An assortment of entrées, including pastas and seafood are priced $4.95 and $11.95.

Lunch served from 12:00 P.M. to 2:30 P.M. daily.

Abbey Pub

3420 West Grace, (773) 463-5808

Buddy Guy's Legends

754 South Wabash, (312) 427-1190

Schubas Tavern

3159 North Southport, (773) 525-2508

The Beat Kitchen

2100 West Belmont, (773) 281-4444

Chicago offers a number of options where you can absorb food for the soul and music for the ears. Abbey Pub serves shepherd's pie, lamb stew, and Irish soda bread to the tunes of Irish bands on Wednesdays and Thursdays, folk, blues, or rock on Fridays and Saturdays, and a weekly Irish jam session on Sundays. Monday is the weekly barn dance, and Tuesday is an acoustic open stage. Buddy Guy's Legends offers the best in blues along with Cajun specialties every night until midnight. If you're less concerned about the food than the music, other good options for grabbing a burger and a band are Schubas Tavern and The Beat Kitchen. Schubas is Chicago's spot for rockabilly and country music. The Beat Kitchen has actually enhanced its bar grub menu with a selection of sixteen individual designer pizzas (priced $7.95 and under), soups, salads, and bayou-style meat loaf.

All open daily. Schubas serves brunch. Full bars.

Saga's Launder-bar and Café/ The Newport Bar & Grill

3435 North Southport, (773) 929-9274

Throw in a couple loads and come around back for a burger, sandwich, or plate of pasta. Sip some suds while you run through the rinse cycle.

Open daily. Full bar.

Nikki & Pete's Fabulous Deli/ We'll Clean

1520 North Halsted, (312) 943-6100

If you're spending $65 to have your car detailed, you can wait while they wash with a sandwich from Nikki & Pete's Fabulous Deli. What's another $5.75 or so when it buys you a Porsche 911 (tuna sandwich), a lamborghini (chicken breast), or a classic '59 'Vette (veggie)?

quick bites

Open daily. Full bar.

Viennese Kaffee-Haus Brandt

3423 North Southport, (773) 528-2220

Live opera Tuesday evenings, jazz on Thursdays, and occasional special performances on weekends—some lasting both nights with all-you-can-eat-and-drink special prices. (For more details see "Oktoberfeast, Ja!".)

Closed Mondays. Full bar.

quick bites

Brew & View at the Vic

3145 North Sheffield, (773) 618-VIEW

When not hosting all-ages concerts marked by a mosh pit of wildly gyrating, gravity-defying young bodies, the Vic becomes the Brew & View, a late-night budget movie theater ($4 tickets) serving a lot of alcohol and specializing in second-run films originally targeted at frat boys. Reasonably priced Bacino's pizza from across the street is a nice alternative to popcorn.

Beer—and a lot of it.

Ravinia Festival

1575 Oakwood, Highland Park, (773) RAVINIA

The Ravinia Festival, of course, is one of the ultimate summer dining and culture experiences, whether you BYOB and graze on the lawn or cough up some bucks to eat at one of the ever-increasing number of on-site dining establishments and later plant yourself in the pavilion. The music starts in June and continues through August. Lawn seats are $10; pavilion seats start at $20.

Wine and beer.

Editor's Note: The price ratings in this chapter reflect the price of meals and not entertainment.

Rib Tips

RACK 'EM UP!

21

Love me tenderloin, love me sweet . . . For years, Chicagoans have been had a love affair with ribs. Yes, there's nothing like a slab in the winter for that warm, contented feeling or a rack right off the grill in the summer heat at the "Taste" dribbling down your Bulls T-shirt and lycra stretch shorts. The debate, however, rages on as to who has the tastiest, the tenderest, the spiciest ribs around. Even after "Rib Tips," the controversy may still exist, except on one point where we should all be absolutely clear—where to pig out for less.

Some history to spare . . . Up to the end of World War II, pork was the principal meat in this country. GIs returning from service, however, had developed a taste for beef in the military messes, and pork was eventually nudged out of its top spot. Pork, though, remains the only meat considered suitable for barbecuing in the Carolinas, Georgia, Alabama, and most of the deep South. Barbecue traditions vary immensely between regions. For example, in eastern North Carolina, the whole hog is cooked and garnished with a vinegary pepper sauce; in western North Carolina, the ribs are cooked, the shoulder is sliced, and all is coated in a tangy red sauce. In contrast, throughout Texas and much of the rest of the Southwest cattle country, beef ribs are cooked and served in a spicy red sauce. Many of Chicago's old-time rib joints reflect the influences of the deep South as much of Chicago's rib traditions were transported north by the Illinois Central Railroad's "Green Diamond," which brought African Americans from the rural backwaters of Louisiana, Mississippi, and Arkansas directly to Illinois Station, Ellis Island of the Midwest.

> "The word *barbecue* may stem from the French *barbe a' queue*, meaning "from whiskers to tail." The expression indicates that the whole animal has been cooked. (And every part is eaten except the piggy's squeak.)"
>
> ***—The Great Food Almanac,* Irena Chalmers**

Where's the beef? Here are some tips if you're going to try it at home or you just don't know what to order. There are three different kinds of pork ribs. Spareribs, cut from just behind the pork shoulder, the shorter back ribs, and country-style ribs, cut from the pork loin. Beef ribs, which of course come from a totally different animal, look much like pork back ribs. The Department of Agriculture defines *barbecue* as "cooked by the direct action of dry heat resulting from burning hardwood or coal for a sufficient period of time to assume the usual characteristics . . . which include the formation of a brown crust." So, if the fat is in the fire, you're broiling; you've got to be smoking to be really barbecuing—the only good argument for smoking we support. (If you don't like that, sooooome!)

Hecky's Barbecue

1902 Green Bay, Evanston, (847) 492-1182

The judgment is in . . . Hecky's is to ribs as the gates are to heaven—you must pass through here to get to the promised (culinary) land. I had this friend, Big John Bednarski, who started every week (or ended every weekend, depending on your point of view) with a slab of Hecky's accompanied by the obligatory slice of white bread and fries for his Sunday night dinner—every Sunday night of his two-year sojourn in Chicago, while ensconced in front of a big-screen TV. Big John was a creature of habit, and, once you've tasted Hecky's, you may well be too. "It's the sauce." Nothing like it anywhere else. You can buy it by the jar—a pint for $4:00 or a quart for $7.25—and transport it to those who aren't fortunate enough to live within Hecky's aura. Hecky's is no frills—purely carryout with the emphasis on the product and no other trappings. This is a serious rib place. A half slab of savory baby backs is $8.85. Rib tips come in snack pack ($4.50 and more than enough for a meal), small ($5.80), regular ($8.30), and large ($11.35). For those who just can't get enough of that sauce, you can savor it on chicken, seafood, turkey, and catfish fillets. Save room for sweet potato pie or peach cobbler—sold by the piece or the whole pan.

Open daily. Carryout only.

The Smokedaddy

1804 West Division, (773) 772-6656

Barbecue and R&B are combined at Smokedaddy where the "WOW" is flashing over the door in neon and in the flavor of the food. The Smokedaddy cooks up peppery "Memphis-Texarkana" pig parts, spareribs, tips, turkey, beef brisket, and veggie burgers in the Little Red Smokehouse, a barbecue pit made in Texas that cost $15,000 and weighs 1,900 pounds. A combination of burning wood, fans, and a stone embedded in the door of the pit helps duplicate the flavor of an old-fashioned brick barbecue pit. A half slab of spareribs is $7.95, and rib tips run $4.95 for a half plate, $7.95 for a full; sandwiches—pork shoulder, brisket, chicken, turkey, or combo—are $4.95 to $5.95. Vegetarian specialties include the vegetarian barbecue sandwich ($5.45). Sandwiches are served with the house Mo-Jo sauce and chow-chow relish. Hot music is available some nights to go with the hot sauce.

Open until 2:00 a.m. Monday through Saturday; Sunday until 1:00 a.m.

Army & Lou's

422 East 75th, (773) 483-6550

At $14.95, Army & Lou's full slab of "meaty baby back ribs" is one of the only selections on the menu that, technically, isn't cheap chow. To bring this tangy treat, with meat so tender it falls off the bone, in under the "fork and knife" limit, share a slab with a friend and then supplement your order with one of Army & Lou's Southern specialties, most of which run under $11—maybe some fried chicken with two sides

($8.75), the catfish filet ($10.95), or the fresh mixed greens steamed with smoked bacon and accompanied by either smoked turkey or smoked ham hock ($7.95). All dinners come with corn muffins and a waitperson with personality.

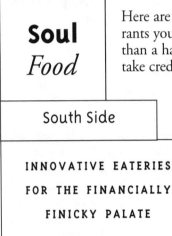

Open Daily.

Soul
Food

South Side

INNOVATIVE EATERIES FOR THE FINANCIALLY FINICKY PALATE

Here are some other Southside soul food restaurants you might want to check out. Most are less than a half mile east of the Dan Ryan, and none take credit cards:

Barbara's Restaurant 422 East 75th, (773) 624-0087. Monday–Saturday, opens at 5:00 A.M.

Jackie's Place I 226 East 71st, (773) 846-1487 and **Jackie's II** 425 East 71st, (773) 483-4095. Specializing in beef short ribs. Jackie's II is open 24 hours.

Robinson's No. 1 Ribs

655 Armitage, (312) 337-1399

Located right in Old Town across from Lincoln Park High School, Robinson's recently remodeled and now has a bright new dining area and an outdoor café. In spite of its yuppie location, Robinson's serves up ribs that rival the best of what the Southside has to offer. Using the *No. 1* sauce recipe that has supposedly been in the Robinson family for more than two hundred years and fourteen generations, Robinson's offers tender tips with a noticeable hickory-smoked tang. A tip appetizer, enough for a meal in itself, can be had for as little as $3.75. There're also good rib tip combos, including the tips and links ($6.45) and the chicken wing combo ($7.50). Both baby backs and beef ribs are available in both full slabs ($14.35) and half slabs ($9.95), a nice option for those of us who would like to pay less in lieu of hauling home a huge doggie bag. Nothing like a day-old rib after it's really had time to gel with its fixin's. For those who aren't feeling partial to pork, there are seafood and fish options, including the grilled Cajun catfish fillets ($7.25) and the half pound of batter dipped fried shrimp ($9.45), and even a veggie burger.

Open daily.

Ribs 'N Bibs

5300 South Dorchester, (773) 493-0400

The Original Leon's Bar-B-Q

8251 South Cottage Grove, (773) 488-4556

1640 East 79th, (773) 731-1454

1158 West 59th, (773) 778-7828

Two Southside originals, you can smell the hickory smoke practically to Lake Shore Drive and in the ivy-covered halls of the University of Chicago. Ribs 'N Bibs is where Hyde Park rib die-hards come for carryout. Maverick Munchies (tips and fries) are $6.90. Chix 'n Tips are $7:00, and the Tips 'n Link combo is $6.90. Leon's is a Southside mainstay where the ribs can be rubbed down and marinated as much as two days ahead of cooking to lock in the flavor. The aroma is the best advertisement money can't buy. Tips come in three sizes—$2.82, $5.87, and $7.23.

Both open daily.

Editor's Note: Price ratings for this chapter are based on an order of tips, not necessarily on the whole menu.

Food For Fast Feasts

Hate to keep going back to the same places, but more good rib tips can be found in "Out of Africa."

N. N. Smokehouse

1465 West Irving Park, (773) TNT-4700

Ditka is gone, and so is his former chef. He (the former chef) now owns N.N. Smokehouse, where smoke from Filipino Narra wood gives these ribs their unique flavor. A regular order of tips with all the trimmings is $7.50.

Open daily. BYOB.

quick bites

Brother Jimmy's

2909 North Sheffield, (773) 528-0888

Take time out for a treatise on North Carolina barbecue. Bring your whole fraternity to feel right at home.

Open daily. Full bar. Music.

Love Bites

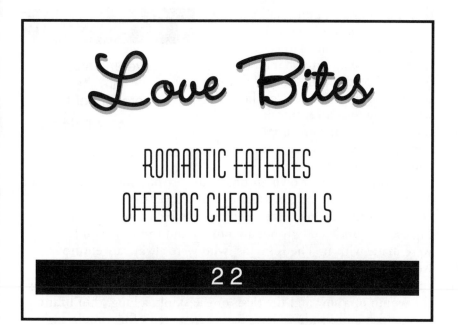

ROMANTIC EATERIES OFFERING CHEAP THRILLS

22

Food and love have had associations since our earliest days. The word *aphrodisiac* has its roots in the name Aphrodite, the name of the ancient Greek goddess of love. Even in the most primitive of times, many foods have been given credit for mood or performance-enhancing attributes. Mandrake root, tiger's milk, and oysters may all come to mind, but some research will show that almost every plant, herb, leaf, or fruit has, at some time, been known for its aphrodisiacal powers.

Certain vegetables were imbued with sexual powers because of their shapes. The ancient Greeks believed the carrot excited passion and facilitated conception. Both Pliny and Athenaus mention the carrot and its romantic qualities, and one ancient thinker once wrote, "the root winneth love." The Kama Sutra advised boiling treacle and asparagus, another phallic vegetable, in cow's milk and glue and adding spices and licorice. The mixture was then eaten once a day to increase sexual power and prolong life.

Fruits also had their place in the bedroom. Introduced into Europe in the sixteenth century from Mexico by the Spaniards, the tomato was known to the English as "the love apple," to the French as "pomme d'amour," and to the Germans as "liebesapfel." Thinking that it encouraged immortality, the Puritans spread the rumor that the tomato was poisonous to discourage them from being eaten. Grapes may owe their place in the history of the boudoir to the Duc de Richelieu who, in the seventeenth century, used to serve bunches at his parties—which everyone had to attend completely naked.

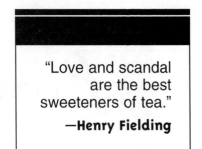

> "Love and scandal are the best sweeteners of tea."
>
> **—Henry Fielding**

Everyone had their own approach to gastronomic seduction. The Moors of Morocco believed honey was a love stimulant and used large quantities in marriage ceremonies, which often became sex orgies. The bride and groom ate honey, and the wine and food were made with it. The Romans, who were always adventurous when it came to food, imported all kinds of delicacies from their conquered territories. Game was considered an aphrodisiac, as was the womb of a sow and the flesh of the skink, a long, thin lizard.

Shellfish and fish have long been given credit for stimulating flagging sexual appetites. The Greeks associated the fruits of the sea with Aphrodite, who was born in the water and who first reached the shores of Greece riding, as portrayed by Botticelli, on a scallop shell. The Elizabethans had great respect for the crab as an aphrodisiac and found it far cheaper than caviar. The ancient Egyptian priests forbade the eating of fish, which they credited with increasing sexual activity.

These days we know the ancients were on to something. Fish is loaded with phosphorus, and a half dozen oysters contain five times the recommended daily allowance of zinc, an important mineral to male testosterone. (Those who didn't like oysters could have tried a turkey leg. The dark meat is also rich in zinc, which may account for how Henry the Eighth was able to make it through six wives.)

A recent survey found that modern Americans' idea of a romantic dinner is based on their pay check; a lobster dinner in a candlelit restaurant is the answer for loving couples—ones who make more than $30,000 a year. Those who are less flush settle for pizza. Whatever your means, take your cookie, your dumpling, your honey, lamb chop, pumpkin, sugar, or sweetie-pie out for something special. Whether it's the general sense of relaxation and well-being good food induces or some real magic, you won't know until you go. Just be careful with those carrots. And the skink.

Jane's

1655 West Courtland, (773) 862-JANE

A tiny, renovated Bucktown bungalow with exposed brick walls and a vaulted wood beam ceiling with skylights, Jane's intimate space is always packed with some thirty-eight beautiful people crammed into tables sardined together so closely that, if you're intent on whispering sweet nothings to your dining companion, you'd better plan on sharing them with everyone seated around you. In spite of its lack of elbow space, Jane's, particularly the tiny tables of two in the front windows, is charming. Food is of a healthy bent—"vegetarian and clean cuisine." In the past few years, prices have gone up, and now only the lighter meals qualify for cheap chow. Pastas include homemade paperdelle tossed with port, marsala, and wild mushrooms with fresh herbs and truffle oil ($11.95). The baked stuffed tofu burrito with roasted vegetables ($9.95) is very tasty, as are the garden burgers and the grilled chicken breast with molinari toscano salami, arugula, and jack cheese on French bread (both $7.95). A full brunch menu is served with most dishes priced at $7.95 and under. Brunch entrées are served with turkey sausage and dill potatoes.

Open daily serving till midnight. Full bar. Sidewalk dining. Brunch.

Café Selmarie

2327 West Giddings, (773) 989-5595

Tucked away in a plaza off of Lincoln, this quiet spot offers a full-service bakery adjacent to a small, brightly sponge-painted dining room with light, eclectic meals. The bakery does a brisk business in wedding cakes, and Café Selmarie hosts cake tastings in January and February. Entrées in the cozy dining room range from vary with the seasons and, a fall menu for example, may range from baked salmon ($8.95) to meatloaf en croute (in a puff pastery, $8.50) to linguine in clam sauce ($7.25). Chicken pot pies and whole wheat calzones are $6.75. The spinach and cheddar phyllo pie in garlic cream sauce ($7.95) is only for those who like it rich. Vegetarians can have a big plate of Creole rice and beans ($7.95).

Open daily. BYOB. Sunday brunch.

Johnny Rockets

910 North Rush, (312) 337-3900

In spite of being in the center of touristville, Johnny Rockets is an enjoyable flashback to those innocent happy days when a big date was a trip to the soda shop for a burger and a shake. The name of the game here is a burger ($3.70 for the original) and fries washed down by a shake or a malt ($3.15). For those who need something healthier, egg salad sandwiches and garden burgers are available. Seating is primarily at one of the counters that runs the length of the restaurant. Your server will give you free nickels to feed the juke box for classic hits like "Midnight Train to Georgia" and "My Boyfriend's Back."

If you're with someone special and in the mood for something hot (and fudge-y), but find yourself a little farther north, try **Margie's Candies** or **Zephyr** (see "Decent American Values") for sundaes you can both dive into.

Open daily. Milkshakes, no alcohol.

Café Zinc

3443 North Southport, (773) 281-3443

With its crêpe warmers, rattan chairs, and the gleaming wood namesake "zinc" bar with brass accents, Café Zinc, the front section of Bistro Zinc, transports you to romance in Paris for just a few francs. Café Zinc serves quiche, crêpes, croques (sandwiches), and salads—all for under $10—allowing you to get a taste of trendy Bistro Zinc without paying its trendy prices. The Café also usually affords you the opportunity to get served an hour sooner than if you wait for a seat in the back. As you might expect in a French café, an extensive dessert menu can make up for all the light bites you ate first. In nice weather, service is "à la fenetre" as diners spill out onto the sidewalk patio.

Open daily. Full bar. Patio.

Verona

1335 West Wrightwood, (773) 935-0081

Verona was opened by the owners of Rose Angelis a couple doors down from their original eatery. A renovated storefront splashed with Renaissance jewel tones and gilt accents, Verona is a tiny wine bar that delivers a relaxing romantic evening at a comfy table or a seat at the bar (for those of us fatally attracted to counter seats), where you can savor a hot espresso or sip a vintage from an extensive list that offers wines by both the bottle and glass. Light entrées priced $6.95 to $9.95 include oven-roasted chicken with herb whipped potatoes, pan-seared pork tenderloin with corn parsnip relish, beef bourguignone with egg noodles, and a pasta of the day. Those waiting for a table at Rose Angelis can order a pizza, an artichoke pesto bruschetta, or one of the other tasty appetizers.

Open daily. Wine and beer.

Grecian Taverna Restaurant & Lounge

4535 North Lincoln, (773) 728-1600

With its airy, whitewashed walls enclosing sunbronzed tiles to create the illusion of a Mediterranean villa, Grecian Taverna is a pleasant alternative to the raucous eateries in Greek Town. Imagine the sea breezes caressing you while you select from a huge menu, with an extensive number of well-priced seafood options, that offer you and your dining companion the opportunity to savor the flavors of the Greek Islands. Various combination plates—the cold appetizer combination ($6.25 per person), hot combo plate ($10.95), special combo ($10.50), and family style plate ($12.95) are a good way to explore. In nice weather, you can take it outside to a tree-shaded patio protected from the surroundings by high, white walls.

Open daily. Full bar. Patio.

Bittersweet

1114 West Belmont, (773) 929-1000

Pastry chef Judy Cotino opened this spun sugar pink eatery to serve breakfast and light lunches. Windows allow diners at the few tables to watch the pastry chefs work on wedding cakes and other decadent sweets. Soup and either a half a sandwich or the quiche of the day is a good deal for

$4.95. The fully-stocked pastry case at the counter, the fruits of the labors in the back room, will tempt you to splurge on treats like raspberry brown butter custard tarts or espresso ganache tarts.

Open daily for breakfast and lunch. No alcohol.

Food For Fast Feasts

quick bites

Albert's Café

52 West Elm, (312) 751-0666

If the last stop on your shopping agenda is Treasure Island on Elm to pick up those special ingredients not found at Jewel or Dominicks, pop into Albert's across the street for a little relaxation and ambiance. Albert's, a European-style patisserie, also offers light sandwiches and salads to be washed down with steaming cups of tea or espresso. An oasis of serenity in the shopping frenzy.

Open daily. Wine and beer.

Pop's For Champagne

2934 North Sheffield, (773) 472-1000

Since Pop's discontinued its Sunday brunch, it's now a club with hors d'oeuvres and desserts instead of a real restaurant. The fruit and cheese or the charcoutrie platter (both $9.50) are good options to nibble while you and that special someone sip champagne to the club's ever-present background jazz. Check out Pop's Bastille Day celebration held in July.

Open daily. Champagne.

Buckingham Fountain Pavilions

Grant Park at Congress and Lake Shore, (312) 742-2474

A front row seat at the lakefront for the fountain's evening light show (summers from sunset to 11 P.M.) Food is courtesy of Gino's East and the Buckingham Café & Grill.

Open only during the summer. No alcohol.

Greener Pasteur

Savor a Vietnamese institution's fresh start

Oh what a difference a fire can make. By 1995, Pasteur, arguably the best known Vietnamese restaurant in the city, had expanded to two locations. There was Pasteur Café, a small storefront on Chicago Avenue known for its cheap lunch buffet, and the original location at Lawrence and Sheridan, which although larger, was still not much more than a storefront itself.

Then, fire swept through and destroyed the original location. The Chicago Avenue effort also closed. But in mid-1997, Pasteur rebounded with the opening of a brand new restaurant in Edgewater north of Argyle Street.

Not surprising from a proprietor who once collected business cards from patrons and followed up with a Christmas card at the end of the year, the new **Pasteur** is as different from its former storefront as an Oak Street retailer is from a thrift shop. It's sleek and fancy and elegant while retaining the quality of food found at the former location—practically the Arun's of Chicago's Vietnamese restaurants.

And, it's lushly romantic. Entering the new Pasteur is like stepping back into the post–World War I era into a scene from Duras's *The Lover*, a shimmering trip back to the waning colonial days of Indochina and the declining sophisticated decadence that marked the French occupation in its latter days.

Pasteur's new building is reminiscent of the rooms of a former colonial mansion. A cozy bar off the entranceway offers visitors the opportunity to enjoy a drink in snug, rattan comfort. Up several teak steps, a more intimate dining room opens off to the side of the main room. The restaurant's main dining room resembles a large, airy courtyard. Warm, peach-colored walls enclose a patio with drop ceiling fans that create lazy breezes. Palms wave over deep-seated wicker armchairs pulled up to tables with snowy white tablecloths. Colorful floor-to-ceiling paintings portraying traditional scenes grace the walls.

The front window panels swivel out to patio dining in the summer. You can almost feel the sultry tropical heat year-round.

Designed for a sultry climate, Pasteur's menu includes many dishes that involve crisp, uncooked vegetables and light sauces, many of which are founded on nuoc mam, a fermented sauce made from small fish and salt that many of the Southeast Asian cultures employ in cooking as the Chinese use soy sauce. Other accents include lime, lemon grass, chilies, purple basil, banana blossoms, shallots, and several varieties of mint. Dishes may start with cuons, rice paper rolls filled with rice noodles, mint, and poached shimp, pork, or other meats. Meals can continue with cold rice noodles that serve as a base for nuong, barbecued meats or prawns. Where some Asian cuisines, Thai for example, emphasize flavors and some, Japanese, stress simplicity and purity, Vietnamese dishes concentrate on texture, mixing cooked ingredients with raw, spicy or sour ingredients with mild, and cold foods with hot.

A food expert once told me that Vietnamese cuisine, with its exotic flavors combined with French influences, tends to be milder but more complex than other Southeast Asian foods. I'm sure that's a matter of a personal taste, but the cooking Pasteur offers stands up to some of the best Vietnamese restaurants around.

The helpful picture books that guided patrons at the old Pasteur in their dining decisions are gone as are, in keeping with the restaurant's new upscale theme, the abundant editorial on the menu—the many "specialty of the house," the claims of authenticity—but all of the old standout dishes are still there. Fragrant chicken sautéed

Pasteur, 5525 North Broadway, (773) 878-1061, is open daily and has a full bar. Meals, for Vietnamese, are on the expensive side, and main courses range from $8.50 to $13.50.

with ginger in a sturdy brown clay pot (ga kho gung) or filets of catfish baked in the same clay pot and simmered with a concentrated sweet-tart glaze made from fish sauce, soy, and caramelized sugar lead the list of old favorites, along with bo cuon la lot, delicate rolls of grilled beef wrapped in grape leaves and stuffed with minced chicken and shrimp, grilled scallops with sesame seeds and lemongrass sauce, and an East-meets-West combination of a seafood noodle bouillabaisse soup. As with most Asian restaurants, there's also a good selection of vegetarians dishes, including a combination of vegetables, tofu, and coconut milk.

Starters include full-length pieces of grilled eggplant studded with garlic and peppers; rice paper spring rolls filled with shrimp, vegetables, rice noodles, and mint; and chao tom, Vietnamese wraps made from charbroiled shrimp paste wrapped around daggers of sugar cane that can then be enfolded in rice paper with vegetables and a savory sauce.

Meals can be washed down with strong French coffee, a memento from the colonial days, iced and sweetened with condensed milk. Just one of the old traditions you can revisit in this snazzy new place.

Chowing Down

All-You-Can-Eat Meals That Will Stretch Your Waistband but Not Your Wallet

23

Gluttony, one of the seven deadly sins. The repercussions of overindulging have been chronicled through the ages. Think of Alice. She could have avoided nearly getting her head chopped off if she had kept her mouth shut and her hands to herself, instead of grabbing drinks and eats off of any available table. Augustus Gloop. Augustus, not Charlie, might have inherited the Chocolate Factory if he had restrained himself from diving into Willy Wonka's chocolate river in an attempt to suck the whole thing down. And then there was Pooh, who got himself into a really tight place after not knowing when to say no. The list of unfortunate examples goes on and on.

Historically, the Romans are credited for establishing the art of pigging out. Romans prided themselves on and derived an obscene sense of power from hosting gargantuan, expensive banquets made up of endless dishes of delicacies, including eels and other elusive sea animals, indigenous species from numerous subjugated countries, and various fried reproductive parts from common herd animals, served to large crowds of politicians and business associates reclining on couches and sofa beds. Things got so bad that the Romans finally passed the sumptuary laws, which restricted how much could be spent on a feast. In addition to honing the exercise of binge and purge, the Romans also invented the napkin, or serviette, which was originally used to carry home leftovers to the wives and families who were never invited to the party.

> "Better a burst stomach than wasted food."
>
> **—Old Pennsylvania Dutch saying**

Although there aren't too many food orgies (at least reasonably priced ones) available today in Chicago, there are still a number of places where you can really shovel it in. The numerous $6.95 (or under!) Polish, Thai, and Indian all-you-can-eat lunch buffets, weekend brunch buffets, and the Friday night fish frys (no surprise in a town both adjacent to Wisconsin and full of Irish sports bars) seem to be the most common opportunities to eat till you're beat. In addition, happy hours—true all-you-can-eat specials where you get endless new plates of piping hot food versus endless chafing dishes of Sterno-ed delights—can still be found. Take your pick, take your time, take your Alka Seltzer, and try them all. But take it easy—remember, Rome wasn't built in a day.

Old Warsaw Restaurant & Lounge

4750 North Harlem (708) 867-4500

Czerwone Jabluszko (The Red Apple)

3121-23 North Milwaukee, (773) 588-5781

No argument, the daily buffet tables at these two Polish restaurants provide the best pig out for the dollar in town. Both provide hot and cold buffets on room-length tables groaning under the weight of salads, desserts, assorted traditional Polish dishes and sides, including sauerkraut, stuffed cabbage, dumplings, roasts, sausages, goulash, cheese blintzes, potato pancakes, fritters, and more. Old Warsaw, where blue hair is the predominant but not mandatory attire, has the better dessert offerings with a huge number of kolacky (fruit-filled traditional Eastern European cookies) pastries, cakes, puddings, and, of course, Jell-O. Old Warsaw charges $5.95 for lunch, $7.95 for weekday dinners, and $9.50 on weekends in the evening. The Red Apple counters with lower prices ($6.95 for dinner), baked apples, and a greater number of authentic dishes, including assorted pork parts (hocks and snouts), and a fullystocked grocery store next door, in case you just didn't get enough and need to take some home. The Red Apple's buffet also includes a beverage, soup, and ice cream, which you have to ask your waitperson for.

Old Warsaw is closed Mondays, while the Red Apple is open daily. Full bar.

Clark Street Bistro

2600 North Clark, (773) 525-9992

Do you ever get up on a Sunday morning knowing that when you're done doing your damage, the only thing you'll be fit for is to go back to bed? Clark Street Bistro has the kind of all-you-can-eat Sunday brunch that leaves you fit for little more than occupying couch space in a vertical position while bleerily focusing on a TV featuring vigorous athletics executed by individuals who have had a whole lot less to eat in the last twelve hours than you have. For $10.95 (a little expensive with a reasonable tip, but worth it), you get the obligatory juice, coffee, eggs, fresh fruit, and other standbys. But, as you graze through the chafing dishes and Sterno cans, you'll also be able to treat yourself to heaps of Italian tasties—assorted hot pastas, cold pasta salads, tangy chicken breasts, Italian sausages, baked artichokes, cold marinated vegetables—dishes that have no business being consumed by anyone who has not been awake for at least four hours. A pleasant and perky little eating option in the restaurant desert of Lincoln Park, Clark Street Bistro's atmosphere still isn't going to be nearly bright enough if you're really intent on doing some damage in the brunch buffet line. If you need to be lean and mobile later, stick to the individual servings on the menu—you'll still probably be walking out with a doggy bag. FYI, free parking is available during brunch hours at Columbus Hospital, two blocks west of Clark Street Bistro on Deming.

Open daily. Full bar. Buffet only served Sundays until 3:00 P.M.

Mongolian Barbeque

3330 North Clark, (773) 325-2300

The Flat Top Grill

319 West North, (773) 787-7676

707 Church, Evanston, (847) 570-0100

Both of these stir-fry grills make hibachi participatory and hip. Straight from those cutting-edge cities of Royal Oak and Ann Arbor Michigan, the Mongolian Barbeque offers a "raw" bar of meats and vegetables for you to mix and match and then stir fry. Chicken, beef, pork, calamari, and tofu are all available to combine with various vegetables and sauces to make sweet 'n sour, curry, garlic, and other combinations (suggested recipes are listed on the wall). A salad bar is also available. An all-you-Khan-eat dinner is $11.95 (one bowl at lunch is $9.95).

The Flat Top Grill offers much of the same in a slightly more upscale atmosphere at a cheaper price. Dinner at the Flat Top is $9.95, and lunch is $6.95. Expect long lines at North Avenue.

Both are open daily. Full bar.

Four Farthings Tavern & Grill

2060 North Cleveland, (773) 935-2060

Four Farthings is one of the best all-you-can-eat options in town, an option made even more attractive by the price: $0. In the comfy atmosphere of its 100-year-old location, Four Farthings offers a complimentary weeknight hors d'oeuvres buffet, along with a free hot dog/chili bar on Saturdays and a free taco bar on Sundays, both served after 3:00 P.M. Weather permitting, you can make as many trips down the buffet line as your stomach can handle from a breezy seat ensconced within Four Farthing's sidewalk cafe.

Open daily. Full bar. Sidewalk seating.

Happy *Gorge*

Spirits with delectable delights

INNOVATIVE EATERIES FOR THE FINANCIALLY FINICKY PALATE

Happy hour spreads are a great source of cheap gluttony. Some good ones include: **Trattoria No. 10,** 10 North Dearborn, (312) 984-1718: This elegant underground wine cellar offers a taste of Italy weekdays from 5:00 to 8:00 P.M. for $7 with a $3 drink minimum. Shrimp, made-to-order pasta, antipasto—you name it. This is the Charlie Trotter's of after-work indulgences. **Brother Jimmy's,** 2909 North Sheffield, (773) 528-0888: Brother Jimmy's lures the crowds nightly from 4:00 to 8.30 P.M. with free "pig pickin's." Rib tips, wings, endless towelettes, and cheap drinks—what some might define as hog heaven. Sundays, Brother Jimmy's hosts all-you-can-eat, all-the-draft-you-can-drink rib tips for $10.95, whole hog ribs for $17.95.

John Barleycorn Memorial Pub

658 West Belden, (773) 348-8899

Just up Lincoln from Four Farthings is another tavern that's been around (the Barleycorn building was built in 1890 and was operated by an Irish immigrant who moonlighted as a Chicago policeman), John Barleycorn serves a different $4 pasta platter four days a week: Mondays (spaghetti), Tuesdays (ravioli), Wednesdays (spaghetti), and Thursdays (fettuccini alfredo). Although not technically all-you-can-eat, the price does include two servings, which, according to the staff, is about all most people can handle. Barleycorn also has a great patio if you can stand the Lincoln Park crowds.

Open daily. Full bar. Patio dining.

FOOD FOR FAST FEASTS

The fish are biting all over town . . .

The Duke of Perth

2913 North Clark, (773) 477-1741

Chicago's premier Scottish pub with the Midwest's most extensive collection of single malt scotch serves all-you-can-eat beer-batter-dipped cod accompanied by peas and chips (that's fries to you colonials) for $6.95 on Wednesday and Friday lunch until midnight.

quick bites

Open daily. Full bar. Patio dining.

Lawry's Tavern

1028 West Diversey, (773) 348-9711

No, not the steak house. An unpretentious little tavern that serves big plates of unpretentious food to neighborhood regulars. Friday nights are all-you-can-eat fried sole, French fries, and cole slaw ($6.25). Wednesdays and Saturdays feature either chicken ($5.95) or pork chop ($6.75) specials. Other nights, all that's offered is orange roughy, shrimp, or pizza.

Open daily. Full bar.

Basement Taste

Gorge on Buca di Beppo's old country cuisine

My friend Tina grew up Italian in Boston. Her whole family lived in a brownstone—grandma and grandpa on the ground floor, aunt, uncle, and cousins in the middle, and Tina's branch of the family on the top. Tina goes back to visit occasionally for weddings and family affairs, and we're always eager to hear her updates. There are the bridal showers, so big they're held in a hall with a DJ announcing the gifts, "We've got another toaster oven here, folks." And the weddings with the white tuxes and black shirts and the groom's sister who nearly lost her spangled tube top as she lunged for the tossed bouquet.

Buca di Beppo might make Tina do a doubletake and ask herself if she'd gone back in time to the old neighborhood. The restaurant pays tribute to the gusto and spice, the bodacious warmth, the stereotypical over-the-top exuberance of southern Italy. Buca di Beppo was designed as a series of connecting wine cellars with oversized colored Christmas lights rimming the ceiling of each room. Every inch of wall space is covered with post cards, black velvet paintings, decorated plates that Tina assures me are still all the rage in her former stomping grounds, and framed pictures —religious imagery, Sophia Loren, relatives, memories from the old neighborhood. Gilded statues sprout from corners, and bathrooms are stocked with creams, curlers, and the assorted other retro paraphernalia that used to make a working girl squirm with excitement to powder her nose. Enough visual noise to leave you moonstruck.

On our first visit, we were graciously given a tour through the kitsch by the friendly waiter Jerry. Besides the main dining rooms and bar, the restaurant has the wine room with a roof of latticed bottles, the Pope's room, which accommodates at least three generations in an intimate setting around a huge, round table with a lazy Susan that spins the food around to everyone, and a table in the kitchen à la Charlie Trotter that seats eight where the action is.

If the decor is Ed Debevic's gone Old World, the food is Leona's on steroids. Meaning "Big Joe's Basement," Buca di Beppo harks back to the restaurants opened by Italian immigrants in their basements that served huge portions, enough for the entire family's Sunday dinner and the rest of the week as well. At Buca di Beppo, towering salads lead into basins of pasta and platters of veal and chicken, matched with signature sides of green beans and garlic mashed potatoes, that should be shared among, at minimum, with your immediate family—and mine and all of our first cousins.

The restaurant's business card pictures a map of Italy that portrays the country as the area between the triangle formed by three cities—Napoli, Calabria, and Palermo—and the flavor focus is the garlic and tomato sauces of southern Italy, where every day is Prince Spaghetti day.

Some of the spaghettis and the fettuccinis can be ordered in two sizes—large and larger, but the rest of the pastas and entrées need to be shared and shared and shared. Meatballs are large enough to be mistaken for sixteen-inch softballs, and thin-crust pizzas are big enough to serve as a welcome

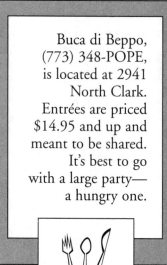

Buca di Beppo, (773) 348-POPE, is located at 2941 North Clark. Entrées are priced $14.95 and up and meant to be shared. It's best to go with a large party—a hungry one.

mat for your front door. Some nice touches like fennel sausage and olives in the red pomodoro sauce baked over homemade gnocchi and linguine with enough fresh seafood to leave a barrier reef picked clean help elevate the food well above Chef Boy-Ar-Dee status.

Appetizers are enough to sidetrack even the most determined diner. Garlicky mussels marina are piled high in a deep bowl, and the monumental Beppo 1893 salad is a king-size bed of greens with olives, two kinds of cheese, mortadellla, pepperoni, peperoncini, onions, cucumbers, and tomatoes. Baskets filled with wedges of focaccia bread incite the diner to sponge up anything on the plate that may have gotten left behind.

Wash down all the fine fare with a fine vintage beverage-poured right from the keg into a bottle for your table. Dessert includes slabs of bread pudding big enough to feed my entire village, and if it's your special day, a birthday cake as big as an ottoman decorated with pastel sprinkles. and topped by the green and red boot of Italy in frosting.

Buca di Beppo is part of a "family of restaurants" (please don't say the word chain) run out of Minneapolis. The restaurant, however, manages to come across as fun and cute versus franchised and touristy, and the reputation of the other locations in Minneapolis and Palo Alto even seems to pull more diners in.

Bagging It

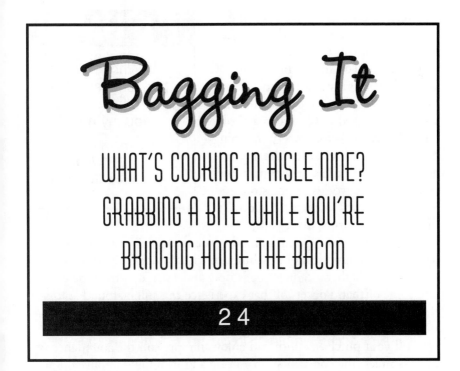

WHAT'S COOKING IN AISLE NINE? GRABBING A BITE WHILE YOU'RE BRINGING HOME THE BACON

24

Making a list, checking it twice . . . If you're like me, you long ago identified the two things in life that are unavoidable and extremely unpleasant—laundry and grocery shopping. For most of us, it's probably easier to postpone shopping than to avoid laundry but at some point, the dirty deed is probably going to have to get done.

So, since Whole Foods is a rare and expensive treat, you're off to Jewel or Dominicks or, if you're particularly intrepid, Cub Foods. You, of course, only manage to get there on Saturday afternoon, ensuring a minimum number of parking spaces and the maximum number of carts in each line. Navigation is only possible through the back of the store, as the endless check-out lines have throttled any movement across the front. No matter how careful you are, no matter how much you try to stick to good intentions, next thing you know, your cart is overflowing, and there's no way you're going to be able to squeeze into the express line (no, four packages of Oodles of Noodles do not count as one big bundle of ramen).

It doesn't have to be this way. No, grocery shopping doesn't have to be an endless trudge up sterile aisles, of not finding ingredients for that recipe you've put off attempting for the last year, and instead buying all kinds of junk you don't need as your stomach rumbles, inexorably driving you to bags of salty snacks and cartons of fat-laden crackers, supplemented with prepackaged meals that practically cook themselves. No, grocery shopping can actually be a relaxing culinary voyage into exotica, a leisurely opportunity to explore new worlds, in the store and later in your own kitchen. (You do know where yours is, don't you?)

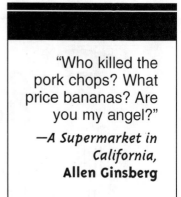

> "Who killed the pork chops? What price bananas? Are you my angel?"
>
> —*A Supermarket in California,* **Allen Ginsberg**

Once upon a time, going to market was a social occasion to look forward to an opportunity to schmooze with the locals, actually learn how to tell whether a cantaloupe is ripe, and stock up on a little of this and some of that. Pockets of that experience can still be found among the faceless superstores that dominate our landscape. Treasure Island—the "TI," our own local retail magic kingdom, with its in-store café (put off your purchases until you enjoy an espresso), the abundance of tasty samples (the constant supply of bread for dipping in olive oil or balsamic vinegar in the Italian section), and its stock of international paraphernalia—long ago recognized the value of enhancing the shopping experience. If you've got a specific food genre in mind, skip the chain stores with the mass market Chun King, the Michelina, the President's Choice Memories of Bangkok. Go back to the neighborhood where you may discover an older world and a store proprietor who is also pleased to be your dining host.

Czerwone Jabluszko (The Red Apple)

3121–23 North Milwaukee, (773) 588-5781

The Red Apple is a fully stocked Polish minimart and deli, adjacent to a sit-down restaurant serving one of the most extensive and cheapest all-you-can-eat buffets in the Chicago area. The retail half of this operation stocks freshly baked breads, over a half dozen different types of pierogis (including the old standards, cheese, meat, and potato, in addition to strawberry, rabbit, and duck), and kolacky (traditional Eastern European fruit-filled cookies), along with a full dairy case and extensive dry goods. One side of the store is taken up with a meat counter staffed by butchers who slice and dice various meats and cheeses in front of a fragrant, wall-length curtain of hanging sausages. Once you've filled your shopping basket with tasty Polish tidbits, you can swing across the hall and indulge in the all-you-can-eat smorgasbord, priced at $6.95, including drinks and ice cream! (For more details, see "Chowing Down".)

Open daily.

La Caridad Foods

3569 West Fullerton, (773) 342-0410

West of the Kennedy on Fullerton at Central Park is La Caridad, a brightly lit, piñata-festooned Mexican supermercado with a full-service diner attached. At La Caridad, loud and bouncy Mexican music accompanies the shopper on the trip down aisles lined with Goya and La Preferida staples, through the meat department where all the signs are in Spanish, around the plantain and banana tree, past the back wall that is completely covered with bags of assorted spices, and finally, to a quick stop in the bakery for some freshly baked cakes and pastries before check-out. Once you've picked up all your supplies to make your own tostadas, you can stop in the diner for a huge plate of huevos rancheros, side of tortillas, chips, salsa, beans, rice, and fresh avocado for $2.95 and wash it all down with a fruit milkshake ($2). If it's too late for breakfast, you can try a seafood platter ($6 and under) or one of the many tacos ($3.25) or enchiladas ($4.50).

Open daily.

Wikstrom's Scandinavian American Gourmet Foods

5247 North Clark, (773) 878-0601

If you're craving some Viking fare, find yourself vilkommen at Wikstrom's, a Scandinavian deli located in the heart of Andersonville. You can enjoy a complimentary cup of coffee while you mosey through the refrigerated cases, selecting between the various tubes of fish roe, Norwegian flat potato bread, gallon cans of lingonberries, and small crates of salted cod. Pick up a couple bottles of Swedish glögg to mix up some festive beverages to wash down your purchases. After you've finished shopping, you can relax at one of the tables at the front of the store and enjoy a freshly made sandwich ($2.50–$3.50) with a bowl of homemade soup. Ja!

Open daily.

Moti Mahal

1035 West Belmont, (773) 348-4393

If you don't want to go all the way up to California and Devon for authentic tandoori chicken, head to this Lakeview branch of one of Chicago's best-known Indian restaurants. A two-room storefront, one side has an Indian deli with cases of baked and fried temptations, along with well-stocked shelves of dry goods including Indian tea, spices, burlap bags of rice, and other necessities imported from the land of the Raj. The retail side of the operation also has tables where you can enjoy your purchases immediately. The other room is a full-service, BYOB sit-down restaurant offering a large variety of bounteous, authentic Indian dishes. Share one of the large combination platters with a friend ($10.95–$13.95) if you don't know where to start.

Open daily. BYOB.

The Vienna Cafeteria

2501 North Damen, (773) 235-6652

Not exactly a hot dog stand, but a full-service cafeteria with a retail sales area. In a city where 1,800 of 2,200 hot dog stands are supplied by one source, when we're talking dogs, we can talk Vienna. The Vienna Cafeteria is located on the first floor of the building that actually houses the plant—the meat mecca where those little casings are stuffed with a variety of pork products. The Vienna line is deli heaven. You name your cold cut, and it's available between two slices of rye. But the real star attraction here is the “hot sandwich” line. Step up for a hot dog and ask the lady who’s been working behind that counter for the last twenty years to “drag it though the garden.” Yes, that’s secret meat speak for “the works.” With that password, you’ll get all the stuff, including the celery salt and the florescent green relish. If you’re not in the mood for something oblong nestled in a long, cylindrical bun, go for the barbecued beef—a mound of fragrant beef shavings, smothered in a tangy sauce and heaped on a hamburger bun. Get there early—reliable sources say the barbecued beef is gone by 11:00 A.M. on Saturdays. Once you’re done eating, stock up for home with extra product. Besides hot dogs by the case, you can buy entire slabs of corn beef and other deli items. Check out the “seconds” bin where slightly “damaged” merchandise is available at a discount. A good deal and (probably) relatively safe to eat.

Although primarily there to serve employees in hairnets, the cafeteria is open to the public every day except Sunday until 3:00 P.M.

L’Appetito

Hancock Building, 875 North Michigan, (312) 337-0691

Huron Plaza, 30 East Huron, (312) 787-9881

Tucked away at the base of the newly renovated Hancock Building is one *mag*-nificent stop for all of your Italian needs. If you’re after some pine nuts, prosciutto, or biscotti for that after-work soirée, L’Appetito is a quick stop that will fill all your needs before you jump on your Michigan Avenue bus home. While you’re filling your basket with focaccia, Nutella, and Chianti, stop for a latte (L’Appetito uses Illy espresso!) and a panini (Italian sandwich on traditional bread, \$4.50–\$7.00), a tostino (a grilled sandwich eaten as a snack, \$4.00–\$5.75), the daily pasta or pizza, or a scoop of the granita of the day. There’s a spacious dining area or, on a nice day, you can sit at the tables in the Hancock Building courtyard. Ciao, bella!

Open daily.

Lunch *Counters*

Eating à la shopping carte

INNOVATIVE EATERIES FOR THE FINANCIALLY FINICKY PALATE

There's been a growing trend among retail health and natural food stores to install counters and juice bars where organically aware shoppers can safely satisfy hungers and quench thirsts built up after a foray into aisles of biologically correct products. Leading the way is **Whole Foods**, 1000 West North, (773) 587-0648. Whole Foods is to health food stores what Treasure Island is to Jewel and Dominicks—a step above the mundane shopping experience. With aisles of organically correct food and personal care products, supplemented by appropriate literature and plenty of tasty samples, Whole Foods is a wellness Disneyland for those who would be aware and sleek (massages are available for the shopped-out). More than just a juice bar, the North Avenue Whole Foods devotes an entire floor to **eden, the natural bistro**, (773) 587-3060, a sit-down restaurant with a full-course gourmet menu, including appetizers, salads, sandwiches, pizzas, and serious entrées serving brunch, lunch, and dinner. Although Whole Foods may be the newest and biggest healthy kid on the block, plenty of competition is out there. Southsider **A Natural Harvest**, 7122 South Jeffrey, (773) 363-3939, is a good-sized health food store with a deli/juice counter set smack in the center of the store. A Natural Harvest makes annual appearances at the Taste Festival, a lone healthy island among the assorted tasty coagulants served by other vendors. A Lincoln Park mainstay, **Sherwyn's,** 645 West Diversey (773) 477-1934, juice bar offers stiff competition based purely on its savvy location across from the never-ending bump and grind of the Century's Chicago Health Club.

Organic Matters

GETTING DOWN TO EARTH AND BACK TO NATURE

25

So, summer ends. You woke up back in April and realized the winter had left you pudgy and unfit to be seen in a tank top and shorts, let alone a bathing suit. You spent a good part of spring and the entire summer getting back into shape. You find yourself cruising into September, and you're looking good. Then, striding into fall, you're at your peak. But for most of us, it doesn't last long. As soon as cooler weather makes its inevitable move back, we start slacking off again. Like bears in hibernation, we sleep more and don't do much else. How to break this seasonal vicious cycle?

Well first, you might look at what you're eating. Years ago, you had a choice of being either a gluttonous carnivore or a smug total vegetarian, a "vegan." But, it has been said, the times they are a-changin'. These days, it's much easier to eat healthy, to eat natural, to eat free—fat free, cholesterol free, calorie free, pesticide free than it has been in the past. In fact, the options to make your diet organically correct have become mind-boggling. You're no longer limited to tofu, beans, and greens. Eggs may be out, but prairie-raised, natural grain-fed lean meat is in. Cheese may now be a lactic death trap, but Italian turkey sausage is the topping du jour for nondairy pizza all over the city. Please pass the tempeh.

> "Cheese: Milk's leap towards immortality."
>
> **—Clifton Fadiman, cholesterol free and lactose tolerant**

Luckily for those of us who have embarked on a mission of culinary awareness, Chicago offers myriad opportunities to abandon our frankly corrupt bourgeois ways and eat like a fit Third World peasant. Ethnic eateries—especially Asian, Middle Eastern, and African—have always had a bonanza of healthy, protein-rich (courtesy of grains, beans, and the almighty tofu) options. But now, everywhere you look, there are a variety of healthy, natural alternatives ranging from the simple to the gourmet.

With all the options out there, "healthy eating" certainly does not have to be tofu, formerly regarded as a dreaded tasteless gelatinous cube. You, however, will notice as you get out and about that the lowly soybean, of which tofu is a by-product, is the foundation of much alternative eating. Tofu is now powering some of the most elaborate dishes around. Healthy burritos and pizza, whole wheat with soy cheese abound. Grilled tempeh, Indonesia's most popular soy protein food, is hot for burgers. With the rising cost of meat and the increasing emphasis on avoiding dairy due to cholesterol, lactose intolerance, and other arterial problems, we're just discovering what other cultures have known for centuries—the soybean is where it's at. Not only is the soybean one of the cheapest sources of protein in the world, but it also provides more protein than any other known crop. In fact, the top five protein sources, of which tofu is one, are all derived from soybeans. Asians, way ahead of us in recognizing the value of the soybean, have so allowed tofu to permeate their lives that it has become part of their culture and language. In Japan, if a situation is hopeless, it's "as futile as trying to clamp two pieces of tofu together." Or, if someone wants you to get lost, he may say "Go bump your head against the corner of a cake of tofu and drop dead."

Whatever your goal, fat and happy or lean and mean, there's a world of healthy opportunity out there. You can start slow, with an occasional lentil burger for your Big Mac, or once in a while forgoing a brat for a tofu dog. You are what you eat. It doesn't have to be a winter of culinary hibernation and discontent. Bean me up, Scotty.

The Heartland Café

7000 North Glenwood, (773) 465-8005

A Rogers Park mainstay for over twenty years and probably the most extensive natural foods restaurant operation in the city besides the Blind Faith business, The Heartland Café offers not only a large restaurant with one of the most colorful and larger outdoor patios around (great to view the interesting street life and interactions of the denizens of Rogers Park), but also live entertainment and an extensive store stocked with juices, books, and all sorts of garments and jewelry manufactured in some Third World country. The Heartland's menu includes poultry, fish, and seafood among its selections of entrées and sandwiches, which range in price from $4.50 for sandwiches, such as the big heart lentil burger or the tempeh burger ($5.95 with melted soy cheese), to $9.95 for the most expensive specials, usually a pasta with seafood. The Heartland has an extensive breakfast menu and, unlike many healthy places, a well-stocked bar. Savor the tall, cold results of fermented yeast while you listen to some music and roll your own meal with the fried-bean plate.

Open daily. Full bar. Patio. Entertainment.

Pattie's

700 North Michigan, (312) 751-7777

Pattie's offers a large variety of sandwiches, pizzas, calzones, and salads, all at $4.95 and under. Pizzas, made with nonfat mozzarella and whole wheat crusts ($3.75–$3.95) are a good bet. The sausage is turkey sausage. For something pizza-like but a little different, try one of the four whole wheat calzones, (veggie and cheese, Spanish rice, spinach and mushroom, or eggplant parmesan, $3.75–$3.95), kind of a pizza turnover. Jerk chicken with red beans and rice ($4.95) is also a popular choice, as are the three kinds of burgers (veggie, $3.85, turkey, $3.65, and buffalo, $4.65) served with low-fat chips (add 3 grams of fat for the chips). As an additional plus, the menu lists the fat content of every item along with the percentage of calories from fat, and the entire menu has been approved by a registered dietitian.

Open every day except Sunday, 9:00 A.M.–6:00 P.M. (Loop hours). Sidewalk seating.

The Lo•Cal Zone

912 North Rush, (312) 943-9060

Can fast be healthy? It can at the Lo•Cal Zone, a healthy little food shack behind 900 North Michigan. Offering a wide variety of vegetarian and vegan options, the Lo•Cal Zone has pizzas, sandwiches, salads, chili, burritos, and Lo•Cal Zones (calzones, get it?). Check out one of the dozen burritos (all $5.75)—a fourteen-inch whole wheat tortilla filled with everything from beans to turkey Italian sausage. The barbecue chicken burrito is particularly tasty, as are the corn tamales and homemade soups.

Open daily. No alcohol. Sidewalk seating.

Karyn's Fresh Corner

3351 North Lincoln, (773) 296-6990

Karyn Calabrese, who's apparently been supplying Fresh Fields, Sherwyns, and the rest of the healthy city with natural sunlight-grown wheat grass, has transformed an old, burnt-out liquor store into a "living foods garden café," complete with patio tables and turf. Food is vegan, and entrées range from mock tuna or turkey to the almond pâté platter to the nori roll (all $9.90). Sandwiches include a veggie burger with lemon tahini sauce and seed-cheese nori roll made with cheese from fermented sunflower and pumpkin seeds (both $6.75). Karyn offers periodic workshops for those who have "strayed." Vegans in the know feel Karyn's food is excellent, but we less selective think healthy is not cheap. Sometimes it's just easier to get a Big Mac.

Open daily. No alcohol. No meat. No preservatives.

Taqueria Mamasita's

3324 North Broadway, (773) 868-6262

Mamasita's vegetarian burrito is the mother of all veggie burritos, the pinnacle that all vegetarian burritos aspire to. A huge mound of tortilla, Mamasita's vegetarian burritos ($3.99) are stuffed with not only the standard beans and cheese, but also those standout ingredients—grilled carrots and broccoli garnished with a dollop of guacamole. Olé! Sheer burrito vegetarian heaven. This vegetarian combination is also available in tacos ($1.65) and quesadillas ($3.50) or in all those forms in combination with chicken or steak. A boring bean burrito ($3.50) can also be had, but why? As an added benefit, Mamasita's prides itself on its fresh ingredients and true vegetarian cuisine. When was the last time you saw a Mexican establishment that advertised "No Lard"?

Open daily. No alcohol.

Chicago Diner

3411 North Halsted, (773) 935-6696

Arguably the best known vegetarian restaurant in the city, the Chicago Diner remains a magnet for the healthy and the out-of-town movie stars, serving a long list of vegan and veggie options including baked grain burgers ($6.25), reubens made with grilled tempeh ($6.95), lentil loafs and tofu loafs ($8.25), and macrobiotic plates ($8.95). Even children can join the fun with their own menu of tofu dogs and grilled cheese (cheddar or soy on seven-grain bread).

Open daily for brunch, lunch, and dinner. Beer and wine.

Heart Wise Express

10 South LaSalle, (312) 419-1329

Heart Wise Express provides a healthy alternative to the fast food you will find on practically every corner in the Loop. Each item on the menu is listed with its "vitals": number of calories, grams of fat, sodium, fiber, and cholesterol.

quick bites

The menu has a solid selection of salads, sandwiches and vegetarian and chicken burritos. House Specials include veggie burgers and vegetarian sloppy joes served with potato wedges.

Closed weekends.

Sun & Moon

1467 North Milwaukee, (773) 276-6525

A café and catering operation, Sun & Moon serves world beat lite bites and sandwiches ($3.50–$5.75), including a veggie melt on focaccia bread and a teriyaki turkey burger with grilled pineapple. Desserts, like the caramel-apple cake, are unhealthily American.

Closed Sundays. No alcohol.

Soul Vegetarian East

203 East 75th, (773) 224-0104

Seemingly an oxymoron, Soul Vegetarian East makes meatless soul food a possibility. Indulge in the vegetable sampler, battered "steak," greens, or peanut-carob cookies while you relax on wicker chairs with kente-cloth cushions on wicker chairs. When you're done, you can browse in the adjoining Boutique Afrika next door.

Open daily. No alcohol.

Faith Once More

Blinded by delight

Once upon a time, the North Center neighborhood, the area between the six corner intersections of Irving Park, Damen, and Lincoln on the north and Wellington, Southport, and Lincoln on the south, was Chicago's most vibrant shopping area outside of the Loop. But, just as State Street decayed and had to be revitalized, so did North Center. Wieboldt's department store, Goldblatt's, and the other big emporiums closed their doors and stood empty, waiting years for the inevitable regrentrification that would turn them into pricey lofts for young professionals returning to the neighborhood.

Oh, some businesses hung in there while the neighborhood quietly slumped. Dinkel's continued to produce some of the city's best baked goods, while Meyer Delicatessen and the Paulina Market continued to stock and slice a wide array of meats and deli products. But, in the empty storefronts interspersed between the old-line businesses, thrift stores and "antique" shops gained ground.

For a while, a restaurant called Mr. Steer anchored the corner at School and Lincoln across from Woolworth's, which closed its doors after a summer-long fire sale. Mr. Steer, a Ponderosa wannabe with its huge sign missing a couple letters that could be seen up and down Lincoln Avenue, eventually shut down too. At one point, it tried to morph into another low-budget eating establishment. A short-lived experiment that didn't work, Mr. Steer sat empty and waited.

Waited for the coming of a new and healthier life. First Wieboldt's across the street evolved into a busy Service Merchandise with expensive lofts upstairs. At the same time, Whole Foods rose from nowhere on the other corner, bringing all natural, free-range grocery products to a neighborhood that had previously subsisted on the everyday average, chemically-induced produce of local bodegas, Jewel and Dominicks. It seemed right, then, that Mr. Steer should take its place in the new neighborhood order as **Blind Faith Café**.

For an "alternative" Evanston institution that has grown from a local college town eatery to a vegetarian juggernaut complete with catering, the spacious confines of the former Mr. Steer offered Blind Faith a launching point to begin to pollinate the urban Chicago market. The cavernous space has been sponge-painted in soft tones of sky blue and peach. Wooden booths and tables are accented with flower arrangements dominated by yellow sunflowers. Baked goods overflow at the counter at the entrance. The huge place looks, well, very Evanston.

The opening of Blind Faith has been greeted with enthusiasm by local residents who have seen both property values and property taxes soar as Service Merchandise, then Whole Foods, followed by Starbucks have opened their doors in a formerly sleepy neighborhood. The new Blind Faith has been discussed from the get-go by neighbors eager for mid-priced eating options. At the Higher Ground coffee house on Roscoe where locals flock on the weekend for gossip, breakfast, and a massage, down the street at Big Hair where a constant stream of walk-ins waits patiently for an $8 hair cut, at J. T. Collins Pub, the former Rexall drugstore where residents stop for a beer on their way home from the El,

Blind Faith Café, 3300 North Lincoln, (773) 871-3820, is open daily serving dinner and lunch and brunch on the weekends. The restaurant has a liquor license and a large selection of baked goods for carryout. Most entrees are priced $9 and range up to $11; sandwiches are less expensive.

all the buzz has been good, really good, better than anyone remembers the Evanston original ever being.

It's been years since I've been to Blind Faith's Evanston locale, so I didn't know what to expect. I was informed by the very helpful staff manning the check-in desk that I had showed up on the second night the restaurant was open. "It's Tuesday, didn't you open this weekend?" I asked. "Not really," I was told. "Those were special cocktail hours and dinners for invitation-only VIPs." So, on the second night for the masses, I began the test drive. Ginger maki tofu, a sublime sushi-like appetizer free of the toxic or bacterial elements that might have attacked me from real raw fish. Followed up with asparagus ravioli in sun-dried tomato cream sauce. So fresh and green, seemingly straight out of the garden patch. The empanada appetizer stuffed with plantains and dipped in a spicy salsa sauce launched me into the Mongolian stir-fry, quick-fried seitan (a wheat by-product that tastes like a nice slice of white meat) in a spicy chili sauce over crunchy rice and noodles.

It wasn't until my third time at bat that I experienced a dull moment. The vegetable pot stickers were fine and crunchy, and my dining companion was happily rooting through her corn and potato enchiladas. I, however, was not as excited by my broccoli shoyu-soba stir fry with pea pods. It was good, but missing a kick. Maybe I should have tried the seitan paella or the pecan scallopini with fresh linguini, marinara sauce, and mozzarella or, perhaps, the spicy seitan fajitas. I'll have to go back and find out. Probably soon.

For those who care about these things, the place is dangerously kid-friendly. Otherwise, there's every reason to keep the Faith.

Late for Dinner

MIDSUMMER NIGHTS' EATS

26

"Well, it's a marvelous night for a moondance . . . with the stars up above in your eyes." Since ancient times, man has been fascinated by the darkness. Folklore revolves around tales pitting day against night, light against dark. Before the days of fluorescent bulbs, the setting of the sun made the familiar potentially unfamiliar. Unusual beings were thought to emerge in the darkness, in nature, and from within ourselves.

The moon has always played a preeminent role in the dark half of our lives and minds. We developed our calendars around the lunar cycle, and today we still celebrate holidays that are rooted in the seasonal celebrations of our ancestors. Although both the moon and the sun are responsible for the movement of the tides, the moon has twice the gravitational pull of the sun. Consequently, the cycles of the moon have a far greater effect on tides and other natural movements. It is said that we even gain or lose slight amounts of weight in sequence with the 28-day lunar cycle.

Since the earliest days, people have attributed human action to the effects of natural phenomena. This philosophy continues in modern times. In spite of our enlightenment, mysteries that align themselves with the darkness still remain. Who can explain why hash browns snarfed well past the Witching Hour bring nearly a supernatural satisfaction never experienced in the morning? Who has ever rationalized the physical phenomenon of waking up starving with a concave stomach after pigging out at 3:00 A.M.? Some mysteries are better left unsolved.

> "Where's a good place for . . .? If I had a book for every time someone asked me that question, I could have written this book from aboard my yacht . . . instead of from inside my cab."
>
> **—Chicago Jack, author of *A Cabbie's Guide to Chicago at Night: All Right, All Night, and After Hours Fun Finder.***

For those seeking late-night culinary excitement, Chicago truly is a second city. Unlike New York and other metropolises that offer night crawlers many opportunities to feed, Chicago is limited in late-night dining if you're not interested in a hot dog stand, a burrito house, or a diner. Being resourceful, however, it's possible to search beyond the cheese fries, the beans and cheese, and beyond the omelets to find a variety of establishments that are open until at least the stroke of midnight. It's possible to discover a full "lunar cycle" of late-night options, including "new moons" (open just till midnight on weekends) to "full moons" (serving until at least 2:00 A.M.) to "lunar eclipses" (open 7 days, 24 hours). Bon nuit, bon appétit. "One more moondance with you in the moonlight . . . on a magic night. . . ."

The Golden Apple

2971 North Lincoln, (773) 528-1413

Not quite as chic as the Nookies with their hordes of beautiful people, the Golden Apple, with its radiant neon apple sign, holds its own with any other diner in the city—any day, any hour. Some six pages of breakfast, lunch, dinner, and dessert, with most complete meals priced at under $6, should satisfy your cravings, no matter what they are, no matter what time. The menu has a Mexican twist, and the breakfast burrito ($4.50), a huge roll of beans, cheese, guac, tomatoes, lettuce, and "taco meat" accompanied by spicy rice, can be an excellent way to start your day or end your evening. One piece of advice—try to avoid the allure of the cream pies in the rotating glass dessert display. Stress-tested at 3:00 A.M., these meringue-coated confections just couldn't stand up to the pressure.

Serving 24 hours, 7 days a week. Sidewalk café.

River Kwai II

1650 West Belmont, (773) 472-1013

Close your eyes, then open them and look around. You're not in Kansas anymore, Dorothy. No, with its low-slung ceiling, overworked window air-conditioner cranking away, open kitchen piled with dirty dishes and red-faced, sweaty cooks, and five small tables, you could have easily been transported to any Chinatown in the world. Then notice the bullet holes in some of the windows and think again—you really could be in Chicago. You're at the River Kwai, one of the few Chicago restaurants that really does remind me of New York. Opening at, say, 9:00 or 10:00 P.M., the River Kwai serves Thai and Chinese stir-fries, noodles, currys, soups, and rice dishes (priced $6.95 and under) until dawn the next day. Helpings are huge (liters of Thai iced coffee are served in soup carryout containers for $1.50). The place is a dump, but everything I've eaten has been safe—so far.

Closed Tuesdays. Opens between 9:00 and 10:00 P.M.; closes 5:00 A.M. weekdays and 6:00 A.M. weekends.

Earwax

1564 West Milwaukee, (773) 772-4019

This Wicker Park coffeehouse has relatively late dining with some extra perks not found in the average café. The service at Earwax is, at best, grudging. If the surly help doesn't bother you, though, you'll enjoy an extensive list of sandwiches and specials oriented to the healthy and the vegetarian, such as Indian lentil stew ($5.50), roasted mushroom and red pepper sandwich ($6.25), and potato sage pizza ($6.50). Earwax's café is combined with a video and record store, giving a new meaning to dinner and a movie.

Serves late on weekends until 12:15 A.M., forty-five minutes before closing.

Tania's

2659 North Milwaukee, (773) 235-7120

A throwback to the days of supper clubs (don't even think about asking for a no-smoking section), this restaurant provides food and entertainment that can be enjoyed until at least 2:00 A.M. Tania's offers a variety of Cuban tapas dishes (among a menu of other more expensive dishes) for between $1.80 and $9.00. Empanadas ($3.95), fried green plantains ($1.95), black bean soup and ham croquettes ($1.80)—rhumba your way through an assortment and then join the conga line in the small, crowded bar where patrons tango, bump, and grind into the wee hours to the merengue sounds churned out by band members in shiny suits with bell-bottoms. There's no cover here—what a deal.

Open daily, serving until 2:00 A.M.

Iggy's

700 North Milwaukee, (312) 829-4449

Iggy's, although lacking live entertainment, does offer an upstairs room complete with outdoor balcony to adjourn to after dinner, allowing you to continue your evening until 4:00 A.M. The dress here is black-haltered, platform-shoed, oh-so-Melrose Place, and the food is Italian trattoria. The quality of food hasn't quite kept pace as the menu's gone increasingly upscale. Cheap chow options are now limited to a couple of vegetarian pasta options (both $6.95), an assortment of late night scrambled egg-based dishes ($6.95–$8.95), and a good selection of salads and appetizers. No matter, if you're hanging out at Iggy's, your priority is probably not what you're eating, but seeing everyone else who's eating and being seen by them.

Open daily. Serving until 2:00 A.M., Saturdays until 4:00 A.M. Patio dining.

Taco & Burrito House

3946 North Broadway, (773) 871-8988

1548 West Fullerton, (773) 665-8389

The Taco & Burrito House, not to be confused with the Taco & Burrito Palace on Halsted, is a small, inconsequential establishment that's packed at all hours (until 5:00 A.M. on weekends) with devotees who worship at the altar of the almighty cheap burrito. Starting at $1.50, you can purchase a complete meal of a junior vegetarian burrito filled with mounds of beans, cheese, tomato, lettuce, sour cream, and the secret sauce. For an additional $.70, carnivores can upgrade to chicken, steak, marinated pork (al pastor), bean and bacon, and homemade Mexican sausage (chorizo). If you're really a glutton, skip over the "junior" and go for the "king," the foot-long version weighing at least twenty pounds and starting at $2.50 for the veggie king. Of course, if you eat here as often as some hard-core fans, you may want to expand your options to the tacos, tortas, tostadas, quesadillas, or chimichangas. But, when it's all said and done, there's really nothing like wrapping your hands around a big burrito.

Open daily and late. No alcohol.

Tecalitlan Restaurant

1814 West Chicago, (312) 384-4285

Out on Chicago Avenue caught between rapidly gentrifying neighborhoods and ethnic enclaves is Tecalitlan, home of the one-pound-plus burrito. A formidable tortilla package that fills the entire plate, Tecalitlan's veggie burrito ($3.95) comes with cauliflower or broccoli, aguacate (avocado) optional. A full-service, sit-down restaurant, Tecalitlan also offers a complete menu with all the old favorites, including fourteen flavors of soft tacos at $1.50 each, along with some specialty dishes to be savored by a certain palate, including the daily caldo de birria (lamb soup) and menudo (tripe soup), which is only served on weekends. Tecalitlan is one of the *Chicago Sun-Times* restaurant critic Pat Bruno's favorite places when he's hankering to leave the white tablecloths behind and take it to the streets.

Open daily until midnight during the week and 3:00 A.M. on weekends. Full bar.

El Presidente

2558 North Ashland, (773) 525-7938

Resembling a Denny's spruced up with Marvel Comic-like pictures of Indian warriors in feather helmets rescuing bosomy Aztec maidens, it's a rare item on El Presidente's menu that tops the $7 mark. The food is acceptable Mexican, and at 4:30 A.M., well, beans rarely taste so good. There are plenty of huevos selections on the menu for those who feel the wee hours should be reserved for and are sacred to breakfast. Try the machacado con huevos, scrambled eggs with dried beef, rice, and beans, $5.95, served "hot" for a really good feeling the following morning.

Open 24 hours, 7 days a week.

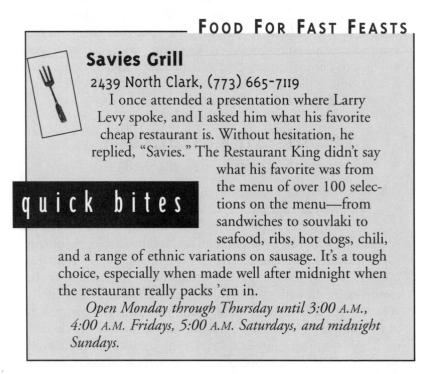

Food For Fast Feasts

Savies Grill

2439 North Clark, (773) 665-7119

I once attended a presentation where Larry Levy spoke, and I asked him what his favorite cheap restaurant is. Without hesitation, he replied, "Savies." The Restaurant King didn't say what his favorite was from the menu of over 100 selections on the menu—from sandwiches to souvlaki to seafood, ribs, hot dogs, chili, and a range of ethnic variations on sausage. It's a tough choice, especially when made well after midnight when the restaurant really packs 'em in.

quick bites

Open Monday through Thursday until 3:00 A.M., 4:00 A.M. Fridays, 5:00 A.M. Saturdays, and midnight Sundays.

Harmony Grill

3159 North Southport, (773) 525-2508

You can listen to good American rockabilly at Schubas and then head next door for good American comfort food until 2:00 A.M. on Fridays and 3:00 A.M. on Saturdays. Sandwiches are $6.00 to $7.00, and entrées are $8.00 to $11.00.

quick bites

Open daily. Full bar.

Kamehachi Café

1400 North Wells, (773) 664-1361

Do you find yourself with a yen for raw fish in the wee hours? Well, at Kamehachi Café, you can satisfy your sushi cravings until 2:00 A.M. An attractive, blond-wood sushi place, graced with a neon martini glass and chopsticks, Kamehachi caters to the Old Town yuppie crowd with its "Beginner Sushi 101" ("all cooked food . . . nothing raw!") including California roll, an ebi (shrimp), and tamago (egg) omelet for $5.50. Standard sushi combo of six pieces and cucumber roll is $9.95.

Closed Mondays. Serving beer, wine, and sake.

Pick Me Up Café

3408 North Clark, (773) 248-6613

Open nightly from 5:00 P.M. to 5:00 A.M. on weeknights and twenty-four hours on weekends, Pick Me Up serves an assortment of Italian options, sandwiches, good vegetarian chili ($3 cup/$4 bowl with thick slices of honey wheat bread), and big breakfasts ($5.25). It's never too late (or early) for the Pick Me Up's brownie sundae.

Open nightly. No alcohol.

Early to Rise

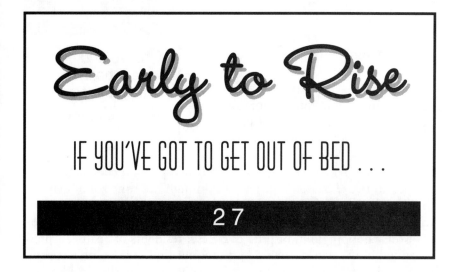

IF YOU'VE GOT TO GET OUT OF BED . . .

27

Breakfast, brunch, petit dejeuner, zaofan—whatever you call it, your first meal of the day is critical. By morning, if you haven't had a little snack during the night, your blood metabolism will have dropped down to 64 degrees, and you'll need to eat again to raise it to a properly functioning 100 degrees. Whether it's something simple on the go (a hot cup of coffee, a steaming mug of tea, a squirt of warm goat's milk) or a more substantial sit-down repast (French toast or waffles, kippers and eggs, lox and white fish) this is the meal that sets you in motion, whether it's off to work or just down to your Sunday paper.

Like much of what we eat, breakfasts foods have evolved under the influences of different cultures. The pancake became a johnnycake when European settlers used corn meal borrowed from Native American Indians to make their pannekoeken. As people moved around, johnnycakes became griddlecakes and then became flapjacks. 'Cakes, crêpes, tortillas, or wonton wrappers, the distinctions sometimes blur, but we like them all. Even with all the borrowing and sharing, typical breakfasts still vary around the globe and even within our own U.S. of A. If we were to zip around the world in eighty words, what would we find as we follow the sun:

Nippon, land of the rising sun, where Tokyo businesspeople in badly fitting blue suits sip steaming green tea and slurp down miso soup, natto (fermented bean), nori (seaweed), shake (grilled fish), and fried eggs.

The bustling port of Hong Kong, also bustling with dim sum carts serving assorted dumpling-ized foods to hungry hordes.

> "Love and eggs are best when they are fresh."
>
> **—Russian proverb**

Viva Roma, where stylish Italians dash into uno caffé for a couple sips of cappuccino and a few bites of panino.

Ah, Paris—city of light, café au lait, and croissants. Nothing sets that Gallic nose a twitchin' like the smell of fresh baked pain au chocolat.

Back in the U.S.A., a quick streak through the time zones may find the denizens of Gotham City chowing on pillow-sized bagels with cream cheese and lox; Southerners sipping chicory-laced coffee with their hoppin' john or grits & cheese; residents of Seattle, espresso capital of the world, shaking off the morning damp with a steaming double latté; and college students everywhere snarfing cold pizza.

So, what do you have to get up for in Chicago? You've got your *Chicago Tribune* and your *Chicago Sun-Times*, and you don't know where to go. Well, wake up and read on.

Jim's Grill

1429 West Irving Park, (773) 525-4050

Jim's, a nondescript, tiny diner at Irving Park and Southport, offers the ultimate dining dollar in a congenial atmosphere. Tables are few, and stools at the small counter, where you can slip into various esoteric discussions between regulars and strangers, can also be hard to come by. But squeeze in 'cause the food is great and the prices are better. Choose between a variety of your standard diner breakfast options, such as an omelet, toast, hash browns, and coffee, or two eggs, bacon/sausage, toast, hash browns, and coffee (each $2.75). Or, branch out to the more exotic Korean selections on the menu. Try the vegetarian pancakes for $3.95, mounds of vegetables stir-fried in a rice-based batter served with a tangy sauce. Or, try one of the $3.95 Korean specials that vary daily—maybe some hot, spicy noodles or vegetarian maki rolls. If you're leaning toward an even more substantial start to your day, try the bi-bim-bop, a kind of Korean fried rice served with a fried egg and stir-fried vegetables (chicken, beef, or pork optional). Go easy on the hot sauce unless you really want to wake up.

Closed Sundays. Open to 4:00 P.M. weekdays and 2:00 P.M. weekends. No alcohol. Jim's sister restaurant, the Korean Buddhist vegetarian Amitabul, is open daily (see "Seoul Food").

Furama Restaurant

4936 North Broadway, (773) 271-1161

So, maybe you get up, and you're still in the mood for something just a little exotic. The run-of-the-mill eggs or pancakes just aren't going to cut it today. Furama may be the answer you're looking for. Seven days a week, dim sum carts wend their way among the countless hungry (both Asian and gwailoh) diners occupying tables with rotating lazy Susans at Furama's cavernous establishments. Choose from a variety of steamed or fried dumplings and rolls costing only $1.75 to $1.90 for a plate. Don't skip the barbecue pork buns ($1.75) or the sweet fried rice ($3.25). Huge plates of roast duck, soy sauce chicken, curry squid, or jellyfish with sesame are $5.25. Polish it all off with an egg custard for dessert ($1.75). Then go home and nap.

Dim sum served daily from 11:00 A.M. to 3:00 P.M.

Bongo Room

1470 North Milwaukee, (773) 489-0690

In its new location on Milwaukee Avenue, Bongo Room is now able to seat three times as many early risers as would fit in its former cramped quarters under the Damen El stop. Although lacking the tiny, jumbled charm of the former location, the new Bongo Room still offers one of the city's best reasons to leave the comfort of the comforter. With a changing menu executed with creativity and flair, Bongo Room turns breakfast and lunch into a decadent culinary affair—possibly as sinful as anything you might have found between the sheets. Calypso French toast stuffed with banana mascarpone cheese and drizzled with mocha cream ($7.50), snow crab benedict with saffron-watercress hollandaise ($8.75), and bittersweet cocoa espresso pancakes topped with butter finger-cashew butter ($5.95) are just some of Bongo Room's treats. Even a simple bowl of cereal, granola served with fresh fruit and raspberry-mint yogurt ($6.50), has more snap, crackle, and pop than most of us are use to handling before 6:00 P.M.

Open daily, brunch is weekdays 7:00 A.M. to 3:00 P.M., weekends 9:30 A.M. to 2:30 P.M. No alcohol.

Cozy Café

2819 North Lincoln, (773) 549-9374

The name says it all—a tiny haven at Lincoln and Diversey seating less than twenty where you can pull up a stool at the counter and enjoy a cup of coffee while enjoying the sounds of the jukebox and watching the cooks grill your order. This is another "fork" kind of place, with nothing on the menu costing more than $5 ($5 items were specials). Biscuits reign supreme here. All selections come with a choice of biscuits or toast (Wonder Bread, anyone?). Or, you can make a meal out of just biscuits alone, gravy on the side, or a double helping of gravy on top (add $.50—you'd better really be a gravy lover). Biscuits can be accompanied by a selection of sides including ham-on-the-bone, pork chops, and corned beef hash.

Open daily but only till 3:00 P.M. No alcohol. Patio seating.

S & G

3000 North Lincoln, (773) 935-4025

A typical diner/breakfast establishment, Sam & George's, S & G, has two standout redeeming features. First, in a dueling diners scenario with its neighbor the Golden Apple across the street, it's open twenty-four hours on the weekends, serving coffee in brown mugs around the clock. Second is S&G's large selection of egg casseroles, meals that combine fried potatoes, eggs, and a variety of fixin's, along with a side of toast, for a real meal for real people (all ranging in price from $4.50 to $5.25). A real favorite of pork patrons (or those with a wicked hangover), the Gypsy has potatoes buried under a layer of eggs, ham, cheese, mushrooms, etc. Those ordering the Sparta—potatoes and eggs with feta cheese and vegetables—might get served the Athenian (add gyros meat). It was all Greek (and tasty) to me.

Open daily, 24 hours on the weekends. No alcohol.

Brett's Restaurant

2011 West Roscoe, (773) 248-0999

Brunch is your opportunity to enjoy the dishes of one of the city's most talented and creative chefs for less than one-third of what you might spend on dinner at Brett's in Roscoe Village. A cozy bistro with wrought iron seating that helps set the atmosphere of eating out on the sun porch, Brett's serves a creative brunch on Sundays with all dishes priced $7.75 and under. Pumpkin waffles with maple syrup ($6.50) and spinach pancakes with corn salsa ($7.75) are both regular breakfast items. If you're not feeling quite so creative, a number of omelets, including one with goat cheese, mushrooms, sun-dried tomatoes, and a fried potato cake ($7.75), are also options. Specials vary by season. A children's menu is also available.

Brunch served Sundays from 10:00 A.M. to 2:00 P.M. Full bar.

Breakfast Club

1381 West Hubbard, (312) 666-2372

A small bungalow has been converted to a pink dining room and the Breakfast Club. Packed with regulars at close set tables, the Breakfast Club serves breakfast and brunch specialties, along with burgers, sandwiches, salads, and some main dishes like pasta and meat loaf (all priced under $8). A.M. specialties include Swedish pancakes with lingonberries ($6.25), potato pancakes with apple sauce ($5.75), French toast stuffed with cream cheese, cinnamon, and walnuts ($6.75), apple-cinnamon oatmeal with honey ($3.95), and omelets like sun-dried tomato with onions and cheese ($5.75). Note, service can be very slow on weekends.

Brunch served daily from 6:00 A.M. to 3:00 P.M. (from 7.00 A.M. on weekends). Full bar. Sidewalk dining in nice weather.

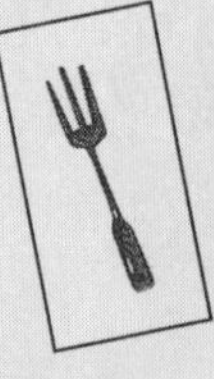

Mike's Broadway Café

3805 Broadway, (773) 404-2205

If you're waking up to the specialness of an alternative type of relationship, Mike's is the place for you. Another typical diner/breakfast–type place, Mike stands out because the food is generally a cut above (certainly better than the Pancake House across the street) the place is open twenty-four hours on the weekend, and no matter who your breakfast partner is, there's always a padded seat waiting for them at Mike's.

quick bites

Open daily and 24 hours on weekends. BYOB.

Ann Sather's

5207 North Clark, (773) 271-6677
929 West Belmont, (773) 348-2378
2665 North Clark, (773) 327-9522
(Just Carryout)
3416 North Southport, (773) 404-4475

Ann Sather's has been serving Swedish breakfasts (and some pretty bodacious dinners) since 1945. Skip the wait at Belmont by heading north to the spacious Andersonville branch. Don't miss the thin Swedish pancakes with the lingonberry preserves ($4.95, add $0.50 for either ice cream or strawberries) and order a side of Swedish potato sausage ($1.75). Cinnamon buns are $7.50 a dozen to go.

Open daily. Full bar including Swedish glögg.

Fresh Toast

Pop into a perky new brunch spot

I believe there's an inverse relationship between parking and meal prices. The less parking, the higher the prices—which is one reason I rarely eat out in Lincoln Park. So many places in those neighborhoods are over-hyped, over-priced, and it can take as long to park as it does to stand in line for a table. An attractive eatery locates itself conveniently within a four-block walk of public transportation or in some neighborhood that offers a legal, albeit small, street parking opportunity, say within a three block radius.

Given this philosophy, it's not often that I'm found in DePaul's Oz Park neighborhood hungry. So, imagine my surprise one night as I strolled west on Webster, and **Toast** popped out at me. Returning the following morning (after successfully wrestling into a tiny space just shy of a crosswalk and only a block away), I found Toast to be the East Side's answer to Wicker Park's breakfast and lunch hot spot, Bongo Room. Both are cozy, sponge-painted fantasies to wake up to. But where the Bongo Room is a cramped and artfully dilapidated little storefront serving brunch fancies to artfully disheveled, black-clad Wicker Park patrons, Toast is a bright piece of real estate twice the size of the Bongo Room dishing up early day taste treats to shiny, happy Lincoln Park people.

Owned by the operators of the oh-so-hip Iggy's, Toast offers culinary depth to a surface motif of cute little toasters, sprinkled throughout the restaurant, and cute waitstaff, one of whom when asked how long the place had been opened replied, "Months. Where have you been?" In spite of this insinuation of gustatory backwardness and motivated by savory, steaming plates piled high and garnished with exotic cheeses and vegetables—names of which the wait staff should really learn to pronounce properly to maintain that aura of chic superiority—my dining partner and I jumped the table line and snagged counter seats where apparently, in spite of long waits, a hostess blithely confirmed for us that possession is nine-tenths of the law.

After admiring the spunky toaster magnets on the refrigerator behind the counter, we brushed the crumbs left behind by the former occupants of our stools off our perky "eat" placemats and debated our options. Should it be breakfast or lunch? Door Number One or Two? On the breakfast side, while my eyes gave an enthusiastic thumbs up to both the eggs benedict with prosciutto and white truffle hollandaise ($7.95) and the French toast filled with either strawberries or mascarpone cheese and topped with seasonal berries ($6.25), my stomach waved a cautionary flag at such indulgences. Omelettes ($6.95) offered a choice of vegetarian (shiitake and oyster mushrooms oozing in gruyere cheese), asparagus and blue cheese, three cheese, or Tijuana jalapenos with onion, tomatoes, Chihuahua cheese and cilantro. Going bare basics, "steel cut" oatmeal with brown sugar and apples struck me as an option for no-nonsense simplicity.

While my partner waded into the rich danger of white truffle hollandaise and slightly dry chicken sausage, I opted for lunch. Although mango chicken chutney and warm couscous shrimp salad (both $5.95) both sounded attractive, I was after something more substantial. I wasn't sure I could do the steak and gorgonzola sandwich ($8.95), served with sweet potato chips, before at least 3:00 P.M. on a weekend. Wasn't feeling nostalgic enough for banana peanut butter and jelly ($3). No, I made a bee line for one of the hottest menu segments out there—the wrap. These days,

Toast, 746 West Webster, (312) 935-5600, is open Tuesday through Friday from 7:00 A.M. until 4:00 P.M. and weekends from 8:00 A.M. to 4:00 P.M.

doesn't it just seem like everybody's wrappin'? I eliminated the vegetarian wrap ($5.95) and the paella wrap ($6.95), narrowing it down to the Thai chicken or the spicy, blackened shrimp and asparagus with red pepper butter in a chile tortilla (both $6.95). Assured by our waitress that "everybody really loves the Thai chicken," fifteen minutes later I wrapped both hands happily around about a pound of Thai fixings and happily munched away while peanut sauce, coconut, and cilantro oozed down over my wrists. I took the other pound home in a doggy bag for a second banquet later.

"It's not what's eating you—it's what you're eating." Toast, I'd recommend a slice or two.

Index

ALPHABETICAL LISTING BY RESTAURANT

C

D

E

F

G

H

I

J

K

L

M

N

O

P

R

S

T

U

V

W

Z

ALPHABETICAL LISTING BY RESTAURANT TYPE

African

All-You-Can-Eat

American

American, Bakery

Vietnamese

ALPHABETICAL LISTING BY NEIGHBORHOOD

Lincoln Park

Lincoln Square

Logan Square

Long Grove

Loop

Mag Mile

Marquette Park

North Shore

Northwest Side

Old Town

Ravenswood

River North

Rogers Park

Roscoe Village

South Side

Taylor Street

Ukrainian Village

Uptown

West Rogers Park

West Side

Wicker Park

Wilmette

Wrigleyville